SBA Hotline Answer Book

Gustav Berle, PhD

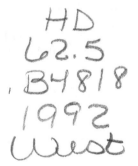

JOHN WILEY & SONS, INC.

New York • Chichester • Brisbane • Toronto • Singapore

Library of Congress Cataloging-in-Publication Data:

Berle, Gustav, 1920–
    SBA : hotline answer book / by Gustav Berle.
       p.   cm.
    Includes bibliographical references.
    ISBN 0-471-54296-2. — ISBN 0-471-54297-0 (pbk.)
    1. New business enterprises—Management—Handbooks, manuals, etc.
    2. Small business—Management—Handbooks, manuals, etc.
    I. Title.
    HD62.5.B4818   1991
    658.02'2—dc20   91-4622

Printed in the United States of America

10   9   8   7   6   5   4   3   2   1

Here is the essence of a million questions on the minds of American entrepreneurs—and the authoritative answers you've been needing! This one book will save you countless hours, hundreds of dollars, lots of frustration. It brings you, for the first time, information, references, and data from inside the U.S. Small Business Administration— categorized and alphabetized for quick and candid understanding.

GUSTAV BERLE

THE ESSENCE OF THE ENTREPRENEUR

The steps to entrepreneurial success are steep and arduous. They include a whole set of possibly new mental attitudes—motivation to achieve and succeed; a constant striving for quality in whatever the product or service, with the knowledge that if the task is not done right the first time, it will have to be done over again, take longer, and cost more; recognition of the need to nurture the customer who, once gotten, is the holy grail of entrepreneurial aspirations; sublimation of the get-rich-quick mentality in favor of the goal of long-term success that will inevitably bring with it market share and profits; cold-shower realization that no man is an island and that group achievement is conservation of the entrepreneurial spirit at its finest; patience and time to train employees in motivation, interaction, and pride in achievement; and in the end, motivation again, because it is the commencement and end-all of entrepreneurship and must pervade all activities from idea-creation to profit-achievement.

The entrepreneur is a dreamer who is also the interpreter of that dream into reality. Once the entrepreneur realizes the steps to success, they must all be wrapped in a mantle of persistence. Setbacks? The entrepreneur gets up again, dusts off, and tries a different tack. Armed with motivation, skill, realism, and persistence, all the other imagined trappings like money and luck will come. Add to the melange enthusiasm and the endless quest for knowledge, and the entrepreneur is an unbeatable economic force.

Contents

Opportunities
Opportunities/SBA Programs

Workshops   172

Appendix   175

Introduction

"Hello, you've reached the U.S. Small Business Administration's Answer Desk . . ."

The dulcet, professionally polished voice of an announcer is at the other end of the toll-free hotline (800 827-5722). The message is repeated at least 250,000 times a year—a million times since this electronic service was instituted by the Small Business Administration (SBA).

It wasn't always thus. Once upon a time, back in the eighties, between four and six SBA employees and occasional volunteers from the Service Corps of Retired Executives (SCORE), Small Business Development Corporation (SBDC), and other SBA-related organizations, would answer telephone inquires "live"—but that was when 50,000 to 85,000 calls were logged annually. With the population explosion, popularity of small business entries, complexity of small business life, and wider knowledge about this SBA service, the number of calls to the SBA Answer Desk grew beyond human ability to field them. To cope with the avalanche of steadily increasing queries, a computerized electronic system was installed. And that's really too bad. It used to be nice to chat with an SBA answer-person on the other end of the line. Now you have to punch different numbers and *hope* to get answers about what you need to know. To say that 250,000 calls reach the SBA's computerized Answer Desk anually is probably a vast understatement. It is quite possible that twice as many Americans call in, but get confounded by the process and discouraged with punching numbers and trying to get answers to questions that do not always fit ready answers or that may need to be approached from a different angle with some kindly human repartee.

This book addresses that potential problem. We have culled the

200 most frequently asked questions and have divided them into alphabetical categories for easy reference. Each question has been polished, researched, and then answered in some detail. The answers here are more detailed than those you might be able to receive on the Answer Desk hotline. They have been checked against the latest available information from the SBA and other government agencies, and scrutinized by government experts.

The result is a cross-section of questions about small business problems evidenced by *vox populi*, as well as the best answers available from the official literature and minds of the experts. Should you not find an answer to your question in this book, you are invited to write the author in care of the publisher or to try once more to elicit an answer from that nice voice on the other end of the hotline.

Of the most frequently-asked questions, one stands out from the rest: "How can I get some money to start my business?" About a decade ago, the U.S. Business Administration issued millions of dollars in loans to just about anybody who had a reasonable idea for a business. Too many of the borrowers were totally unqualified and lacked equity, incentive, and motivation. Somehow, many of them forgot that loans, even those from Uncle Sam, had to be paid back. Well, it wasn't long before the SBA's pot o' gold dried up. Beautiful ideas like free money from Uncle Sam die hard. Today most callers to the SBA's Answer Desk still want to know about loans, but the answers have changed.

The cold realities of the nineties is that the SBA does not usually lend money but only guarantees loans made by banks, and then only after very detailed scrutiny by at least two bank officers and an eagle-eyed staffperson at the SBA. The millions of dollars that had been lent out previously (and frequently forfeited) were, after all, the People's money. The loans represented tax receipts and the SBA was only the custodian.

Still, as we said before, such perceptions of easy money die hard. Perhaps this book will help to set the record straight. We hope it will assist you when going into a business of your own, help you to prevent problems with, or expand, the one you already have.

A SURVEY OF SMALL BUSINESS

Here are some approximate figures to give you an overview of small business in America: There are about four million businesses in the United States, which employ around 90 million people. As a group, about 99 percent of all businesses have fewer than 250 employees. But of this, 90 percent have fewer than 20 employees, and 53 percent of the companies are very small, having four or fewer employees.

Statistics can play tricks. The SBA, for instance, draws the line at 500 or fewer employees. Any company having fewer than 500 workers is considered a "small" company and thus elegible for SBA assistance and attention. OSHA, the U.S. Occupational Safety and Health Administration, on the other hand, defines a small business as a firm with fewer than 10 employees. The EPA (Environmental Protection Agency) bases its studies on companies with fewer than 50 employees, and our subsequent figures are based on the EPA's middleground. For the record, however, OSHA's firms include 75 percent of all American companies, the SBA's figures encompass 99.6 percent, and the EPA's figures 91.5 percent of all firms.

Whatever definition is used, most businesses are small and the number of small businesses is around 3,900,000. It is from this group that many of the questions in this book have arisen, and it is to this group that the answers are directed.

Small businesses in the U.S. were grouped into nine categories by the SBA's Small Business Data Base. We have rounded the figures for convenient comparison:

Type of Business	*Number of Businesses*
Agribusiness	95,000
Construction	500,000
Finance	250,000
Manufacturing	350,000
Mining	30,000
Retailing	1,200,000
Services	900,000
Transportation	130,000
Wholesale Trades	450,000

Because profit is the end to the means, it is illuminating to learn from the SBA's files that, depending on size, small business firms gross between $300,000 and $1,200,000 a year. Average profits (return on equity) is 12 percent, although this varies from 17 percent for firms under 10 employees down to 9 percent for firms with more than 100 employees. Conversely, of course, company assets increase as the size of the business increases—ranging from $150,000 for small firms with fewer than 10 employees to more than $6,000,000 for the top-ranked firms with more than 100 employees.

OK—the phone is ringing and it is time to start answering some of the quarter million questions that pour in annually to the Answer Desk. Remember that the question topics are alphabetical and will sometimes be cross-referenced. If you still cannot locate the exact question for which you seek an answer, pick up your phone and dial 800 827-5722 (800-U-ASK-SBA). It works from all over the United States and the price is right. It's free.

ACCOUNTING—*Selecting Software*

Q: *"Frankly, I'm scared to turn all my records over to an accounting firm where everything is now done on a computer because I feel I'll lose control over my business records. Are my fears justified?"*

They are justified only insofar as you have not yet learned the way computers can work for you. There are financial management services in probably every city of any size that can provide reasonably priced services, software, and explanations. Your first step is to determine what information you need for your particular kind of business. Generally, each business needs a *general accounting system* that can be expanded through the addition of optional modules as your own needs and expanded business demand.

Additions could be an *accounts receivable* module that provides you with a list of customer charges, a cash receipts journal, general journal, posting of finance charges, A/R general ledger, listing by customer of account status, and statement printing. There may be other features, if you desire them—aged account analysis, historical information on accounts, customer lists, and even mailing labels. The same goes for your *accounts payable*. Then there are modules to handle payroll records and inventory processing. There are many options, but they make sense only if you need them, if you can understand them, and if you can afford them. To determine the answers to those "ifs," you do need an understanding, knowledgeable, and sympathetic accountant or advisor. Don't allow the computer system to develop beyond your needs or understanding.

ADVERTISING—*Do I Need It?*

Q: *"Most small businesses spend between two and ten percent of their gross income on advertising. I should think that if I had quality mer-*

chandise, the public would beat a path to my door and I could put the savings into price reduction."

Some businesses have historically gotten along without advertising. Hershey Chocolate and Reader's Digest were two famous examples. But somewhere along the line even these companies changed once they realized that to maximize their growth and profit, they needed a wider customer base. Word-of-mouth advertising, which used to be regarded as the best and soundest form of promotion, was no longer adequate to the fast-track business world of our age.

To start with, look at advertising as an investment rather than as an expenditure. If advertising is produced well, researched candidly, and analyzed continually, it can help you sell more and do so at a lower cost. Its results are often subtle, but advertising can open doors and create a positive company image—an image that not only helps bring you customers, but also good employees who want to work for you and suppliers who want to deal with you. Like any other business function, the direct value of advertising is not always apparent (except in mail order advertising). As the old saying goes, "If you've got it, flaunt it." Advertising will help put a spotlight on your products and services.

Like any other business activity, it must be professionally executed and appear in the right medium to reach your particular audience. Much money can be wasted by advertising in fits-and-starts, by using the wrong media, and by using media that cost too much per audience. Advertising that was prepared on the kitchen table by some budding genius can be costly in terms of wasted dollars and damaged image. Advertising is truly expensive only when it's done poorly.

ADVERTISING—*How Much?*

Q: *"How much money should I spend for advertising to be most effective?"*

There are many variables that affect the amount of money that a business should allocate to advertising. The term "allocation" or "investment" is preferred, because that's what good advertising should be—an investment, not an expenditure. You should always expect something back from your investment, or it is not worth making. The message and graphic presentation of your ad, its placement in appropriate media, and its timing are as important as the amount of money you invest. As in accounting or law, you are best off dealing with a professional when creating your advertising or selecting the right medium for your particular product or service. Your aim should be to gain optimum exposure for the dollars invested. As for the amount that should be allocated, various industries have averages, which should be spread out over each year's advertising program in accordance with seasonal variations. Here are some of them:

Industry	*Percent of Sales*
Agricultural products	2.1
Bakery products	1.5
Books	4.0
Bottled/canned drinks	6.6
Commercial printing	1.2
Construction/contractors	1.9
Foods, related products	5.2
Footwear	4.5
Hardware	6.3
Computers, mini/micro	6.5
Furniture	2.6
Records, tapes	9.1
Retail department stores	3.5
food markets	1.4
fashions	2.5
jewelry	6.2
Mail order houses	13.2
Real estate	1.5
Motels, hotels	3.5
Restaurants	3.7
Recreation, amusements	4.7

ADVERTISING—*The Advertising Consultant*

Q: *"I've been trying to get an advertising agency to do my work, but because I can budget only $20,000 a year at this time, the agencies aren't satisfied with just a 15% commission. Are there any alternatives?"*

Most advertising agencies feel that they cannot make money on an income of $3,000 a year—which is 15 percent of your $20,000 budget. The alternatives, remuneration charged by the hour at a mutually agreeable rate, or a cost-plus method in which the agency gets its 15 percent from commissionable media, and bills you for work that they feel is over and beyond that income, might be discussed. Then there are two other possibilities: 1) You might be able to make a connection with a creative and experienced person in an agency who wants to moonlight your account, that is, work on it after normal working hours, while you arrange with various commissionable media to place advertising directly or through a dummy or "house" agency and thus earn the 15 percent commission. Or 2) you can find a consultant who advises you on your marketing strategy and creative processes, while you let an art studio handle the production of advertising material and place the media yourself directly with the publication, printer, electronic medium, billboard, etc. The more you understand about the advertising business, the closer you will come to a satisfactory *modus operandi* that works for you. Perhaps your advertising involves only direct mail, in which case you can have work done by a direct mail specialist or creative print shop. Because there is no commission involved, you merely pay the bills against approved estimates, postage, and handling.

ADVERTISING—*Direct Mail*

Q: "*Direct mail is getting so expensive that we're wondering how we can control the spiraling cost of this form of marketing?*"

Total delivered cost of a direct mail piece is nearly $1.00 today, counting time, all physical costs, address maintenance, and postage. The old blitzkrieg approach of saturation bombardment of an area or group with mailing pieces is slowing down considerably. Today, direct mailing must be done not bigger, but smarter, and the computer is helpful in achieving better record keeping, efficiency in handling, and filtering of unproductive names. But it still takes people to direct computer programs. Some of the requirements for keeping direct mail costs in check include:

- Making sure that all departments involved in the marketing process keep each other informed so that records are kept up-to-date. The old saying "garbage in, garbage out" certainly applies here.
- Using all the tricks of the trade to make your mailings more attractive and attention-getting, including computerized name insertion.
- Addressing the envelopes directly instead of applying commercial-looking labels. The same goes for postage.
- Focusing your mailing lists on specific interest groups, which will react more positively if the mailing appeals to their special interests.

Computerized direct mail will get more accurate as time goes by. Clever techniques will make junk mail harder to throw away. Smart mail, rather than direct mail, might be the solution of the future.

ADVERTISING—*Educational Media*

Q: *"We sell most of our goods to a youth market. Using television or youth-oriented radio is fine but our budget is too limited and the media are too scattered. Do you have any advice on that?"*

You might set up an appointment with your local SCORE or SBDC counselors and discuss your situation. You could also explore the field of educational public relations, which is making great strides both nationally and locally. On a local level, one shopping center, for instance, had good-quality bookcovers printed up that included class schedules with space for a student's name and distributed them to several area schools. They reached nearly 10,000 students at a cost of about $1,000. The national youth market today represents $250 billion in business. One company, Whittle Communications, has created Channel ONE, which brings a daily 10-minute news program, including two minutes of sponsored commercials, into more than 7,000 schools. This fairly subtle PR program is being challenged by those who do not like the commercial intrusion into schools, but thus far most of the local school boards have acquiesced to it. They realize that the contributions of equipment and educational aids by the sponsors more than compensate for any possible negative impact. Perhaps such commercialism is even beneficial, in that it acquaints students with the real world they will face upon graduation. If properly handled, such programs can also help sell business to students who are usually quite ignorant of the commercial functions of our society. Keep in mind that the school's first job is to educate young people—then wrap your company promotion program around that need and present it to the school's administrators.

ANSWER DESK

Q: *"What is the Answer Desk anyway and what does it do?"*

The Answer Desk is run by the SBA's Office of Advocacy and has answered close to a million calls since its inception in 1982. This hotline is the only national toll-free service set up to provide information on small business problems. The number, perhaps one of the most popular ones that the government has, is 800 827-5722.

In the old days, about two or three years ago, a battery of SBA employees and volunteers used to man the Answer Desk phones and give callers personal and direct information. The growth of the nation and a tremendous increase in small business interest forced the Answer Desk to go electronic. As soon as this system was completed, the logged calls shot up to around 250,000 a year. Today, when you call the Answer Desk, you get a 10-step response by a dulcet recorded voice:

1. Hello, this is the Answer Desk.
2. Punch 1 for a directory of services.
3. Punch 2 if you know what you want.
4. Punch 3 if you want to hear about upcoming events.
5. Respond "yes" if you want to start a business . . .
6. If you want financing information . . .
7. If you want the nearest SCORE office for counseling . . .
8. If you request other SBA services . . .
9. Facts about small business and other data . . .
10. Missed something? Punch this button if you want recorded messages repeated.

The Answer Desk, an information and referral service, fields about 600 different types of questions. This book has attempted to cull the 200 most vital and most often-asked and answer them in some detail, which is of course not feasible in a brief recorded message.

BONDING

Q: *"Is it possible to obtain bonding through the SBA?"*

Through its Surety Bond Guarantee Program, SBA helps to make the bonding process accessible to small and emerging contractors, including minorities, who find bonding unavailable to them. SBA is authorized to guarantee to a qualified surety company up to 90 percent of losses incurred under bid, payment, or performance bonds issued to contractors on contracts up to $1,250,000. These contracts may be for construction, supplies, manufacturing, or services provided by either a prime or subcontractor for government or nongovernment work. This Surety Bond Guarantee Program is administered through SBA's 10 regional offices and participating surety companies and agents throughout the United States. A list of SBA offices, locations, and phone numbers can be found in the Appendix.

BREAK-EVEN POINT

Q: *"In preparing a business plan for presentation to my bank, how can I determine the break-even point in a business that I haven't started yet?"*

The break-even point is reached when your expenses balance your income, but you are still at the zero point in earnings. It is true that most business planning fails to include *all* expenses in making up a projection. For that reason caution dictates that we should always factor in a percentage for unforeseen expenses. There are so many areas that no amount of experience and crystal-balling can anticipate. If you are sure that you have accounted for all expenses in opening and operating your new business, then take a look at the areas that cannot be foreseen at the time you make up your projections:

- Increase in taxes
- Slower repayments by customers
- Difficulties in attracting new business
- Changes in management on the part of your "sure" customers or clients
- Changes in styles, preferences, and demand
- New competition in your market that siphons off some of the income
- Price increases from your suppliers
- Unforeseen obsolescence for your product or equipment
- Accidents to you, your employees, or best customers that reduce productivity
- Departure of a key employee such as a productive sales representative
- Fire, flood, or other unforeseen damages to your property
- Illness to you or family member that reduces your availability
- Increases in insurance, utility costs, or vital supplies (like oil/gas)
- Lawsuits that cost money for defense or fines

There are certainly other reverses that can affect your break-even point, none of which may be your fault but which nonetheless are part of the risk of doing business. In making projections, you need to take even remote probabilities into account to avoid the possibility of failure.

BUSINESS COSTS

Q: *"What does it cost to operate a business?"*

This is a commonly asked question that has no specific answer. If anything, it indicates that the questioner has only a limited idea of the nature of his or her chosen business. Some businesses like supermarkets wind up with one to three percent in profit, because it costs 97 to 99 percent for merchandise and overhead; however, gross volume for such businesses might go into the millions. In comparison, you could operate a personal consulting or professional service out of your house and have neither inventory nor employees. Your expenses could range from 10 to 20 percent and your profit from 80 to 90 percent—but you may do only $30,000 to $50,000 in annual business. Trade associations generally maintain and make available (sometimes only to members) typical costs of operating businesses in their field. Perhaps a counselor at your local SCORE chapter has had specific experience and will pass this on to you at no cost. Gustave Berle's recent book, *Raising Start-Up Capital for Your Company* (John Wiley & Sons, Inc., 1990), offers some details and typical costs in various businesses.

BUSINESS FAILURES

Q: *"I have been thinking about going into a business of my own, but, frankly, I'm afraid of what I hear is the high percentage of failures. Does the SBA have any advice on how to prevent that?"*

Volumes have been written on this subject. It is true that as many as 80 percent of all new businesses will no longer be alive five years after start-up. According to Dun & Bradstreet, which has furnished business information since 1841, nearly 93 percent of business failures are due to the three "in" factors: inexperience, incompetence, and instability. The chief reason is not lack of financing, as so many entrepreneurs believe, but rather lack of management experience. The SBA offers management assistance through its more than 100 field offices and the more than 380 offices of SCORE, the Service Corps of Retired Executives. Since both SBA and SCORE services are usually free, it would be foolish not to take advantage of them—especially before problems arise. SBI, SBDC, and other SBA-affiliated agencies are also available, as are local chambers of commerce, business associations, and specific trade and professional organizations. The SBA has dozens of helpful, inexpensive booklets available, and every library of any size has shelves of business books and often the entire collection of SBA-produced management aids. But the most important preventative to business failure is the owner's personal preparedness. All the above suggestions should be explored prior to spending the first dollar on a new enterprise.

BUSINESS PLAN

Q: *"Everybody talks about the need for a business plan. How can I get some help in making one up for a business that I am planning to start?"*

A business plan is like a blueprint for building a house or a road map when you venture into uncharted territory. It is absolutely necessary in any professional approach to business start-ups or management, and especially if you plan to borrow money from a financial institution. Since a business plan is a very detailed and difficult document, it requires the coordination of the entrepreneur, competent counsel, and often professional assistance such as an accountant or attorney. Counselors from a local SCORE office can help to execute a proper business plan. There are numerous books in the library that go into great detail on the subject. The author of this book wrote one entitled *The Do-It-Yourself Business Book* (John Wiley & Sons, Inc., 1989), which contains a very detailed outline of a practical business plan and explanation. The SBA has published booklets on the subject that can be obtained at your regional SBA office or through the local SCORE office. They may also be ordered (check or money order) from U.S. Small Business Administration, P.O. Box 15434, Ft. Worth, TX 76119. The wonderful thing about a complete and well-executed business plan is that it opens the entrepreneur's own eyes to his plans and operation, and makes him or her look professional in the eyes of counselors and bankers. Business planning publications produced by the U.S. Small Business Administration are available from the SBA regional offices, SCORE chapters, or direct from the SBA Publications section as follows:

> Developing a Strategic Business Plan (publication MP 21)
> Business Plan for Small Manufacturers (publication MP 4)
> Business Plan for Small Construction Firms (publication MP 5)
> Business Plan for Retailers (publication MP 9)
> Business Plan for Small Service Firms (publication MP 11)
> Business Plan for Homebased Business (publication MP 15)

BUSINESS START-UPS—*Ideas*

Q: *"I've got this great idea for a business that I am sure will work. With whom can I discuss it confidentially?"*

The SBA has an affiliated association called SCORE, which stands for Service Corps of Retired Executives. It has about 750 offices and satellite locations throughout the U.S. and possessions (see locations in Appendix). SCORE executives come from all trades and professions. Perhaps there is one at your nearest SCORE office who has had the specific experience you need to help you get started. The counseling is free and confidential. A couple of general considerations that need to be determined in launching a new business are

1. Accurately pricing the product or service, delivered to the customer.
2. Peripheral costs such as packaging, advertising, shipping, financing, commissions.
3. Competition, direct and indirect, including the competition's pricing and past success.
4. Obsolescence and breakage factors.
5. Should or can the product be patented, trademarked, or copyrighted.
6. What follow-up servicing does it require and what is the estimated cost of such service.

BUSINESS START-UPS—*Low Cost*

Q: *"I want to start up a business of my own, perhaps part-time at first, until I can build up enough capital without going into a lot of debt. Do you have any suggestions on low-cost small businesses?"*

Any business that can benefit from your experience, skill, and contacts will be among the easiest and least expensive to get started. You might also want to make an appointment with the nearest SCORE office and discuss your ideas with a counselor—a service that is free and confidential. Read some of the small business magazines like *Success, Entrepreneur, INC., Small Business Opportunities,* and *New Business Opportunities,* which are full of ideas and case histories. Some businesses that are spotlighted by *Entrepreneur* magazine, for instance, that are claimed to require less than $5,000 in start-up capital, include

Imprinted advertising specialties—usually sold from samples and catalogs.
Typing and word-processing service—depends heavily on quality and prompt delivery as promised.
Herb farming—can be started small, servicing area groceries and better restaurants with fresh products.

Home services—like pool cleaning (requires some knowledge of water chemistry) or doing an environmental audit (knowledge of variety of environmental problems and products).

Detailing cars—requires strength and perhaps a crew of energetic young part-time workers.

Agenting—representing temporary specialty workers, baby-sitters, nannies, tutors, etc. for a 25% fee of their services.

BUYING A BUSINESS—*Where to Start*

Q: *"I want to go into a business of my own but believe that I would prefer to buy a business rather than to start one. What suggestions can you give me?"*

A good starter is the SBA brochure "Buying and Selling a Small Business" (MP 16). Also useful would be "Locating or Relocating Your Business" (MP 2) and "Choosing A Retail Location" (MP 10). A (free) consultation with a counselor from your local SCORE office will be helpful. See also the other entry in this category. The most important considerations in buying any business are your own management ability, adequate financing, and the existence of a need for the business or service. If the business is already established, the reason for selling the business is very important and needs to be investigated thoroughly and honestly—without pressure from the seller or his broker, or without being blinded by your own enthusiasm and anxiety. Don't be rushed into buying an "emergency" without detailed investigation and consideration and, preferably, seeking outside opinions from neutral sources, such as SCORE and SBA counselors, bankers, noncompetitive fellow-merchants, suppliers, newspaper representatives, and outside salesmen. It is amazing how you can piece together this mosaic of information and often come up with a picture that is at variance with your original conception. Often such knowledge will make the buying of a specific business much more realistic—and on considerably more favorable terms.

BUYING A BUSINESS—*Buying after 50*

Q: *"I am already over 50 but want to get into my own business. I am considering buying an existing business rather than starting my own from scratch. Can you give me any advice?"*

Buying an existing business is indeed a shortcut to getting started. If the business is sound, it has a better chance of survival than a brand new business, providing the new management is capable and adequately financed. In buying someone else's business, one stands a chance of buying a pig-in-a-poke or a chance in a lifetime. There are three major considerations that must be examined with a magnifying lens: 1) Why does the seller want to get out of the business? 2) How accurately can the buyer determine the true value of the business being acquired? 3) What are the real future prospects of the business?

SBA's affiliate, SCORE, has counselors who can be of help in offering a "second opinion" and guidance in the purchase of an existing business and its continuing operation. The SBA's booklet, "How to Buy or Sell a Business" can serve as a brief guide. Lawrence W. Tuller's *Buying In: A Complete Guide to Acquiring a Business or Professional Practice* (McGraw-Hill/Liberty, 1990), treats the subject in great detail. A complete 24-point checklist when considering the acquisition of a business is contained in Gustav Berle's *The Do-It-Yourself Business Book* (John Wiley & Sons, Inc., 1989), as well as in his *Planning and Forming Your Company* (John Wiley & Sons, Inc., 1990). Business brokers, accountants, and attorneys can be helpful as well, but at a price.

CERTIFICATE OF COMPETENCY

Q: *"Do I need a Certificate of Competency from the SBA before I try to get a federal procurement contract? And what happens if I don't get it?"*

Getting a Certificate of Competency (CoC) is necessary if a supplier wants to be a contractor or subcontractor to a federal agency. If the federal agency turns the applicant down, then the applicant can turn to the SBA for help. Congress has empowered the SBA to work with rejected applicants and to help them achieve acceptable status. The criteria that are judged include

- Capability
- Competency
- Credit
- Integrity
- Perseverance
- Tenacity

A specialized SBA field team with technical, engineering, and financial capabilities works with the applicant-company for each procurement contract. The team will examine the company's credit ratings, past performance, management capabilities, management schedules, prospects for financing, and equipment that might be needed in the performance of the contract. The SBA's assistance program may include management, loans and counseling, legal, technical, and financial reviews. If the CoC Review Committee's review is affirmative, a letter is issued certifying the applicant's eligibility, and the certificate is then sent to the purchasing agency for a contract award. This checks-and-balances system is designed to help small business and protect the purchasing agency that is spending the government's money.

COMMUNITY PROBLEMS

Q: "Our small town lost its major industry and if we cannot effect a turnaround, we stand a chance of becoming a ghost town. Is there any assistance available in such a case?"

Many small communities are buffeted by economic reversals, usually caused by the closing of a major industry, a major natural disaster, or a dramatic shift in consumer use of local products or services. It happened to Strawberry Point, a small town in Iowa located about halfway between Dubuque and Waterloo. The 1,300 citizens of the town found themselves economically stranded as a result of the closing of its major industry. After local bootstrap efforts failed, someone suggested contacting the Dubuque chapter of SCORE. A group of retired business executives from the city decided to rise to the challenge. They formed a team of marketing, management, and finance experts and drove to Strawberry Point. After looking around the town and formulating some ideas, they met with the town's leading citizens and laid their ideas on the table. It took some months of working together to start a turnaround, but it worked. U.S. Senator Charles Grassley, who represents Iowa (including Strawberry Point, of course), lauded SCORE's success in helping to revitalize the community.

COMPUTERS—*Bookkeeping Applications*

Q: "Everybody's talking about, and evidently using, computers to help run small businesses. Do you have any guidelines on how computers can help with bookkeeping and accounting?"

A basic booklet, "How to Get Started with a Small Business Computer" (publication MP-14), is available from the SBA for one dollar. Most SBA offices will also have a booklet titled "Life Line: A Small Business

Guide to Computer Security" (publication LF-001), which treats the important issue of safeguarding records from inside and outside abuses and errors (see next question). Computer applications fall into eight categories:

- Accounts receivable
- Accounts payable
- Inventory control
- Payroll
- General ledger
- Planning
- Nonaccounting functions
    correspondence
    record storage
    promotion response records
    commission versus sales ratios

The booklets mentioned above detail these functions as they apply to small business operations.

There are numerous accounting software packages that can be added to any computer. Discuss your specific needs with your own accountant, who can advise you on what to get, or with a knowledgeable computer store salesperson. The most important computer use will be in keeping your general ledger. The most important factor to remember is to keep your eye on your own specific needs and your own ability to operate the system and understand it. Unless a computer saves you time and increases the efficiency of your operation, it is merely a gadget.

COMPUTERS—*Security*

Q: *"Computer security is becoming a problem with us. How can we make sure our information is safeguarded?"*

The SBA has published a brochure entitled "Life Line: A Small Business Guide to Computer Security" (publication LF-001). Your own computer company and accounting firm might have further information on the subject. Some aspects of computer security, especially those that involve your own employees, are somewhat nebulous and subject to legal interpretation. Basically, if you have a good back-up system, personnel that are carefully screened, and an intelligent entry code known only to a limited number of trusted people and clients and changed periodically, you have accomplished the major protective steps. Eight steps you can take, specifically, to cut down on what has become a $40 billion crime, are as follows.

- Use a password or code known only to those who are authorized to use your computers
- Train employees to use computers carefully; change passwords often and at irregular intervals
- Maintain a meticulous log of computer entries and check it at odd times against your instructions
- Establish a log-in and log-out procedure for employees using computers
- Establish a separate category for accounts payable personnel; they should not be those who record transactions on the computer (sign checks, etc.)
- Keep vital diskettes in a safe place and shred other material when no longer needed
- Have back-up material of all important entries and store them securely
- Spot-check computer usage to ascertain possible abuses and to keep employees aware of your alertness

CONTRACTS—*DUNS Identification*

Q: *"I see a 'DUNS Identification' mentioned in contract applications. How do you get that?"*

DUNS stands for Data Universal Numbering System. It is required by Federal Acquisition Regulations for the purpose of identifying each plant or location of government contractors.

To obtain a DUNS number call the Dun & Bradstreet office at 215 776-4388 in Philadelphia and ask for a number. Give the firm name and complete address of the plant for which a number is desired, providing no number has been previously assigned to that plant. There is no charge for this service. If portions of the government contract are performed at different locations, then each location should have an identifying DUNS number.

CONTRACTS—*Language*

Q: *"When considering bids to the government, I've noticed the use of certain initials like IFB, RFP, and RFQ. Can you explain them?"*

IFB means *invitation for bids.*
RFP means *request for proposal.*
RFQ means *request for quotation.*

You have to be on a federal agency's bidders' list in order to receive an IFB. Those on the bidders' list receive a package that contains Form 33, which includes instructions and specifications for preparing bids. It includes a description of specifications for the product or service to be bought. These requirements must be filled exactly, and no "just-as-good" substitutes can be offered or the bid will be considered "non-responsive." It will also include a delivery schedule and packaging/shipment requirements, which must be met exactly as stated. For any bid to be considered, all conditions must be met exactly. If any questions or discussions are needed before returning the bid, the issuing contract officer is the first contact.

Other enclosures will be a payment schedule and terms, which must be executed accurately, as the contract officer has no authority to make alterations in the price or in compensating for mistakes. Standard contract provisions and clauses that are binding will be presented relating to defaults, changes, and disputes. Deadline for submitting bids, date and time of bid opening, and date of contract award will also be stated. All bids are opened in public at the agency contract office.

RFP and RFQ are used when the federal purchase office buys by negotiation rather than by sealed bid. This method is used when adequate specifications of a product or service are not possible to draft; when the product or service is experimental, developmental, or of a research nature; or when the purchase is small—that is, a "set aside" for small businesses, amounting to less than $10,000.

To receive an RFP (request for proposal), a firm also has to be on the agency's bidders' list. The "Commerce Business Daily," a government information newspaper, lists such bids every day (see separate entry on this publication). Federal installations also post such bids daily. Otherwise, all specifications for such small bids (RFPs) are similar to IFBs.

If you decide to answer a request for an RFP, this is what you need to answer:

1. A price quotation
2. Description of the products or services
3. Resources to be used in performing the work
4. Capabilities (yours) to complete delivery
5. Contract terms

If your price falls into the range of the contracting agency's needs and all other specifications are acceptable, the process of negotiation commences, confirming all of the above items.

The contract award is made to the bidder whose final offer is considered the most fair and reasonable to both parties. It is not required that the recipient of the award have the lowest price.

A Request for Quotation (RFQ), used by all federal agencies, is called Form 18. It is designed to obtain price, delivery, and related information from suppliers. It may be used for small (under $10,000) and large purchases. Furnishing a quotation to a government office is not an offer and cannot be accepted by the government as a binding offer. The contract becomes reality only when the supplier accepts the government agency's offer, its terms and conditions.

CONTRACTS—*Minority Assistance 8(a) Program*

Q: *"We are a small, minority-owned company and want to get in on the federal government's procurement. Can you tell us how we can best go about that?"*

In 1968 the Small Business Act was introduced. It contains a clause referred to as Section 8(a), the purpose of which is to help small start-up or operating companies run by socially and economically disadvantaged persons. The 8(a) program has representatives in every SBA office who will help foster business ownership for disadvantaged entrepreneurs, promote their competitive viability, and encourage the procurement by federal government departments of products and services from such disadvantaged companies.

To be eligible for the Section 8(a) program, the applicant

- must prove that he or she owns at least 51 percent of the company
- must be a citizen of the United States
- must be able to prove ethnic prejudice and cultural bias that places his or her business at a disadvantage

One of the first steps should be to contact your nearest SBA office and obtain Fact Sheet 36, which explains this special situation in detail. Financial assistance is also available to successful applicants—contrary to normal SBA loan procedures—including advance payments for labor and material that might be needed to complete a government procurement contract.

CONTRACTS—*Payments*

Q: "I have heard that government contracts can sometimes take a long time to get paid. How can I get faster action?"

The government has a system of progress payments. These are made to the contractor when he or she can show progress in completing the contract, usually based on provable costs up to the point of the payment request. A clause in the government's solicitation will give notice of the availability or unavailability of progress payments. If you bid on a government contract, this request should not be part of your bid. However, once you get a government contract, you can file a separate request with the contracting officer to include such a request with your bid. It normally takes about four months to get a payment. If you claim that you are unable to fulfill the contract because of insufficient working capital, or that product delivery might be affected, progressive payments will be considered.

CONTRACTS—*Preparation*

Q: "Can you tell me what I should know before applying for a minority defense contract?"

Every federal agency, including the Defense Department, has an office that helps small and disadvantaged business to get a fair share of federal contracts. The Defense Department has the Defense Logistics Agency (DLA) that publishes a booklet entitled "Pre-Award Survey Information for Prospective Government Offerors." The people in these offices who are available to assist you are called Small and Disadvantaged Business Utilization Specialists. The office of the DLA can be contacted at Cameron Station, Alexandria, VA 30461; phone 703 274-6471. For a complete list of all 32 Offices of Small and Disadvantaged Business Utilization (OSDBU) see the entry OSDBU-Procurement Assistance-Contract Listings.

CONTRACTS—*Problems/Resolutions*

Q: "What assistance can SBA provide in resolving technical or production problems that come up in trying to get government business?"

Problems of production, technical, or contract matters may be referred to organizations allied with the SBA, such as SCORE, the Service Corps of Retired Executives. The SBA is prohibited by law or limited by its own personnel resources from entering into situations that involve claims against other government agencies. The SBA can, however, assist in locating appropriate agencies within the government that are set up to render technical advice and information.

CONTRACTS—*Protest Procedure*

Q: *"What is the procedure if I want to file a protest against the award given to another company?"*

Once a government bid for products or services is announced, any protest against this award must be filed by the 5th day after the award is announced. It should be in writing so that an answer may also be received in writing after the 60 to 90 days it takes to investigate the protest. Protests must not only be timely, but also be as specific as possible, and hard facts must be included in the allegation. The General Accounting Office (GAO) receives most protests from disappointed bidders or offerors, by potential bidders, or by others who have some legitimate interest in the particular action. GAO attorneys will call a conference of all concerned parties, hear the case, and report within 90 days, in writing, to all parties.

CONTRACTS—*Specifications*

Q: *"How can I get accurate specifications for a government contract?"*

Government contract offers are usually accompanied by detailed specifications and, where necessary, especially in military specifications, by drawings, standards, and technical data. If for some reason they are not complete, detailed specifications can be obtained from the Commanding Officer, U.S. Naval Publications and Forms Center, 5801 Tabor Avenue, Philadelphia PA 19120.

CONTRACTS—*Termination*

Q: *"If I find that I cannot complete a contract with a government agency, is there a penalty?"*

Like other contractual obligations, a government contract to produce materials or render a service is a legal instrument and an obligation. To start all over again seeking another contract could cost the government agency more money and loss of time. Such additional costs penalize the taxpayer ultimately—and the contractor who accepted the bid and then defaults on it can be held responsible for damages and additional costs. The contracting officer can charge the defaulting con-

tractor the difference between the original contract price and the ultimate cost to the government.

DISASTER LOANS

Q: *"Our area is subject to spring floods. I have heard that emergency
loans are available from the government to help affected businesses
get reestablished."*

Disaster loans are available through special SBA offices and trained
specialists. These loans are applicable to small business damage as a
result of natural disasters, hurricanes, floods, tornadoes, and earth-
quakes that cause hardships with which the business cannot cope. The
area must be declared a disaster area by the president or the SBA
administrator before either physical disaster loans or economic injury
disaster loans can be issued. Although four regular field offices (listed
below) are maintained, the SBA usually establishes an on-site office in
the area of the disaster to help with loan information, processing, and
loan disbursement. The local SBA or SCORE office may also be contacted for information and assistance. The four regional disaster area
offices are

Regions I and II:
    15-01 Broadway, Fair Lawn, NJ 07410; 201 794-8195,
    800 221-2093

Regions III, IV, and V:
    120 Ralph McGill St., Atlanta, GA 30308; 404 347-3771,
    800 334-0309

Regions VI and VII:
    2306 Oak Lane, Suite 110, Grand Prairie, TX 75051; 214 767-7571,
    800 527-7735

Regions VIII, IX, and X:
    1825 Bell St., Suite 208, Sacramento, CA 95853-4795;
    916 978-4578, 800 468-1710

ENTREPRENEURIAL PERSONALITY

Q: *"Sometimes I wonder if I have the right kind of personality to go
into a retail or service business. I know that I will be the one the business*

must depend on. How can I find out without resorting to a psychoanalyst's couch?"

This is a very wise question, especially when one considers that good management is the number one requirement for business survival. Lenders, from banks to venture capitalists to SBA guarantors, consider this factor as most important. Many books and articles have been written that try to define the entrepreneurial character. There are some acknowledged common denominators: educational background, family influence that provides encouragement and role models, proof of previous experience in one's chosen field or something akin to it, perseverance, and pleasant personality. The SBA's booklets that are available from your local office can be illuminating:

"Small Business Decision Making" (MP 19)
"Techniques for Productivity Improvement" (MP 24)
"Techniques for Problem Solving" (MP 23)
"Effective Business Communications" (MP 1)
"Personal Qualities Needed To Manage a Store" (SMA 145)

The Do-It-Yourself Business Book by Gustav Berle (John Wiley & Sons, Inc., 1989) has a 20-point test that is supposed to determine your E.Q., that is, your Entrepreneurial Quotient. It also provides a YOU-checklist to help you determine your personal readiness.

ENVIRONMENT—*Laws*

Q: *"What impact will the new environmental laws have on small business, like properties, loans and storage tanks?"*

One problem today is that banks are reluctant to lend mortgage money on industrial and commercial properties unless they have received environmental clearances. There have been a number of cases in which banks have acquired properties through purchase of collateral collections that were in gross violation of environmental regulations—such as leaking underground storage tanks or hazardous wastes buried on a farm—and then got stuck with huge cleanup bills. If you have such a suspect property for sale or are planning to buy such a property, it would be advisable to obtain an environmental audit of the property. Only when you can prove that there is no significant environmental threat can you buy or sell a commercial or industrial property without fearing some future repercussion. (See also the section SELLING A BUSINESS in this book.)

ENVIRONMENT—*New Opportunities*

Q: *"I keep reading about new business opportunities that will come as the result of the Federal Clean Air Act. What are some of the opportunities that the SBA has identified?"*

The Environmental Protection Agency is charged with administering the currently revised Clean Air Act, Clean Water Act, and others that are designed to stop the pollution and in many cases reverse the damage done to our environment by industrial, agricultural, and people pollution. The EPA estimates that the enforcement of the various clean-up measures will create a $100 billion a year growth industry. Many states also have introduced clean-up measures and some (Virginia, for example) have even offered tax credits to those who can prove remedial actions. Municipalities also have introduced recycling and other clean-up programs that involve private individuals and companies, and they have created and are continuing to create entire new businesses. Many small mail order and manufacturing businesses, and retail stores as well, have sprung up to sell only environment-friendly products that are biodegradable or recyclable or made from recycled products. The conversion of trash-to-cash is not only an environmentally beneficial activity, but also a boon to big companies and small entrepreneurs. Large companies like IBM and Marriott have made hundreds of thousands of dollars by training their administrative employees to sort and recycle tons of office paper. A lawyer in Washington started a business that, while cleaning up at a stadium, collects thousands of empty cans, plastic bottles, tons of newsprint, and recyclable glass. A 27-year-old computer studies graduate found that $100 replacement laser cartridges could be rebuilt and resold for $39 to $49 and thus joined a thousand other entrepreneurs who are today selling recycled cartridges that benefit the environment, customers, and themselves. There are literally thousands of new opportunities in the wake of the world's awakening concern about the globe's ecology. The magazine *In Business* is devoted almost entirely to these opportunities. Consumer education goes hand-in-hand with environmental business opportunities, simply because, as Pogo said in the comic strip, "I have met the enemy—and it is us." Entrepreneurs taking advantage of the business opportunities offered by environmental measures must also become educators in order to maximize their opportunities.

EXPORTING

Q: *"We are a small manufacturer doing business only in the United States through representatives. We'd like to explore export opportu-*

nities. Can you give us some general advice on whether it's worthwhile or not?"

Many companies that do business overseas show surprising profit figures, usually greater than from domestic sales. The U.S. government is encouraging exports, especially by the many smaller businesses. The SBA and Department of Commerce especially have many valuable publications, conferences, and expositions that are low-cost, educational, and afford great networking opportunities with other experienced and novice exporters. It would also be useful to contact your nearest SCORE office to see if an international trade expert is on staff to consult, free of charge and in confidence, with you. Some general advice when considering exporting:

- Sell only quality products that will encourage repeat business and require little or no maintenance.
- Make a decision to get into exporting for a long time, not just for a short trial period.
- Make use of all the government help available—both federal and state—and do as much networking with other, noncompeting manufacturers as you can.
- Take time to establish a good, active, honest distributor abroad and be careful of signing any agreements whose interpretation might be different from what you expect in the U.S.
- Factor in the use of a professional export agent and rely on his expertise.
- Have any promotional literature and letters translated by professionals.
- Use rapid means of communication because speed is often of the essence in consummating an overseas deal. Use of a fax or telex is important, even if you have to lease time on them from an outside office.
- Transfer of money prior to commitment or shipment is vital. Rely on a local bank that has export facilities and expertise and include that cost into your price.

Get SBA's free information sheet 7 on "Opportunities in Exporting" for more information. A sound investment will indubitably be a subscription to *Business America, the Magazine of International Trade,* published every other week by the U.S. Department of Commerce. It is $49 a year from the Superintendent of Documents, U.S. Government Printing Office, Washington, DC 20402 (order no. S/N 703-011-00000-4). Another useful booklet is "Exporter's Guide to Federal Resources for Small Business" also from the preceding source (order no. S/N 045-000-00250-1).

FAMILY BUSINESS

Q: *"When my kids grow old enough, I would like to think that they'll come into the business and eventually be able to take over. I don't want them to be fighting about their roles in the business. What can I do early on to make such a move smooth and friendly?"*

To build up a business and pass it on to one's children and then be able to retire, or mostly retire, with a continuing income, is the dream of many entrepreneurs. Sometimes these plans work; sometimes they are shattered by jealousy, ineptitude, and in-law children who come into the family. The term "family businesses" no longer connotes the optimistic expectations that it once did. There are few entrepreneurial dynasties at the end of the twentieth century. However, it is still possible to create a continuing family business if you lay the groundwork as carefully as you would for a partnership. For example, it is considered advisable that the heir-apparent go to work for another preferably competing company prior to joining the family business. Gaining experience there, rather than in the cushiony family business, will serve the prospective head of the business well. Other problems to consider early in long-range planning for family businesses:

- Possible charges of nepotism from your unrelated key employees and the necessity for extra efforts on your part to be fair with everyone in terms of salary and responsibility.
- Sibling rivalry among children who are also working in the business, or even who are not working in the business.
- Protecting yourself in case of illness or retirement: have a qualified impartial lawyer draw up agreements to offer you that protection unequivocally, including a way of protecting yourself if the continuing sibling reneges on the family agreement. Consider this scenario: you've retired after 60 or 65 and expect the business to pay you that expected "pension," but junior says the business can no longer afford that plus allow him to send his kids to college. How can you remonstrate? Such catch-22 situations are all too common and are making some lawyers rich (and entrepreneurs poor!)
- Making provisions for the "child's" departure, if he or she should decide to leave, yet keeping the door open and family relations intact.

- Setting a policy for earning shares in the business and for compensation (e.g., requiring the sibling to earn raises just as do unrelated employees), and establishing the policy for other siblings or relatives to enter the business or to limit the latter's entry into it.

A family business can be a potent and satisfying organization, if it works. Realistic advance planning, sometimes with the help of a dispassionate outside counselor, can make it so. However, a "prenuptial" agreement is even more vital than in a mature marriage. Although blood may be thicker than water, money is a very divisive agent.

Remember that only one-third of all family-owned businesses remain family-owned past the first generation! Read also the SBA's booklet, "Problems in Managing a Family-Owned Business" (publication MP-3).

FINANCING—*Accounts Receivable (A/R) Financing*

Q: *"I need to raise some cash and want to look into accounts receivables financing. Can you tell me roughly how that works?"*

There are three ways to obtain quick cash from your accounts receivable: 1) Get an advance of 70 to 80 percent (depending on age and size of accounts) from a bank or commercial finance company against your A/Rs. Arrangements can be made on a notification basis (when your customers will be informed to send all remittance to the accounts-receivable financier) or on a nonnotification basis (when customers continue to send payments to you but then you need to make payments to the lender—providing you have adequate A/Rs covering the loan). 2) Construction loans for the construction of commercial property are drawn as the building progresses and repaid from ultimate permanent financing, usually through a bank or savings and loan association. 3) Commercial paper is a financing tool mostly for larger companies. Smaller companies with a good track record and sound banking relations can often obtain surrogate backing from their bank by means of a payment guarantee or an irrevocable letter of credit. There is usually a one to one-and-a-half percent fee for the latter service.

FINANCING—*Asset-Based Loans*

Q: *"Our small company needs occasional infusions of seasonal funds. Money supply is tight but we have a sizable investment in property and equipment. What do you think is the best way to borrow short-term money?"*

Asset-based lenders might be your best bet. These lenders make loans based on accounts receivable, inventory, real estate, and equipment. They look beyond the traditional numbers of balance sheets, financial statements, and traditional credit analysis. The asset-based lender accepts a pledge of a borrower's assets. An asset-based lender can be helpful especially when you have problems with timing and cash flow. Businesses that are cyclical or seasonal in nature can benefit from this source especially. Asset-based lenders usually work faster. They don't have the cumbersome bureaucracy and regulatory restrictions to contend with. They can tailor loans quickly to the specific requirements of the borrower in order to take advantage of seasonal lulls or discounts on sudden purchases, make rapid acquisitions, or recover from momentary setbacks. It is likely that an asset-based loan will cost a little more than a bank loan, but its advantages at the time you need it may outweigh that slight differential in cost. There are about 240 such lenders, and your bank can lead you to them—many of them are owned by banks. Asset-based lenders consider themselves more as partners than bankers or creditors. It will be useful to you to establish a personal and long-term relationship with one.

FINANCING—*Blue Sky Laws*

Q: "What are Blue Sky Laws that affect selling stock?"

Blue Sky laws are laws of the various states in which a company wishes to sell its securities. These laws require that a company's attorneys file a registration in each state. Often these state laws are different from the national SEC regulations. Of course these laws add to the cost and time of going public, but they are necessary and give each state some prerogatives in how the sale of stock to the public is handled. For more detailed information, see the entry FINANCING—*Going Public.*

FINANCING—*Business Loans*

Q: "What kind of a deal can we look for in getting a business loan for our company? We've been in business for more than five years but realize that we must move forward."

The SBA has a program of loan guarantees for qualified small businesses that backs up to $750,000 in borrowed capital through thousands of

SBA-approved financial institutions. As an example, there is a savings bank in South Florida that specializes in professional loans to entrepreneurs who own their own building and/or equipment. Their loan offerings include

- 25-year no-balloon loans on real estate
- 7- to 10-year no-balloon commercial loans
- Financing up to $900,000 with $750,000 guarantee by the SBA program
- Fees under two percent of the total loan with no prepayment penalties

The latter provision can be important if the loan enables a business to expand more rapidly and accumulate assets quicker than planned. It is certainly kinder than the more persistent involvement of venture capitalists. Another good deal to consider is a link with a Certified Development Company. There are about 400 of them throughout the U.S.—they are public-private investment groups composed of local lenders, banks, and the SBA. The local CDCs are interested in fostering business in their communities. The major criteria for a favorable CDC loan is that for each $15,000 lent, the borrowing company must create one new job or prove the retention of an old one that might otherwise have been lost. Minimum loans are $50,000; averages are $1 to $2 million. Borrowers typically put up 10 percent of the loan, backed by property, machinery, equipment, or fixtures.

FINANCING—*Delinquency*

Q: *"Frankly, I'm almost embarrassed to ask this question, but I have a SBA-guaranteed loan and my business has slowed so much that I am hard put to keep up payments. Is there anyone with whom I can discuss my situation?"*

It is better to discuss possible delinquencies and bankruptcy than to wait until it is too late for rescucitation. The SBA-affiliated association, SCORE, has had considerable successes in hardship turnarounds. As an example, in San Francisco during 1988, about 30 businesses were registered with SCORE as being in trouble. The local SCORE (Service Corps of Retired Executives) put together an ICU (Intensive Counseling Unit), which usually includes a former accountant or financier and does in-depth consulting with the business that has encountered problems it can no longer solve by itself. Out of these 30 cases, 10 went bankrupt and had to be liquidated, because their status had so far deteriorated or they came to SCORE's attention too late. But of the other 20, all are still in business. They either have paid off their loans in full, are current in their loan payments, or are still making payments as best as they can. This kind of experienced, pragmatic, but cost-free counseling can be of inestimable value. It is completely confidential, but should commence as soon as signs of problems become apparent.

FINANCING—*Financial Planning*

Q: *"I know what I'm taking in but I never have anything to show for it at the end of the month. I don't know where the money goes. Is there anyone I can consult to get me straightened out?"*

It appears that what you need is to consult a personal planner or an accountant who can analyze your cash flow. One of the first steps to take on your own is to do a cash flow statement so that you can accurately keep track what's coming in and what's going out. The SBA's booklet "Understanding Cash Flow" (publication FM-4) will be a good start. You can begin right now. Pick a time period, for example, the next three months. Put down every single expenditure for your business and what you take out of it. Budget balancing is a detective job: trying to find all those little leaks, all those seemingly insignificant trips to the till or the checkbook that add up to big red figures at the end of the month. Busy people have excuses that they need to reward themselves for working hard by eating out more often, taking costlier vacations, spending extra for conveniences. That's how you can get on a treadmill—work harder, spend more, have less to show for it all. If you keep track of *all* expenses you will get a better handle on the problem. Somehow, in black-and-white, those figures will begin to look more realistic and enable you to make rational decisions on where to cut expenses, how to reorder your priorities, where to charge more, or stop wasting productive time. And perhaps a $10 dinner will taste just as good as a $25 one?

FINANCING—*Going Public*

Q: *"What is involved when a small but fast-growing company wants to go public?"*

The most critical factors in determining whether to go public—that is, sell stock to outsiders in order to raise working capital—are the sizable costs involved. There are at least six areas of expenses that need to be considered:

1. Underwriters' fees
2. Legal fees
3. Accounting fees
4. Printing costs
5. Registration fees
6. "Blue sky" filing fees

As in the operation of any business, a key factor in a company's ability to go public is its public image. That image is determined by its management. The first people to whom the company's image needs to be sold are the lawyer, the accountant, and the banker, all of whom should be knowledgeable about security sales requirements and convinced that your company can indeed successfully meet all the many demands of issuing public stock.

The next group that needs to be contacted and convinced is the Securities and Exchange Commission (SEC). A registration statement needs to be filed with this agency and needs to be cleared before any stock shares can legally be sold. The next step is the selection of the underwriting firm that will actually advertise the stock to the public, and sell it, evaluate the issuing company, and suggest changes in company structure that will make the stock offering more attractive. All this will take from 60 to 90 days, and possibly longer if additional questions are asked and further information and substantiation of claims demanded.

A preliminary prospectus called a "red herring" is usually distributed by the prime underwriting company to other underwriters. It is a networking move that will help sell the stock through other brokers—something like a multiple-listing in real estate. While this presale activity goes on, attorneys may prepare a "Blue Sky Memorandum" that goes to each state in which the stock issue will be offered. It is necessary to comply with regulations within the state that might be different from the SEC's national regulations.

All these reviews, filings, and printings will take at least an additional 60 days between the time the registration statement is filed and the signing of the formal and final agreement between the company and the underwriter, upon which information dissemination and sale can begin. Two hundred fifty thousand dollars in costs for the entire process is not unusual. The very complexity and cost involved in the process of going public demand much advance study and preparation and a team of experienced advisors on your team.

FINANCING—*IRA*

Q: *"I have a small business and don't really have enough left over to have a pension fund. How much would I accumulate through an IRA plan?"*

A federal tax-deferred savings plan, like the IRA plan, allows you to save $2,000 annually, taken out of earnings. Based on average current interest rates, you would save the following sums over the stated periods of time:

After 10 years	$32,096
15 years	60,986
20 years	104,324
25 years	169,330

After you reach age 59½ and before 70½, you have to plan taking specific sums out of the IRA account. These withdrawals will be taxable during the year of each withdrawal.

FINANCING—*Over-the-Counter*

Q: *"What does it take for a small company to be listed on the OTC?"*

The OTC, or Over-the-Counter stock exchange, is an automated trading system information network that provides price and volume information on securities traded over the counter. It is operated by the National Association of Securities Dealers and is listed as NASDAQ. There are about 300 members. It costs $1,000 as a one-time entry fee plus additional fees that vary with the size of the offering. Since listing on the New York Stock Exchange costs $37,470 as a starter, the OTC listing is composed primarily of smaller companies.

FINANCING—*Venture Capital*

Q: *"What are venture capitalists and how do they work?"*

Venture capital firms are privately owned investment groups that seek to invest money in fast-growth businesses that produce high rates of return. These groups might be conglomerates of wealthy individuals, institutions, licensed Small Business Investment Corporations (SBICs), or subsidiaries of lending institutions. Venture capitalists expect a return on their portfolio of 25 to 30 percent because many of their investments are in new ventures that are prone to a high failure rate. There are venture capital groups that focus on high-technology businesses, on environmentally oriented companies, and on new and established companies that want to market a promising and possibly innovative new product.

From the entrepreneur's viewpoint, the high price of such money should also bring with it specific expertise in your field. Many venture capitalists will insist on becoming equity partners and will thus de facto as well as de jure be your partners. This could become a burden or, if they are experts in your field, a great asset. Other venture financing can be in stages—as you need money to bring a new product from the R&D stage to marketing and profiting. Or it could be a lump-sum deal to finance a major expansion. It is very difficult to structure such a deal and will take considerable experience and often outside counsel. It can make money for both parties, or become the proverbial Faustian deal with the devil.

FINANCING—*Venture Capital Variations*

Q: *"What are various ways venture capital investors put money into small companies with big potential?"*

There are lump-sum investments, used primarily for expansion of a business by acquisition or building; stage investments, which release part of a committed larger sum as the product progresses to market; debt obligation financing, which usually has a conversion-to-equity clause in its contract; and equity financing, which is more speculative but carries the possibility of partial ownership for the investors. The topic is discussed in some detail also in the preceding entry FI-NANCING—Venture Capital. See also the "Directory of Venture Capital Clubs" at your library (or contact P.O. Box 1333, Stamford, CT 06904) or the directory of the National Association of Small Business Investment Corporation (618 Washington Building, Washington, DC 20005), or National Venture Capital Association directory (1225 19th St., NW, Washington, DC 20036).

FRANCHISING—*Evaluations*

Q: *"Should I go into business with a franchise, and how can I be sure I buy a good one?"*

The remarkable survival record of franchised businesses has helped the growth of this form of entrepreneurship by leaps and bounds. It seems as if almost every business that can grow into three units wants to franchise itself and grow rich. Franchise opportunities should be studied as carefully as going into a business on your own. There is plenty of help, however. In every major city, franchise fairs offer the opportunity to meet representatives of franchisors, see examples and displays, and get details on entry costs and continuing fees, advertising, and training support. The SBA booklet "Evaluating Franchise Opportunities" (publication MP 26) is one place to start. Make an appointment with a local SCORE counselor or see what you can find out about a specific franchise from the chamber of commerce or from a franchisee in a nearby town. The U.S. Department of Commerce publishes the "Franchise Opportunities Handbook" that gives you a complete checklist of questions to ask, a franchise contract, and details about the Federal Trade Commission's disclosure statement. Contact the International Franchise Association at 1350 New York Ave., NW, Washington, DC 20005, for available information, including attorneys that specialize in franchise contracts. *Entrepreneur* and *INC.* magazines are also good sources of information. Remember that to buy a franchise demands an upfront fee of $500 to $100,000 and proof of financial liquidity of four to five times that amount.

FRANCHISING—*Headstarts*

Q: *"I have $65,000 available to start a business, but I don't have a financing or accounting background. Do you think buying a franchise will afford me a better chance than starting a business of my own?"*

Franchises do have a better chance of succeeding and staying in business, because of the experience, name-recognition, and training provided by the franchisor. However, buying a franchise is not accompanied by a guarantee for success. You need to have a well-honed business sense, do considerable research, learn in a hurry what the franchise business is all about, and have a temporary partnership with an experienced accountant and lawyer who will make sure your franchise agreement is affordable and will give you everything you expect. One of the best ways to assure that you are buying the right franchise is to talk to franchisors who are already operating such a franchise, but in areas that are noncompetitive with the one in which you plan to open shop. The International Franchise Association in Washington, DC, is growing by leaps and bounds because more and more companies are looking to the franchise route for expansion of their businesses—i.e., using other entrepreneurs' money to expand their own operations. Of the $65,000 mentioned above, probably not more than 10–25 percent should go into the franchise fee. The rest can be divided into halves— 50 percent for acquisition of merchandise or materials, 50 percent for overhead until the business starts producing income. These are general figures subject to many variables, but especially predicated on your ability to learn quickly, pick the right location, and do intelligent marketing.

FRANCHISING—*Information*

Q: *"I have heard that franchise businesses have a much higher rate of success than independent businesses. How can I get some unbiased information on franchises?"*

The survival rate of franchised businesses compared to independent businesses is phenomenal. One or two percent of franchised businesses go bankrupt during the first few crucial years, whereas independent businesses suffer an 80 percent bankruptcy rate during the first five years. The reason for this is that the franchise business is based on a proven principle and method of operation. It has built in a great deal of quality control, training, promotion, recognition factor among the public, and, frequently, continuing support beyond the grand opening. It is also likely that some of the better-known franchises will not want to see one of their franchisees go broke, and they might step in with fresh management help, or even buy out the old franchisee and replace him with a more competent one. Buying a franchise, however, is not for everyone. The entrepreneur is not always inclined to follow in someone else's footsteps or have his modus operandi dictated by a stranger. It often takes considerable up-front money to buy a franchise and continuing fees and royalties to maintain it—a fact of life resented by many franchisees once their business seems to be running well. Although every major city will have periodic franchise shows at which franchisors display their products and try to parlay their advantages into contracts, you should go beyond that introductory level and investigate the large body of information that has been written on this modern merchandising phenomenon before you invest the first dollar or sign any agreements. There are attorneys and accountants who can be consulted and whose fees will be well-earned in comparison to the cost of buying a franchise. The local chamber of commerce and SCORE office will have additional information. Studying an actual operation of your franchise choice, or asking pertinent questions of a current franchisee who is located in a noncompetitive area, will bring the surest and most pragmatic information. The following government and privately printed publications offer partial reference to the growing library of franchising information:

"Evaluating Franchise Opportunities," (publication MP 26) SBA
"Starting and Managing a Small Business of Your Own, Volume 1." (publication 0-370-969:QL3 SBA). Available from Superintendent of Documents, U.S. Government Printing Office, Washington, DC 20402-9325

FTC Rule 436 (disclosure information that franchisors must divulge) and "Advice for Persons Who Are Considering an Investment in a Franchise Business" (Consumer Bulletin No. 4) from the Program Advisor, Franchise and Business Opportunities Program, FTC, Washington, DC 20580 or phone 202 326-3128

Franchise Opportunities Handbook, U.S. Department of Commerce, at libraries or U.S. Government Bookstores

Planning and Forming Your Company, Gustav Berle (John Wiley & Sons, Inc., 1990) includes the chapter "How to Buy a Franchise," which has 47-point checklist and 20-point disclosure statement checklist (Chapter 4)

FRANCHISING—*Pitfalls*

Q: *"I have talked to the owners of many different franchises and have heard a mixed bag of problems and complaints. Do you have a checklist of pitfalls to watch out for?"*

Take a close look at the answers to the other Franchising questions in this book to get a feel for the pros and cons of buying a franchise—either from a franchisor or from an existing franchisee. Here is a brief checklist of caveats that you need to keep handy for further investigations and negotiations:

- Cost is the first consideration. Can you afford the franchise? Will you have enough capital left over to operate the business? How does the cost of the franchise relate to your potential profits? What are the post-contract costs?
- Continuing expenses can be incurred by building a structure for the franchise, buying products from the franchisor at an increased cost, and paying a percentage to the franchisor for national promotion that might not be commensurately beneficial to you locally.
- Find out how much support you will receive from the franchisor. Will it train you and your employees? Be sure you know the responsibilities you will have to each other. For instance, will the franchisor guarantee the loan on your mandated building, when you alone might not be able to get such a loan commitment?

- When talking to other, noncompetitive franchisees for the same company try to determine the actual net profit they earn. What percentage goes to the franchise? Who works for whom?
- Find out if your location-to-be is protected by a noncompete agreement which prohibits the franchisor from selling to other franchisees within a specific radius. Has the franchisor stuck to this promise with previous franchisees?
- Do your homework thoroughly, ask all the questions up-front while you are still in the driver's seat, and then have an experienced attorney on your side to negotiate the best possible deal for you.

FRANCHISING—*A Team Effort*

Q: "*I am bothered by the fact that a pretty large sum of money is paid up front to get a franchise. How do I know what I'll be getting after I make the payment and sign on the dotted line?*"

There is no doubt that a sound, well-established franchise operation can give new businesses a faster start and assure greater longevity. As when purchasing anything of that magnitude, you need to check out the deal *before*, not after, the fact. There are two very important steps in your presigning survey: 1) Talk to existing franchisees who have been in business for a while—especially those in nearby communities who do not consider you a potential competitor. Observe how well their business is doing and how happy they are with their franchisor. 2) Visit the franchisor at their home office or company-owned location(s). See how smoothly they operate; how well they mesh with your own philosophy and desire to do business; how well you think you can work under their banner. All this investigation can go on prior to any serious contractual negotiation. Training-time and effort and continuing management assistance, spelled out in the franchise agreement, are very important. That, after all, is part of the value of buying a franchise: getting high-powered, proven business expertise at the crucial start-up time. It's like a booster rocket that can be jettisoned after you safely reach your orbit. See also the SBA booklet "Evaluating Franchise Opportunities" (publication MP 26); *How to Buy a Franchise That's Right for You* by Steven Raab (John Wiley & Sons, Inc., 1988); *The Insider's Guide to Franchising* by Bryce Webster (AMACOM, 1988).

FRANCHISING—*Types of Businesses*

Q: "*What types of franchises are the most popular? I am interested in buying a franchise.*"

The type of franchise business to buy—or, for that matter, the start of any business—should depend primarily on your ability, experience, and interest. Here is a statistical breakdown of franchise firms' share of the market in percent of all franchises:

Type of Business	*Percent of all Franchises*
1. Restaurants	23.4
2. Auto products and services	14.5
3. Home improvement, Cleaning, Construction	13.4
4. General retailing	11.8
5. Business aids and services	10.9
6. Convenience stores	10.0
7. All others	16.0

GOVERNMENT—*Information (Toll-Free Numbers)*

Q: *"Occasionally, we want to check with other federal agencies. Don't most of them have toll-free numbers that one can call?"*

Most federal agencies have so-called hot lines that are toll-free from anywhere in the United States. A list follows. However, you can often get a satisfactory answer about small business problems from a local SBA or SCORE office; about taxes from a local IRS office; or answers to many questions even from the reference librarian at your local library. The nearest office of your elected U.S. senator and congressman can frequently be of great help. However, if no local resource can satisfy your needs, formulate your requirements clearly and call one of these toll-free numbers on the following page.

GOVERNMENT—*Publications*

Q: *"The government publishes reams of books and pamphlets on just about any business subject, I hear. How can I see what is available and what they cost?"*

We are glad you asked. Getting information is the first step in any business move. Your nearest SBA or SCORE office has lists of available

U.S. Government Toll-Free Numbers

Agency	Number
Agriculture Fraud Hotline	800 424-9121
Commerce Department Fraud Hotline	800 424-5197
Consumer Product Safety Commission	800 638-2772
Defense Fraud Hotline	800 424-9098
Energy Inquiry and Referral (Energy Department)	800-523-2929
EPA Hazardous Waste Hotline	800 424-9346
EPA Industry Assistance Hotline	800-424-9065
EPA Small Business Hotline	800 368-5888
Export-Import Bank	800 424-5201
Fair Housing and Equal Opportunity (HUD)	800 424-8590
Federal Crime Insurance	800 638-8780
Federal Deposit Insurance Corporation	800 424-5488
Federal Home Loan Bank Board	800 424-5405
Flood Insurance	800 638-6620
General Accounting Office Fraud Hotline	800 424-5454
Health Info Clearinghouse (HHS)	800 336-4797
Highway Traffic Safety Administration	800 424-9393
Housing Discrimination Hotline (HUD)	800 424-8590
Interior Department Fraud Hotline	800 424-5081
Internal Revenue Service	800 829-1040
Labor Fraud Hotline	800 424-5409
National Consumer Co-Op Bank	800 424-2481
National Health Information Hotline	800-336-4797
Overseas Private Investment Corporation	800 424-6742
Small Business Answer Desk	800 827-5722
Talking Books Program (Library of Congress)	800 424-9100
Veterans Administration (by state)	(ask operator)
Women's Economic Development Corps	800 222-2933

publications that are either free or available at nominal cost—ask for SBA Form 115A. The government also runs bookstores all over the country where you can inspect and buy every conceivable book. See the complete list of U.S. Government Bookstores in the Appendix of this book. The U.S. Government Printing Office, Superintendent of Documents, Washington, DC 20402, has more than 15,000 titles available free and for purchase. Write for free "Subject Bibliography" Forms SB-307 on Small Business and SB-090 on Federal Government Forms. In addition, the federal government maintains 42 information centers throughout the United States. For the complete list and their toll-free numbers, see Appendix C, Federal Information Center Program.

GOVERNMENT PROCUREMENT—*Bidding*

Q: *"What is this Form SF-129 that you need in order to sell to the U.S. Government?"*

Standard Form-129 is the Bidder's Mailing List Application. It is for individuals or firms who wish to be added to a particular agency's bidders' list for equipment, supplies, materials, and/or services. This completed form should be filed with each agency with which you wish to do business. Two publications will be useful in completing this form as well as understanding how to do business with the U.S. government:

> "U.S. Government Purchasing and Sales Directory"
> "Selling to the Military"

If the local SBA or SCORE office does not have them, you can order the first from the Superintendent of Documents, U.S. Government Printing Office, Washington, DC 20402, and the second one from the Publication Section, Department of Defense, Washington, DC 20301.

Another useful reference is a book written by a former procurement officer, *The Entrepreneur's Guide to Doing Business with the Federal Government*, by Charles R. Bevers with Linda G. Christie and Lynn R. Price (Prentice Hall, Inc., 1989).

GOVERNMENT PROCUREMENT—*Directory*

Q: *"How can I locate the specific agency and purchasing officer for my products?"*

As you can imagine, the government's procurement operation is a gigantic one. More than 20 million purchases are made each year, totaling around $17 billion during an average twelve months. You will have to do a little digging through their Directory (see below) to come up with the specific information you seek; however, it will no doubt be worth the effort. Check the alphabetical listing for the title of your product or service category. Try to find the broad classification in which it is most likely included. Each is followed by one or more numbers. The purchasing office—military or civilian—designated by these numbers can be identified by referring to the appropriate listings in the Directory.

Then turn to Part II of the Directory for the listings of military purchasing offices, or the listings of civilian purchasing offices in Part IV.

The Directory also contains other information on selling to the government, local purchasing, research and development, specifications, government property sales, a listing of government offices, and various forms. "The U.S. Government Purchasing and Sales Directory" can be purchased at any U.S. Government Bookstore (of which there are 24; see APPENDIX E for U.S. Government Book Stores) or ordered from the Superintendent of Documents, U.S. Government Printing Office, Washington, DC 20401.

GOVERNMENT PROCUREMENT—*General Services Administration (GSA)*

Q: *"I understand that a great deal of procurement for various government offices is done through the GSA. Where can I get information on what the government is buying and how to execute contracts?"*

Many SBA and SCORE offices throughout the country have knowledgeable counselors who will advise you free of charge on government procurement procedures and contracting opportunities. The GSA itself maintains 13 Business Service Centers in addition to the national office in Washington, DC. Each office covers a district encompassing several states. The complete list is printed below. See also other entries in this book under the heading GOVERNMENT PROCUREMENT for further information.

GOVERNMENT PROCUREMENT—*Procurement Automated Source System (PASS) Registration*

Q: *"As a subcontractor, should I join the PASS registration?"*

PASS offers smaller businesses an additional opportunity to be contacted by buyers. PASS is the Procurement Automated Source System that enters firms who register with it into a computerized system. This system is called upon by buyers when they need to find small business resources for their buyers' lists. To be included in the PASS system, a firm should register with one of the SBA procurement specialists. The central Office of Procurement and Grants Management is located at 409 Third St., S.W., Washington, DC 20416; phone 202 205-6460. All regional offices also have procurement specialists who may be called upon to assist in the proper registration. The service is free.

PASS was designed in 1978 to establish a centralized computer-

U.S. General Services Administration Business Service Centers

Region	Address	Telephone
National Capital Region Washington, DC 20407	7th and D Sts., S.W.	202 472-1804
1. Boston, MA 02109	John W. McCormack Federal Building	617 223-2868
2. New York, NY 10278	26 Federal Plaza	212 264-1234
3. Philadelphia, PA 19107	9th and Market Sts.	215 597-9613
4. Atlanta, GA 30303	75 Spring St., S.W.	404 221-5103
5. Chicago, IL 60604	230 S. Dearborn St.	312 353-5383
6. Kansas City, MO 64131	1500 E. Bannister Rd.	816 926-7203
7. Fort Worth, TX 76102	819 Taylor St.	817 334-3284
8. Denver, CO 80225	Building No. 41 Denver Federal Center	303 234-2216
9. San Francisco, CA 94105	525 Market St.	415 974-9000
10. Los Angeles, CA 90012	300 N. Los Angeles	213 688-3210
11. Seattle, WA 96174	915 Second Ave.	206 442-5556

based inventory and referral system of small businesses interested in being a prime contractor or subcontractor for federal requirements. Using computers and remote video terminals, PASS furnishes sources by matching keywords that small firms have used to describe their capabilities, by SIC codes (Standard Industrial Classifications), Federal Supply Codes, or by DUNS numbers (see CONTRACTS—DUNS Identification in this book). Small business registered in this PASS system can also be found by geographic regions, specification, minority status, and quality assurance programs. Over 150,000 firms are registered. The SBA suggests, however, that PASS be used only to augment a company's regular marketing and sales efforts.

GOVERNMENT PROCUREMENT—*Set-Asides*

Q: *"What are small business set-asides?"*

"Set asides" are bids for government product and services limited to small businesses who are in a competitive situation. Where two or more small firms are available to furnish a product or service to the government, such a competitive situation exists, and firms are eligible to apply for set-aside contracts. If one small business has a monopoly on an item or service, this procedure does not apply. Usually the procurement officer determines if the criterion for a set-aside is met. SBA can intercede and assist the contracting officer in making a determination. Here are the 11 regional offices you can contact for help:

States/Region	Address/Phone
New England	60 Batterymarch, 10th Floor, Boston, MA 02110, 617 223-3162
NJ, NY	26 Federal Plaza, New York, NY 10278, 212 264-7770
Mid-Atlantic	Suite 646, West Lobby, 231 S. Asaphs Road, Bala Cynwyd, PA 19004, 215 596-0172
Southeast	1375 Peachtree St., 5th Floor, Atlanta, GA 30367, 404 881-7587
IL, IN, MI, MN (east), OH, WI	219 S. Dearborn St., Rm. 858, Chicago, IL 60604 312 886-4727
AR, LA, MI, MN (west), OK, TX	8625 King George Drive, Bldg. C, Dallas, TX 75235-3391, 214 767-7639
IA, KS, MO, NE	911 Walnut St., 23rd Floor, Kansas City, MO 64106, 816 374-5502
Mountain States	1405 Curtis St., 22nd Floor, Denver, CO 80202, 303 837-5441
AZ, CA (south)	350 S. Figueroa St., 6th Floor, Los Angeles, CA 90071, 213 688-2946
CA (north), HI, NV	Box 36044, 450 Golden Gate Ave., San Francisco, CA 94102, 415 556-9616
Northwest and AK	4th & Vine Bldg., 2615 4th Ave., Seattle, WA 98121, 206 442-0390

GOVERNMENT PROCUREMENT—*Small Purchase Opportunities*

Q: "How do I find out about small purchase opportunities and procedures?"

The Federal Acquisition Regulations (FAR), Section 13 contain Small Purchase Procedures, under which the federal government purchases supplies, equipment, and services under $25,000. The purchase is invariably preceded by an informal oral or written solicitation from one to three potential suppliers. In order to become part of this small busi-

ness network of suppliers, firms interested in selling to the government
under FAR, Section 13, should either 1) make a personal visit to the
procurement offices of the federal agency with which they wish to deal,
or send a letter and brochure or catalog to that agency, attention Small
Purchase Section or, if they know a specific name, to the individual
buyer. There are federal facilities and installations all over the country.
The local SBA or SCORE office can be helpful in locating them, if you
do not already have their addresses. Ask for the SBA's brochure PA 3
(publication GPO 1988 0-216-005:QL 3) titled "Procurement Assistance." (See also SELLING TO THE GOVERNMENT.)

GOVERNMENT PROCUREMENT—*Subcontracting*

Q: *"Frankly, I don't think I am equipped to deal directly with the U.S.
Government, but I'd like to look into becoming a subcontractor. How
do I go about that?"*

Subcontracting is one the great opportunities for small and small disadvantaged businesses. Contracts that are less than $1,000,000 in the
construction of any public facility, or less than $500,000 in the case of
all other contracts, can be subcontracted directly with the prime contractor. However, when the contracts are more than these amounts,
even the subcontractor has to submit a production plan that becomes
part of the primary contract. When the prime contracts go over $500,000
and $1,000,000, respectively, the major contractor will arrange to
designate a Small Business Liaison Officer who administers the subcontracting program. "The Commerce Business Daily" is useful in identifying firms that offer subcontracting opportunities. The SBA also
publishes a directory of all these prime contractors, which includes
their address, description of product lines, and the name and telephone
number of an initial contact point for a small firm with subcontracting
interests and capabilities. This directory is available at all SBA regional
and field offices. (See also GOVERNMENT PROCUREMENT—PASS
Registration.)

HOME BUSINESSES—*Potential Problems*

Q: *"I want to start a business that I can run out of my home. My
spouse doesn't think it will work. Can you give me some advice on
how others have made out?"*

There are millions of men and women who start and often run successfully a small merchandise or service business from home. The

problems are less the location than the temptations to operate in an unbusinesslike manner. Quite aside from such considerations as zoning and permits, there are many personal facets whose impact and importance only you can assess. For instance,

- Do you have adequate space without interfering with your and your family's living space?
- Will your spouse and/or your children cooperate with you and the possibly rare occasions when a customer or client calls or visits?
- Do you have the self-discipline to actually work to get things done? To ignore the temptations of the refigerator? Other diversions? Visitors? Gossippy telephone calls?
- Are you a self-starter? Could you stand the occasional isolation? Will you get off your duff to go out and make customer or client calls?

You'll find more advice in the SBA information sheet 8, "How to Start a Home-Based Business," and "The Business Plan for Homebased Business" (publication MP 15). Also, "Starting and Managing a Business from Home" (USGPO 1988, 216-273/0); *The Home Office* by Peg Contrucci (Prentice-Hall/Spectrum); *The Do-It-Yourself Business Book* by Gustav Berle (John Wiley & Sons, Inc., 1989)

HOME BUSINESSES—*Personal Problems*

Q: "*My wife and I want to start our own business, operating from our home. What are the chances of our success?*"

The chances of succeeding with a home-based business are about the same as the chances of any other small business. About 80 percent of small businesses do not survive beyond the first five years. Home business are probably even more vulnerable. There are too many temptations (see HOME BUSINESSES—Potential Problems); a husband and wife working together could get on each other's nerves; customers or clients might not regard a home-based business with a great deal of respect or seriousness. While you might be able to conquer the first pitfall with good work habits and discipline, the second depends squarely on the husband-wife relationship before the home business is started. Remember the popular aphorism, "I married you for better or for worse, but not for lunch."

The third pitfall depends on the type of business you are planning to conduct and how important or unimportant it is for you to put up a businesslike, or professional, front. Many doctors, dentists, and professional services have done quite well when operating businesses from their homes—particularly in the suburbs or very small towns. The fiscal and time-saving advantages of the latter operations are substantial and, for many, worth the comparatively small risk. Pay particular attention to the personal relationship, because that will impact all other problems.

IMMIGRANTS' PROBLEMS

Q: "I came from Russia not long ago and want to become a capitalist. I have heard that the U.S. Government helps us go into business."

Many of the thousands of immigrants from around the world have business ambitions and have received advice and assistance from various local and national government departments. One specific instance occurred in the spring of 1990 in the town of Haverhill, Massachusetts. The local SCORE chapter was a participant in a job fair conducted by the town. More than 180 recent immigrants attended. They came from many walks of life—engineers, computer programmers, ship designers, and cabinet makers. They all spoke Russian and some English, as well as at least one other language, and all had one ambition: to go into a business of their own, something that had been denied them in their previous life in the USSR.

The local SCORE (Service Corps of Retired Executives) chapter, which is affiliated with the SBA, made four of their counselors available for a series of counseling sessions, both one-on-one sessions and workshops for groups of up to 40 attendees. Through these meetings, the immigrants learned about going into businesses in America, utilizing their talents, and how to watch out for the many pitfalls that entrepreneurship imposes in return for the possibility of independence and profits.

INCUBATORS—*Getting Information*

Q: "Can you tell me how I can get information on entering an incubator program to start a new business?"

Incubators are relatively new forms of small business. As the term implies, it is a way of nurturing a fledgeling business under the guidance of a larger, sponsoring organization. The following entry gives you more details. One of the greatest byproducts of being able to become an incubator business is the survival rate. It is considerably higher than trying to go it alone. In a recent survey, incubator businesses showed a survival rate of 83 percent over the first five years. As new-job creators, incubators were found to generate additional employment at less than $800 per new employee. More information and a useful newsletter are available from the National Business Incubation Association, One President Street, Athens, Ohio 45701, Dinah Atkins, executive director. Numerous state incubator associations also exist, as well as one organized by the National Rural Electric Cooperative Association in Washington, DC.

INCUBATORS—*How They Work*

Q: *"I've heard of business incubators. How do they work and where can I get more information on them?"*

Business incubators, like those used in baby nurseries and chicken hatcheries, help new and young businesses grow. These growth environments began only in 1984. The SBA helps the development of these business incubators through its Office of Private Sector Initiatives, located at 409 Third St., N.W., Washington, DC 20416. Most incubators focus on technology firms, which is one reason they are often located within or near universities where physical and academic services are easily available. It won't be long before a thousand incubator businesses will be in operation—sponsored by private and public investors in just about equal proportions. Often university professors and graduate students participate in the management of an incubator company, frequently made possible by substantial government funding. Incubator businesses are usually part of an informal group of entrepreneurs that share physical facilities, office and promotional purchases, professional services, shipping and warehousing facilities. Rentals in a common facility are reasonable, but often limited, because once the incubator company can fly on its own, it needs to leave the "nest" and make room for another start-up.

INFORMATION—*Federal Information Centers*

Q: *"As a taxpayer, I resent the vastness of our federal government. How can I get information with a minimum of confusion?"*

The vastness of the federal bureaucracy is merely a reflection of the vastness of our country. When our country was formed, only a few million people lived here. Today we are nearing the quarter-billion mark. Even the SBA had to computerize its popular "Answer Desk" because the number of calls, like yours, jumped from 50,000 to 85,000 to 250,000 in just a few years. (See ANSWER DESK as well Appendix E, titled U.S. GOVERNMENT BOOKSTORES.) The federal government, in response to its citizens seeking information, has established a large number of primarily toll-free telephone numbers. On the other end will be specialists who can help you find your way through the federal bureaucracy, reduce your time spent chasing information, and save your money. Here is a list of no less than 42 numbers, including a general, national number and even a number for the hearing-impaired citizen. Be mindful of the proximity of your elected federal representatives, your U.S. senator and U.S. congressman/congresswoman, who maintain offices in your state capital and can sometimes perform miracles in tracking down information.

A list of federal information center follows.

Turn to the Federal Information Center with your government question, no matter how simple or complex. If you would prefer to write, please mail your inquiry to Federal Information Center, P.O. 600, Cumberland, Maryland 21502.

If your metropolitan area or state is not listed below, please call 301 722-9098.

Users of telecommunications devices for the deaf (TDD/TTY) may reach the Federal Information Center by calling a toll-free number, 800 326-2996.

Alabama
Birmingham
Mobile
   800 366-2998

Alaska
Anchorage
   800 729-8003

Arizona
Phoenix
   800 359-3997

Arkansas
Little Rock
   800 366-2998

California
Los Angeles
San Diego
San Francisco
Santa Ana
   800 726-4995
Sacramento
   916 973-1695

Colorado
Colorado Springs
Denver
Pueblo
   800 359-3997

Connecticut
Hartford
New Haven
   800 347-1997

Florida
Fort Lauderdale
Jacksonville
Miami
Orlando
St. Petersburg
Tampa
West Palm Beach
　800 347-1997

Georgia
Atlanta
　800 347-1997

Hawaii
Honolulu
　800 733-5996

Illinois
Chicago
　800 366-2998

Indiana
Gary
　800 366-2998
Indianapolis
　800 347-1997

Iowa
From all points
　800 735-8004

Kansas
From all points
　800 735-8004

Kentucky
Louisville
　800 347-1997

Louisiana
New Orleans
　800 366-2998

Maryland
Baltimore
　800 347-1997

Massachusetts
Boston
　800 347-1997

Michigan
Detroit
Grand Rapids
　800 347-1997

Minnesota
Minneapolis
　800 366-2998

Missouri
St. Louis
　800 366-2998
From elsewhere
　in Missouri
　800 735-8004

Nebraska
Omaha
　800 366-2998
From elsewhere
　in Nebraska
　800 735-8004

New Jersey
Newark
Trenton
　800 347-1997

New Mexico
Albuquerque
　800 359-3997

New York
Albany
Buffalo
New York
Rochester
Syracuse
    800 347-1997

North Carolina
Charlotte
    800 347-1997

Ohio
Akron
Cincinnati
Cleveland
Columbus
Dayton
Toledo
    800 347-1997

Oklahoma
Oklahoma City
Tulsa
    800 366-2998

Oregon
Portland
    800 726-4995

Pennsylvania
Philadelphia
Pittsburgh
    800 347-1997

Rhode Island
Providence
    800 347-1997

Tennessee
Chattanooga
    800 347-1997
Memphis
Nashville
    800 366-2998

Texas
Austin
Dallas
Fort Worth
Houston
San Antonio
    800 366-2998

Utah
Salt Lake City
    800 359-3997

Virginia
Norfolk
Richmond
Roanoke
    800 347-1997

Washington
Seattle
Tacoma
    800 726-4995

Wisconsin
Milwaukee
    800 366-2998

INNOVATION—*Finding New Products*

Q: "We have a small technology company and know we need to expand. Can you give us some resources where we can locate innovations *and patents that can be obtained by transfer or reasonably purchased or licensed?"*

There are many resources that offer just what you are looking for. Two useful booklets from the SBA are

> "Can You Make Money with Your Idea or Invention" (publication PI-1)
> "Introduction to Patents" (publication PI-2)

These booklets list information and additional resources. The government's former Bureau of Standards, now called the National Institute of Standards and Technology, has a system of transfering useful technology to American businesses. You might want to visit them, especially their high-technology workshop, or write for information: Room A-617, Gaithersburg, MD 20899; or call them at 301 975-4009.

Another remarkable resource is the Directory of Federal and State Business Assistance, a very useful 170-page guidebook available at the library, the SBA offices, or directly from National Technology Information Service, U.S. Department of Commerce, Springfield, VA 22161 (PB88-100011/AAW).

INNOVATION—*Opportunity For*

Q: "Is there still opportunity to build the better mousetrap? It seems everything has already been invented."

This question was asked, no doubt, before Edison invented the light bulb or Ford put a production-model automobile on the road. Innovations are always in season, and as long as the human brain uses only a small portion, that other, larger part will come up with new and better mousetraps. In just one single year recently the following innovations were noted:

- Scientists have come close to devising a no-fault gene, and although they do not yet effect cures, they have improved diagnostic tests that can lead to proper treatment and eventual cures.
- IBM, not a Japanese lab, created a 4-million-bit memory chip that can hold more than 100 pages of typewritten material.
- Black and Decker converted a steam iron into a steam wallpaper stripping machine. It was a "first" that nobody else had thought of before.
- Campbell marketed a soup 'n sandwich combo that can be 'cooked'

in a microwave oven in seconds, because consumers had been ordering this combination in restaurants.

- A company revived the old periscope toy and made it into a sophisticated $50 sportscope that you can use in crowded stadiums, on hunting trips, and for just plain snooping.
- Sony has come out with a 28-oz. camcorder and Compaq with a 6-lb. laptop computer that has a truly visible screen working off a 3-hour battery.
- Zelco now makes an alarm clock that you can shut off merely by hitting a large pad, even with your eyes closed, and Samsonite is marketing a suitcase that piggybacks others and can go up and down curbs and stairs.
- Hanco redesigned the traditional squeegee into a handier, more effective one for use at gas stations, by window washers, and home users.
- Motorola has a working wristwatch pager, à la Dick Tracy, and on the other end of the innovation spectrum, Mary Anne Jackson, a mother of two girls, created health-conscious foods that are assuredly additive-free and sold in supermarkets as well as chain toy stores.
- Don Beaver's little company, New Pig Corp., devised electrostatic dustcloths for circuit boards and grease absorbing mitts and socks for janitorial crews—just because they were needed.
- Sometimes innovation means going backward to neglected truisms. Take Gerber Foods. They got into all kinds of diversifications before deciding that baby food is what they make best and are known for—and went back to concentrating on that. Profits now are better than ever. That, too, is innovation.

Yes, there is always room for a better mousetrap. Sometimes it is as simple as giving yourself a little time off to think, or to put two or three brains together in a little brainstorming, or putting up a suggestion box and a couple of incentives, and watch ideas come in from the builders of your own, but as yet hidden, better mousetraps.

INTERNATIONAL TRADE—*Expanding into Foreign Trade*

Q: *"I want to expand my business into foreign trade, export and direct import as well. How can the SBA help me get started?"*

As the government has become increasingly conscious of the need for more U.S. export activity, and because of the growing globalization of our world, foreign trade programs are also increasing steadily. There are a number of aids available directly and indirectly through the SBA that will help small businesses enter foreign trade. These include 1) publications, 2) conferences, and 3) referrals to outside information, both governmental and in the private sector.

1) Obtain the SBA booklet "Market Overseas with U.S. Government Help" (publication MT 10). "The States and Small Business" is a directory of programs and activities, including foreign trade, offered by the 50 States; it is published by the SBA (order 045-000-00257-8 from the GPO, Washington, DC 20402). "The World is Your Market" is a very useful export guide for small business, published jointly by the SBA and AT&T as a private/public sector initiative. An earlier book by the same team is the "Exporter's Guide to Federal Resources for Small Business." The U.S. Department of Commerce's International Trade Administration has published "A Basic Guide to Exporting" available also through the GPO or at U.S. Government Book Stores (GPO no. 242-320/04073). All the above resources and further study of government-sponsored publication lists will reveal many more valuable publications.

2) Conferences are held by both the SBA and the Department of Commerce, as well as by smaller agencies like the Export-Import Bank and OPIC. Organizations like SCORE and SBDC also conduct occasional workshops focusing on this topic, as do some larger chambers of commerce, trade associations, and trade publications. The value of such conferences and workshops is not only in listening to speeches and picking up literature, but in networking with those attending these events.

3) Referrals by SBA foreign trade experts also are valuable. Most major SCORE offices, for instance, have one or several counselors that are familiar with foreign trade and can help expedite your entry and progress in the field. Other sources worth checking out in your area are the chamber of commerce, foreign trade associations, universities giving foreign trade courses, bankers who do foreign trade business, other exporters and importers who handle noncompetitive products and services, consulates, and local offices of the Department of Commerce.

INTERNATIONAL TRADE—*Letters of Credit*

Q: *"How do I get a letter of credit to pay for merchandise I want to buy in Europe? And does the SBA help in any way to get me started?"*

A letter of credit (L/C) is in a way a loan from a commercial bank that handles this kind of business. It is a system of international credit that dates back to the old Rennaissance trading families of Italy. Virtually all of the nearly 20,000 small companies in the U.S. engaged in export and import use letters of credit. Basically, getting an L/C is like applying for a bank loan—it is in effect a short-term loan supported by documents showing details of the transaction and your collateral that assures the bank that they will be able to get their money back per your agreement. L/Cs usually go from your bank to a big bank that is known internationally. The creditworthiness of two banks thus assures that you will get paid—or vice versa, that your supplier will get paid. Between the time that an L/C is finally approved and the time the goods you ship arrive at the foreign destination, many weeks can pass (or vice versa in the case of imports). The terms of the L/C must be met exactly and any changes require new documentation. Today all such transactions can be made electronically once a relationship is established with your corresponding banks. You can obtain detailed help from the bank's international trade officer, from your local SBA field office, or from a SCORE counselor who is familiar with export-import procedures. The SBA also has an instrument called Export Revolving Line of Credit Program (ERLC). Under this system the SBA can guarantee up to $750,000 in credits (85 percent of the loan). With the Export-Import Bank as coguarantor, this loan can even be increased to $1,000,000. As on all loans, tight collateral is required and a ¼ percent user fee is charged on short-term loans of up to 12 months. Collateral must be located within the United States. It is doubtful that such short-term loans supporting letters of credit will go beyond one year, but if they do, there will be a charge of 2 percent on the balance of the loan guarantee. The U.S. Government is anxious to support export efforts and regional SBA officers will be available to see you through the seemingly mountainous obstacles of international trade until you get the hang of it.

LEASING

Q: "To lease or not to lease is my question. What are the tax advantages of each?"

A frank discussion with your accountant will show you the pros and cons at this time. Situations may change with current tax laws, with your capital availability, and with the operating needs of your particular business. A discussion with a SCORE counselor will be productive. Then, too, are you talking about leasing a building vs. buying a property? Leasing equipment vs. buying it outright? Even leasing employees vs.

hiring permanent ones? Each situation has pros and cons and must be analyzed individually and in terms of your own needs and preferences. The SBA booklet "Should You Lease or Buy Equipment?" (MP 8) provides a handy checklist of options. In general, leasing conserves limited capital funds. In the case of equipment, an open-end lease offers opportunities for having current equipment as it comes on the market, without having to worry about depreciation schedules, obsolescence, and resales. If equipment or property has a substantial equity value at the end of a lease term (5 to 10 years), then owning might be more advantageous—providing you have the cash to invest in the property in the first place. There are many variables that need to be calculated carefully. Because advantages and disadvantages are often subtle, the options must be carefully considered. A discussion with your financial advisor prior to signing any lease can offer your biggest saving.

LEGAL MATTERS—*Antitrust Problems*

Q: "*I have a small business that is being squeezed out by a big new chain. Is there anything I can do under the antitrust laws to prevent my going under?*"

Rendering such legal advice on the phone or by mail is quite impossible. You would need to consult a local attorney who can study the ramifications of your specific case. However, here is some general information that could be useful. The first step would be to obtain the SBA's booklet, "Antitrust for Small Business," published by the SBA's Office of Advocacy and available at SBA field offices, FTC offices, or Antitrust Division offices of the U.S. Department of Justice. A list of all offices is contained in the Appendix A of this book.

The Federal Trade Commission (FTC) and Justice Department (Antitrust Division) appear to be overlapping in their functions. The Justice Department alone can bring criminal sanctions against a violator of these laws; the FTC prosecutes civil cases. Both are concerned with preventing collusion among competitors and the abuse of market power. They attempt to provide an economic climate in which large and small firms alike can compete on the basis of their ability to serve American consumers.

There are four basic federal antitrust laws that have been enacted during the past century. The Sherman Act (1890) prohibits any "contract, combination, or conspiracy in restraint of trade and any monopolization, attempted monopolization, or conspiracy or combination to monopolize." Prosecution under the Sherman Act is only for "unreasonable" restraint of trade. Proven violators can be fined up to $100,000 individually and up to $1,000,000 for corporations.

The Clayton Act (1914) supplements the Sherman Act by applying its terms to lease and sale restrictions, as well as some mergers and acquisitions. Suits can be brought for up to triple damages.

The Federal Trade Commission Act (also 1914) prohibits "unfair methods of competition and unfair or deceptive acts or practices." It gives the Sherman Act more teeth.

The Robinson-Patman Act (1936) prohibits certain discriminatory practices, including pricing, services, and allowances in dealings between merchants. Discounts are allowed in order to meet competition, of course, and plaintiffs under this act must prove that discrimination may "substantially lessen competition or tend to create a monopoly." Criminal sanctions can be imposed upon violators if the purpose of violations is to destroy competition.

There are also state antitrust agencies that can bring "parens patriae" suits against violators under the various federal antitrust laws. If a suspicion exists that unfair trade practices might have seriously injured a local business, a first step would indeed be to check with the local state attorney general's office.

LEGAL MATTERS—*Business Organization*

Q: "I want to start a new business, but how do I know which legal structure is best for my needs?"

Basically, there are three options: sole proprietorship, partnership, or corporation. Each has its advantages and disadvantages. Your own lawyer or accountant can acquaint you with all of them and can, for a fee, prepare the proper papers and requirements under the laws of your state. A looseleaf compendium is available for each state, published by Oasis Press and probably available in the business section of a major local library. The SBA publishes "Selecting the Legal Structure for Your Business" (Management Aid Publication 6.994 or publication MP 25). Details are spelled out in *Planning and Forming Your Own Company* by Gustav Berle (John Wiley & Sons, Inc., 1990). The sole proprietorship is of course the simplest, requiring usually only a local license. It is easy to establish and costs little. Decisions can be made quickly, unilaterally, and flexibly. All the profits are the owner's. However, so are the liabilities, the responsibilities, the limited opportunities for raising money and, yes, the occasional loneliness "at the top." As sole proprietorships grow, they can be changed into the other available legal forms. Partnerships are like marriages and are fraught with the same problems and dangers, as well as comforts and advantages. Since most states have adopted a Uniform Partnership Act, it will be wise to check this out in your state. Business persons entering into a partnership should by all means prepare Articles of Partnership that spell out in great detail and clarity the duties and contributions, remunerations, and terms of withdrawal of each participant in the agreement. Corporations are artificial "beings" that eliminate or limit the liabilities of the firm's members. They are more complex and expensive to establish and subject to more rules and restrictions. *Planning and Forming Your Own Company*, has a table for each of the 50 states that details costs and addresses for corporate charter applications. Banks will often favor corporations in loan applications. In the legal formation of a business, it must also be realized that if the firm employs 10 or more people, it comes under the scrutiny of OSHA, the Occupational Safety and Health Administration. OSHA information can be obtained by writing to their Publications Office, Department of Labor, 200 Constitution Ave., NW, Room S1212, Washington, DC 20210. For legal information on income taxes, the IRS has a Business Tax Information Program that can be reached through a national toll-free line 800 829-1040.

LEGAL MATTERS—*Cost of Legal Service*

Q: *"I probably need to consult a lawyer in order to start up my business and get continuing legal advice, but I'm afraid of the high cost and whether I can afford it. Do you have any suggestions?"*

While the SBA does not provide legal advice except in the case of loan applications, some counseling can be obtained in general areas from SCORE or SBDC. There are many books at your library that are helpful—even if only to prepare you better to discuss your requirements intelligently with an attorney. Since lawyers usually work on a time basis, the better you are prepared, the less it will cost you. SBA's booklet "Selecting the Legal Structure of Your Business" (publication MP 25) and others listed in the SBA "Directory of Business Development Publications" (Form 115A) can be of help. Because even lawyers are not infallible, it is always wise to know a little about business laws, pertinent documents, and to have a clear understanding of what you need. This will be especially true in setting up a partnership or corporation, executing a lease, or creating an agreement with a key employee or representative. When setting up a relationship with an attorney, present your needs as candidly and clearly as you can, and find out in advance what costs are entailed and how they are determined. This will prevent future unhappiness and, worse, legal problems in the very matters in which you seek protection.

LEGAL MATTERS—*Free Service*

Q: *"Can SBA provide free legal counsel for the formation of my business?"*

SBA attorneys do not counsel on routine or general problems. For such counsel you need to turn to a legal aid society, your own family lawyer, or your banker's recommendation. The SBA's legal staff and its affiliated agencies can advise you on the various forms of business organization, however, and guide you in preparing certain details of loan applications. Legal counsel by SBA sources is very limited.

LEGAL MATTERS—*Incorporation*

Q: *"Should I incorporate my new small business? What are the pros and cons?"*

Look at the entries under LEGAL MATTERS—*Business Organization and Cost of Legal Service,* for references and suggested booklets. Whether to run your business as a personal proprietorship or corporation depends on financial and managerial questions. A corporation costs more to organize and requires more paperwork but provides a protective umbrella that safeguards your personal assets. If you need to borrow money or raise capital, a corporation is definitely preferred. If the kind of business involves some risk—such as a restaurant, food sales and service, drugs and pharmaceuticals, public transportation, or any area that could develop lawsuits against your business—then a corporation is mandatory. Of course, there are books that promise you incorporation for $50, but your local attorney might be preferable and surer. If you are at all unsure about this and want to get some second opinions, make an appointment with a counselor from the nearest SCORE office (it's free and confidential) and/or your state's office of business development or state department.

LEGAL MATTERS—*SBA Counseling*

Q: *"Does the SBA provide legal counsel to small businesses?"*

Only in cases involving loan applications. The SBA is mandated to help small business as well as the tax payer who furnishes the funds.

To make sure the small business applicant gets a fair hearing and, if warranted, loan guarantees that will enable him or her to go into business, the SBA legal staff works with the prime lender (usually a bank) to protect all parties involved. The SBA cannot become involved in the several hundred thousand cases that come to its attention each year, but suggests that family lawyers handle such situations. The SBA has several useful booklets that offer guidance, available at SBA and SCORE offices or by mail. As a starter, obtain the booklet "Selecting the Legal Structure for Your Business" (publication MP 25); "Curtailing Crime —Inside and Out" (publication CP 2); "A Small Business Guide to Computer Security" (publication CP 3); and "Introduction to Patents" (publication PI 2).

LEGAL MATTERS—*S Corporations*

Q: *"What is an S corporation? How is it different from a regular one?"*

The S corporation is more like a partnership. As a business entity it pays no income taxes, but earnings are passed on to its shareholders, who are then taxed in proportion to their holdings. Not all earnings need to be distributed, even though all earnings are taxed. The tax rates, too, are a little lower than regular corporate rates, being the same as individual proprietorships and partnerships. The same applies to capital gains taxes and losses. If losses occur, the shareholders can take those losses on their individual taxes. Because the S Corporation pays no taxes in itself, it can conserve capital during the start-up years and during recessive periods. Wealthy individuals, too, favor involvement in S corporations because they can take losses or pay a slightly lower tax than their corporations would. The complexity of this legal organization makes it desirable that a knowledgeable attorney handle incorporation and filing of such an entity.

LOANS—*Discrimination*

Q: *"How come the big guys can borrow millions and I have a hard time getting a small loan to start a business?"*

That's one of those loaded questions that's like wading through a snakepit. Big business people usually have a track record of successes or a lot of collateral like other property. Sometimes the property declines in value at a future time and then the loan collateral becomes endangered. If a national credit crunch compounds the problem, then a lender might sometimes call in the loan or force the big borrower into bankruptcy. No loan is 100 percent foolproof. Bankers, however, try to make sure that repayment sources are established beyond doubt and that the management expertise of the borrower is well proven. That's why banks sometimes appear as tough ogres and why the SBA at times tries to help out small business applicants by guaranteeing a loan. A banker or other lender will generally insist on certain basics from a potential borrower—just as the SBA now does—and these steps include:

1. A well-prepared business plan that proves that the borrower knows what he or she is doing, has a viable idea for a business, and can adequately manage that business.
2. Repayment of the loan within a stipulated time frame is what the bank and the SBA are ultimately interested in.
3. Collateral must exist that is realistically appraised as to its current cash value.
4. Personal and business credit must be above reproach and the backing of an SBA guarantee reinforces such a loan.

LOANS—*For Exporters*

Q: "We are considering exporting our products and heard that the SBA has a loan program especially tailored to promote exporting of American products. How does that work?"

Export Revolving Line of Credit (ERLC) loans are available only under the SBA's guaranty program to provide financial assistance to small business exporters. This program assists exporters in financing the manufacture or purchase of goods and services for export or for development of a foreign market. The borrower can make any number of withdrawals from his ERLC account and make repayments within the dollar and time limits of the loan. As a new exporter you will not be eligible, though after having been active in exporting for 12 months or more, you will be eligible by filing an application with your nearest regional SBA office. Loan proceeds can be used for materials and as well as services, professional assistance, foreign travel, and participation in trade shows. ERLC loans are limited to 18 months in length. Collateral has to be available—usually assignment of contract proceeds, accounts receivables, letters of credit, or other business and personal assets located in the United States. Guaranty fee for an ERLC loan is .25 percent of the guaranteed portion of the loan plus .25 percent for a lender's fee, providing repayment is made within 12 months. For maturities beyond 12 months, regular guaranty fees apply.

LOANS—*Pollution Control*

Q: *"Under the recent EPA laws, I might well have to replace a couple of underground tanks at a cost of $40,000. Can I borrow that from the SBA or get an SBA-backed loan?"*

Yes, the SBA has a Pollution Control Loan Program that provides financial assistance to small business for the planning, design, or installation of a pollution control facility. Loans are to be made only through lenders participating in the U.S. Small Business Administration's guarantee loan program, and will be guaranteed by the SBA. This program applies to all small businesses, except those engaged in rental real estate or newspapers, magazines, and schools. SBA will guarantee up to $1,000,000 of a loan to any one borrower, less any loan that might already be outstanding under the regular SBA lending program. Applications must include detailed plans, specifications, estimates, and copies of pertinent local regulations and EPA regulations. Check with your local SBA lender or SBA office for more details or contacts.

LOANS—*Proposals*

Q: *"Raising money for a small business is probably the toughest job. How should I go about writing a loan proposal that the bank regards seriously?"*

New business formations and small business expansions invariably require some outside financing, though that is not as universal as commonly believed. Many businesses are started very small—some service businesses with as little as $1500—or with financing gathered from family sources. If you go to an outside source such as a bank or investment group, you need to go through a complex and often frustrating process. Naturally, a professional, like a well-versed accountant, will be very helpful, but could also be expensive. A sum of $2,000 to $5,000 would probably be required to have a knowledgeable CPA prepare a professional loan proposal. There is much that you as the entrepreneur can do to accomplish this task yourself or to make the outside professional's job easier and less expensive. Follow these steps:

1. Explore all personal money sources first—your own mortgageable or collateralizable assets, friends, family, credit union, charge card limits, pension, or IRA/Keogh assets.
2. Determine exactly how much money you really need. The more

unneeded money you borrow, the more interest you will have to earn and the longer it will take to pay it back. Maybe you won't need as much as you think, or a line of credit will be sufficient.

3. Make a list of all assets, such as valuables, stocks and bonds, real estate, and other paid-up equipment and vehicles. Determine a realistic current value for them and then take 75 percent of that value. That is probably how much real collateral you can come up with.

4. Do you need the money for a short term or long term? Can the accounts receivable you have or will have be used as collateral or for factoring?

Once you have all the answers to these preparatory questions and you still want to draft a business loan proposal, the following information needs to be included in such a proposal:

1. General information: business name, principals, addresses, social security numbers; purpose of the loan exactly; how much money do you need and when and for what purpose.

2. Business description: detailed history of the business, employees, current assets, and proof of your legal structure.

3. Management profile: include each principal staff member, skills, accomplishments, and financial interest, if any.

4. Market information: product and market description, details on competition, profiles of your customers.

5. Financial information: balance sheet, income statement (for three years, if you have been in business that long), or a projection for the above if you are just starting out; personal financial statement for all owners; and a list of available collateral.

A crucial question that the loan officer will ask and that your proposal needs to answer: does the business have enough cash flow to make the monthly payments on the loan request?

A good resource for counseling to keep in mind: the nearest chapter of SCORE, the Service Corps of Retired Executives, where you can get free and unbiased counseling on the preparation of the loan proposal. Ask SCORE or your local SBA office for information sheet OBD #1 "How to Raise Money for a Small Business." It is free.

LOANS—*SBA Loan Guaranty Amounts*

Q: *"Are SBA loan guarantees still limited to half a million dollars?"*

No, SBA loan guarantees were increased to $750,000 a couple of years ago. SBA-guaranteed loans usually carry interest of up to 2.75 percent over prime and have maturities that vary from 12 months to 10 years, though loans for buildings can be extended to 25 years. In the cases where the borrower qualifies for a direct loan, a ceiling of $150,000 exists. The various loan programs to which these parameters apply include regular business loans, veterans' loans, handicapped loans, contract loans, seasonal line of credit loans, 7(a)11 loans, small general contractor loans, qualified employee trust loans, solar energy and conservation loans, and certified development company (CDC) loans.

LOANS—*Small Loans*

Q: *"I don't need or want a lot of money, but $25,000 would enable me to buy some new equipment that can allow me to continue in business and make some money. Yet banks don't want to talk about small loans like that. What now?"*

The SBA has a $50,000-and-under guaranteed loan provision that some banks might not be familiar with. It is not a separate program, but rather an inducement to lenders to make loans of $50,000 or under. Under this program the SBA splits its two percent guarantee fee with the participating lender. Check with your nearest SBA office and get a list of local banks that are SBA-approved lenders. Make sure that you have a good business plan and projection to prove that this loan will indeed do what you expect it to do—and how and when you can pay back the loan. Another source for loans, if this is an equipment loan, is through an approved Certified Development Company. Again, the nearest SBA office should have a list of the currently active ones in your area.

LOCATION—*Site Finding*

Q: *"How do I go about finding the right location for my planned retail business?"*

Most chain stores and franchisors, which are highly experienced in site finding, look at high-traffic locations, visible corners, and shopping malls as primary requisites. Although the rent in such select locations is considerably higher than off-street locations, the traffic generated by prime locations is worth the difference in rent. You have to look at rent payment as a certain percentage of total expected volume, not merely as one dollar figure compared to another lower dollar figure. Businesses that do not rely on prime locations are rare in retailing. Usually, if a customer has difficulty finding a store location, the entrepreneur has to advertise more heavily or pay more for an attention-getting sign, thus paying more than what he or she might otherwise have paid in higher rent. Be mindful also of three vital considerations in choosing a location that is suitable to your needs and type of business—that is, zoning, lease terms, and competition. You will need to add to these considerations a number of other criteria that have to be checked out one-by-one: road access; parking facilities; convenience of services such as delivery, utilities, and transportation; restrictions and costs of existing merchants associations; available publicity media; local labor availability; local taxes; weather protection; condition of the physical premises; reputation of the landlord; limitations on your own signage; other needs such as banks, restaurants, post office, automotive services, telephone availability; security provisions; and local municipal services like police and fire protection. One very important aspect that needs to be considered right up front: the demography of your customers. You have to consider who your customers are, where they come from, what specialized cultural or ethnic preference they have, what is their income and educational level—and then you have to match up all these facts with the kind of merchandise and service you plan to provide. A good way to start is to get a booklet from the SBA entitled "Locating or Relocating Your Business" (publication MP 2). Once you have studied the latter and answered all the questions of the previous criteria, you can talk to your realtor like a professional. Before you sign the lease—and it could be the single biggest commitment of your business life—be sure you know every single facet of your impending obligations. An eagle-eyed lawyer with experience in contracts and real estate could be worth his fee—in gold.

MAIL ORDER—*Motivation*

Q: "I started a small mail order business and have used low-cost classified ads in a number of publications. But I bombed out pretty much across the board. Can you advise me on what I evidently did wrong?"

One of the first steps would be to contact a local SCORE office and see if one of their members has experience in mail order selling. Such a consultation will be valuable and it is free. Mail order selling is like any other business and requires considerable investment, shrewd buying or producing, a markup between your total cost and your net returns that is generally higher than in traditional retailing, a mailing list that is current and has proven responsiveness, and a detailed record system that tells you how much a medium costs (such as magazines with mail order sections) vs. the returns you get from it. Since your ad or letter is the only contact between you and your potential customer, the words in that message must do a complete selling job that you would normally do in person. Few mail order ads can depend entirely on straight facts—or on reason. Most mail order copy must appeal to the emotions, because more sales are made for *imagined* or emotional reasons than for reasons of logic or necessity. Sears Roebuck and Company sells goods because the reader has specific needs. A casual reader who happens to glance at your ad in a magazine or receives an offering in the mail will respond more likely because of emotional appeals. Always sell the prime benefit of your product or service; don't confuse the casual reader with too many facts and rationales. Make it easy to order. Keep checking and testing and be flexible. And keep reading what the experts have to report.

MANAGEMENT—*Banking*

Q: *"We are a small-town financial institution and want to do something locally to bring the thrift ethic back to our customers. Do you have any case histories that could be useful?"*

A good place to start is with children. If you get them used to the idea of saving, of putting something away regularly, they will keep that habit for life. Not only that, but chances are that the children will influence their elders and thus become the pebble tossed into a pond of sound habits. You might discuss a savings plan with the principal of your local elementary school or schools. Set up a minimum weekly contribution, ask one of the teachers to act as the agent within the school, make a presentation at the school assembly as well as before the PTA group. Establish small awards for the individual or class that has the biggest savings account. Show graphically what a child can achieve by saving—one dollar a week buys a used bike; two dollars a week a new one. A savings account for the six years of upper-grade school helps to assure going to college. It is a wonderful way to teach economics to children and instill a lifetime habit—even encourage parents and relatives and potential employers to make cash contributions to the youngsters' bank accounts.

MANAGEMENT—*Big Competitors*

Q: *"A big discount store has come into our town and the competition it has generated is threatening to put me out of business. Can you advise what I, and other small stores like mine, can do in situations like that?"*

All across America the incursion of large, well-managed discount stores has changed the face of retailing. Now, not only in retailing, but in most other businesses—newspapers, auto dealers, groceries—it's the giants—multi-newspaper chains, the giant auto showrooms, the Southland Corporation with their thousands of 7-11s—that have come to prominence. The personal "crackerbarrel" store has become a dinosaur, but there is a pendulum that swings back. There is increasing proof that more and more small businesses are springing up and many are surviving, especially in the service sector where personal skills, one-on-one relationships, and small investments are often more vital than gigantic public corporations managed by computers and push buttons. Some stores are closing in the old downtowns, but reopening in the strip centers dominated by that big ogre, the chain discount store. There evidently are still a lot of people who want that personal touch, that exclusive brand, that relationship between two human beings that an impersonal self-service store or a disinterested sales clerk cannot provide. Small retailers will have to concentrate on this personal service, buy smarter, merchandise like the major operators, analyze their variable internal expenses, and operate more efficiently. The Wal-Marts of America are smart operators, but they have no exclusivity on smarts—and nostalgia is often an unaffordable luxury. Small entrepreneurs, please note!

MANAGEMENT—*Burnout*

Q: *"Our company is doing pretty well, but I just don't feel that I have the usual zip anymore and want to get out of it. Is this typical of many small businesses? What can I do about it?"*

Psychologists call this feeling of uselessness or disinterest *burnout*. It happens with a lot of human activities—including running a business. Entrepreneurial activity is usually a very concentrated and demanding one. Starting and running a business takes one away from family, social activities, and avocational pursuits. One can get tired even of eating steak or dancing with a movie star. What to do about it? Plan your business activities in greater moderation. Compromise with the demands of the business by alternating tasks and time spent in the business. Learn how to delegate some jobs that could be done by employees or family members. Be less of a perfectionist. And make sure that you reward yourself by getting away from the pressures of the business occasionally. One entrepreneur *planned* a vacation every three months and flew off to a Caribbean island or took a cruise where no phone could reach him. Another reactivated an old hobby, stamp collecting, and spent evenings at this calming avocation. While burnout is the primary reason for small business leaders' cessation, there are others, cited in this order:

- Lack of operating and growth capital.
- Lack of interest by the children to eventually take over and run the business.
- Too much financial and personal demand by business in relation to remuneration possible.
- Advancing age and poor health.
- Desire to try something new.
- Insecurity about taxes, economy, and interest rates.

MANAGEMENT—*Construction Business*

Q: *"The construction business is known for its ups and downs. As I look around our area and at my competitors, I realize that much of our problem is unbusinesslike operation and too much lowball bidding. Can you give me some positive advice?"*

Like any business, you need to have a professional plan of operation. Just as you wouldn't build a house without a blueprint, you wouldn't want to run a business without a firm plan of operation. The SBA's booklet "Business Plans for Small Construction Firms" (publication MP-5) will be a good start. If you need independent, cost-free outside counsel, why not call the nearest SCORE chapters to see if they have a counselor experienced in the construction business? A primer for any business, but especially for a contractor, to follow, is this six-step plan:

1. Quality work
2. Timely completion of projects
3. Adequate financing
4. Good understanding of sound business principles, not just technical expertise
5. Competent, reliable people working for you
6. Fair treatment of customers—your bottom line

And now, a caution on bidding, because it is here where many construction companies, even large ones, come up short: Don't ever low-ball a job. You cannot figure any building job too tightly. Each job has to have some fat in it because the unforeseen will occur. Estimate your job accurately and then add 20–25 percent to it for your final bid figure. Should you come in under bid, you can always refund all or a part of it and make a lifelong friend. In the real-world of dealing with subcontractors and frequently itinerant employees, unions and weather, plan changes and material variations, and even excluding mind-changes by clients (which can be covered by contracts), deviations from original bid plans are more likely than not to happen. And when the building business slows down in recessive times, renovations, remodeling, and rebuilding increase. If you are flexible enough to see and to react to these trends, you can make a lot of money in the construction business. Many of America's largest midlevel fortunes have been made in the building industry—and there appears to be no end to its need, especially in the affordable housing phase of it.

MANAGEMENT—*Consultant's Checklist*

Q: "To become a management consultant, what kind of checklist would I need to cover all bases?"

Management consulting is a very complicated field that requires knowledge in about 16 separate subjects. At the SBA, business development specialists—not always just one person—will cover all 16 subjects with about 215 distinct questions. SCORE's checklist (with a slightly modified introduction) appears below. It will help owners and outside consultants evaluate their businesses.

MANAGEMENT CONSULTANT'S CHECKLIST

The subjects covered are:

   I. The firm's market
  II. Asset adequacy
 III. Adequacy and use of accounting records
  IV. Financial condition
   V. Location analysis
  VI. Layout analysis
 VII. Proper legal form of organization
VIII. Sales development program

   IX. Pricing policies
    X. Merchandising of lines of goods
   XI. Seasonal variations and their implications
  XII. Purchasing and inventory control
 XIII. Expense analysis and break-even chart
 XIV. Credit policies in effect for sales and purchases
  XV. Risks and protection provided
XVI. Personnel policies

I.   For Evaluating Markets

1. Is the firm's major problem lack of sales?
2. What has been the trend of sales in recent years?
3. What factors can be determined as responsible for the trend of sales?
4. Was a *proper* market survey made when the firm started?
5. If so, what were the predicted results in sales volume?
6. If not, should such a survey be made now?
7. Have the basic sources of market survey data been studied?
8. Does population growth, new competition, or competitor change in methods justify new ways of serving this market?
9. Has the character of the population in the trading area changed, aside from general growth or decline? Has this affected sales?
10. Has the ratio of population to number of firms in this trading area changed since the firm was established? If so, what has been done by management to keep current with these changes?
11. What is the nature and form of competition?
12. Does the future look good, medium, or bad for this firm in this market?

II.   For Evaluating Asset Adequacy

1. Does the firm lack any assets that would improve its capacity for service, its image, or its profitability?
2. Are its store fixtures, office fixtures, and/or machines modern? Would newer ones improve image, service, or profitability?
3. Are present fixed assets consistent with the floor plan, available additional space, and customer comfort?
4. Does the firm have the necessary capital to finance its own receivables? Should this be done?
5. Are cash balances and working capital adequate for the volume of business being done?

6. Do growth requirements of the immediate future suggest the need of any other current or fixed assets? If so, are plans satisfactory for their acquisition?
7. Could the firm expand sales and profits with more assets in its present operation? How?

III.   For Evaluating Adequacy of Accounting Records

1. Does the proprietor have monthly statements easily available?
2. Does a complete accounting system exist?
3. Does the present system involve excessive posting?
4. Would a combined journal-ledger system reduce the work of the system?
5. Can the owner tell quickly the amounts owed by credit customers? (Is there an accounts receivable ledger of some kind?)
6. Can he quickly ascertain the balances due to creditors? (Is there an accounts payable ledger of some kind?)
7. Can sales easily be broken down into departments, chief lines of merchandise, or special items?
8. Does the system in effect provide a means of telling the profitability of individual departments or lines of merchandise?
9. Do the monthly adjustments include properly the charges for depreciation, amortization, and new inventories?
10. What types of information, not now easily available, does an owner need?
11. Does the firm take advantage of purchase discounts? Do the records provide adequate notice of discount periods?
12. Do procedures include a regular aging of accounts receivable?
13. Does the system easily produce meaningful control reports?

IV.   For Evaluating Financial Condition

1. What is the relationship of assets and liabilities?
2. What is the relationship of current assets and current liabilities?
3. Are the current assets truly current?
4. Are the liabilities properly classified?
5. What is the working capital? Is it adequate?
6. What is the current ratio? What is the quick ratio? What is the proprietorship ratio?
7. Is the firm trading on too thin an equity?
8. Does it have trouble paying its current bills? Why?

9. Have the accounts receivable been aged recently? What is the firm's policy on charging off uncollectible accounts?
10. How much of current profits is going to pay for fixed assets?
11. Are any ceditors witholding credit because of the company's debt-paying habits or its other financial problems?
12. Does the firm need additional investment capital? Are any sources available?
13. Is the inventory turnover a cause of financial stress? Has it been reviewed for slow-moving merchandise lately? Are there other problems?
14. Is the gross margin consistent with that of comparable firms? If not, why not?
15. Are operating expenses in line? If not, why not?
16. Do company policies indicate that the financial condition will be improved? How?
17. Are any other financial weaknesses apparent?
18. Does the company have meaningful management controls reports?
19. Are financial reports produced timely?

V. For Evaluating Location

A. *For Retailers*

1. Is the firm located in a high-rent or a low-rent area? Should it be? Is the rent paid by the firm competitive?
2. If in a low-rent area and competing with firms in high-rent areas, how does it compensate in attracting customers?
3. Is the location good from the standpoint of meeting competition?
4. Is the total traffic in the area adequate?
5. Do neighboring stores draw potential customers?
6. Is there a parking problem for customers? Would it be worthwhile to pay for customer parking?
7. Is the location good for development of sales via promotion?
8. Is the location appropriate to the principles of location for convenience, shopping, and specialty stores?
9. Is there a better site available in the area?
10. Is the going-home side of the street or the sunny side of the street important to this firm? Does it have that advantage?
11. Do the community and general area suggest adequate payrolls, population trends, living habits, and attitudes to encourage firm development here?
12. Are any other disadvantages of this location observed?

B. For Wholesalers

1. Is the location economically accessible to its market?
2. Are shipping costs in receiving inventory the lowest available? Would additional rail, truck, or air facilities improve efficiency and reduce costs?
3. Do competitors have advantages in costs of delivery to customers due to better location?
4. Do customers visit the plant in person or call in orders by phone? If they visit, is the accessibility and customer convenience satisfactory?
5. Does this location make possible the best layout of merchandise to expedite order filling and minimize labor costs?

C. For Factories

1. Should this type of factory be close to its markets or to its raw materials? Is it?
2. Do the facilities at this location make possible the best use of the appropriate production layout?
3. Is the location appropriate to hiring the types of labor required? Is adequate labor of the type desired available?
4. Are utility costs consistent with those available at other potential locations?
5. Are adequate shipping and receiving facilities available at competitive costs? Would additional competition by shippers be helpful?
6. Are government attitudes and community facilities encouraging?
7. Do alternative locations offer reduced costs or better profits? Why?
8. Are there environmental problems with the location?

D. For Service Firms

1. Is customer visitation an important part of the business? If so, are facilities for customer comfort adequate?
2. Is the location consistent with the type of clientele sought and its habits in buying this service?
3. Does the firm need a high-rent location? Is it in one?
4. If efficient working conditions for employees are important, do they exist?
5. Is the firm paying an expensive rental for space when most of its business comes via telephone? Is this necessary?
6. Is drop-in business important? Does it exist in adequate quantity? Can it be developed by advertising?

VI. For Evaluating Layout

A. *For Retailers*

1. Is the present layout encouraging to sales because it reflects buying habits of customers?
2. Could it better reflect a good "selling machine"? How?
3. Is merchandise attractively displayed?
4. Is merchandise displayed to facilitate easy comparisons and easy examination?
5. Is customer comfort properly provided to meet the particular shopping habits of the firm's customers?
6. Are associated lines of merchandise displayed adjacently?
7. Does the layout reflect maximum use of light, ventilation, and heat?
8. Is maximum view of store space by customers, employees, and managers desirable? If so, is this view now possible?
9. Are selling and nonselling activities properly separated?
10. Are convenience, shopping, and specialty goods properly located in the floor plan?
11. Does the image of the store reflect colors, fixtures, and displays that are compatible with the type of customers sought?

B. *For Wholesalers*

1. Does the layout make order-filling easy?
2. Are most popular lines of merchandise located adjacently?
3. Is maximum use made of rolling equipment in filling orders?
4. Do customers visit the firm often? If so, is the image proper?
5. Are receiving doors convenient to inventory stacks? Are more doors needed?
6. Is the line of travel from merchandise collection for orders to location of loading deliveries direct? Could it be shortened to reduce costs or order filling?
7. Are aisles wide enough for efficient operation?
8. Can the height of merchandise stacks be reduced in the present space?

C. *For Factories*

1. Does the firm now use a process or a product layout?
2. Is maximum use made of the advantages of the present layout?
3. Can the unproductive movement of raw materials, goods in process, or finished products be reduced?
4. Are testing and quality control stations located in the best spots

on the production line? Should there be more quality control locations?

5. Are materials to be placed in production located close to the point of introduction into production?
6. Are material-receiving areas located as close to storerooms as possible?
7. Are luncheon areas, rest rooms, drinking fountains, and other employee areas located for maximum efficiency?
8. Are there efficient methods of moving materials used?

VII. For Evaluating Legal Forms of Organization

1. Under what legal form of organization is the firm now operating?
2. What are the major risks to which the firm is subjected?
3. Does the legal form of organization give the firm proper protection against these risks?
4. Does the firm supplement its legal form of protection with public liability insurance? Is the amount adequate?
5. Is unlimited liability a serious potential problem for the owner(s)?
6. Has the present form limited financial needs in any way?
7. Has the owner considered changing the legal form?
8. What is the relative incidence of the major risks of the firm?
9. Are there tax advantages available by changing the legal form of organization?
10. Is the owner fully aware of the management advantages of the alternative legal forms available for his firm?
11. Are the features of a Subchapter S or 1244 corporation known? Would you recommend them in this case?
12. Is the firm utilizing all the advantages of the present legal form of organization?

VIII. For Evaluating Sales Development

1. Has the firm properly distinguished between established demand and promoted or created demand for its goods?
2. Has the owner considered all the direct and indirect sales promotion methods?
3. Are the applicable sales promotion methods being used in effective quantities?
4. Is the present advertising program being checked for its effectiveness?
5. Is the present sales volume consistent with the potential for the firm in this trading area? If not, how could it be increased?

6. Do customers generally reflect a feeling of satisfaction in doing business with the firm?
7. What is the firm's image in the community that it serves?
8. How could it be improved if deficiencies are found?
9. Is personal selling by employees consistent with the best practices?
10. Do any suggestions seem apparent for improving sales promotion?
11. Is the sales force producing at economic levels?

IX. For Evaluating Pricing Policies

1. Do prices now produce an average gross margin consistent with the sales volume for this type of firm? If not, why?
2. Is the firm's pricing policy influenced by fair trade laws, nationally advertised prices, or competitor prices?
3. Is market strategy employed in setting prices?
4. Is the owner reluctant to adopt less-than-average markup prices when good judgment dictates their use?
5. Do prices reflect attempts to sell slow-moving merchandise?
6. Are proper methods used in moving slow merchandise?
7. Is style merchandise a factor in markups and markdowns?
8. Does original markup policy reflect normal markdowns, employee discounts, damaged merchandise, and shortages?
9. Does the firm use adequate markups to produce desired results?
10. Are markups based on cost or retail prices?
11. Have loss leaders ever been used? Were they necessary or productive?
12. Does the firm's overall pricing policy reflect a dynamic management?
13. Do above-average markup sales cover sales in less-than-average markup items?
14. What are the prices and pricing policies of the competition?

X. For Evaluating Merchandising

1. Does the owner recognize the differences in convenience, shopping, and specialty goods?
2. Does he properly place his merchandise inventory into these categories?
3. If sales effort is primarily in one category, does his merchandising policy properly reflect this fact?
4. Is the merchandising policy generally in line with the majority of customers in his trading area?

5. Are selling policies and services in line with his products (credit plans, delivery services, etc.)?
6. If selling industrial goods, does the firm recognize the differences in merchandising its goods and consumer goods?
7. Is the location consistent with the type of merchandise sold and the price policies in effect?
8. Are employee capabilities and qualifications consistent with the needs of the type of merchandise being sold?

XI. For Evaluating Seasonal Variations

1. Does the firm have distinct variations in sales in different months and/or seasons of the year?
2. Is the management using accepted methods of adjusting operating expenses to these variations?
3. Is purchasing policy consistent with the noted variations?
4. Would the addition of different lines of merchandise or different products help to even out the seasonal variation in sales?
5. If seasonal variations are drastic, would it be better to close the business entirely for some period in the year?
6. If a manufacturing firm, would it be more profitable to use the slack periods to build up inventory and to cut down factory overtime in the busy seasons? What are the trade-offs?

XII. For Evaluating Purchasing and Inventory Control

1. Are the proper sources of supply now being used?
2. Is the firm taking advantage of all purchase discounts?
3. How are minimum inventories and ordering points determined?
4. Has the firm suffered from stockouts of finished merchandise or raw materials?
5. What is the record for quality, service, and price of its present suppliers? How about dependability and assistance in periods of sellers' markets?
6. How does the firm set its minimum and/or economic ordering quantities?
7. Has buying policy been guilty of buying too large quantities that were not justified by carrying costs?
8. What is the cost of carrying inventories in stock until needed?
9. Does the firm owner know what his best average inventory is and use it to guide his purchasing policy?

10. Could more effective purchasing contribute profits to the present results of operation? How?
11. How many times does the inventory turn over each year? Is this consistent with industry average?

XIII. For Evaluating Expenses and a Break-Even Chart

1. Have fixed and variable expenses been thoroughly determined?
2. Are there advantages to altering the present relationship of fixed and variable expenses? Is this possible?
3. Has the firm produced a break-even chart for annual operations?
4. Has this chart been reduced to monthly periods?
5. Could the break-even point in sales be lowered? How?
6. Can any fixed expense be made variable in order to reduce risks?
7. How would profits change with a 10 percent increase in sales?
8. How would profits change with a 10 percent reduction in fixed expenses?
9. Is the firm approaching 100 percent of capacity in its present quarters?
10. Is the present percentage of capacity known? Can it be increased?
11. Is each expense dollar providing a productive return to the firm?
12. Can semivariable expenses be controlled any better?

XIV. For Evaluating Credit Policies

1. Is the firm financially equipped to carry its own accounts receivable?
2. What types of credit accounts are available to customers now?
3. Should other types of accounts be made available?
4. What is the cost of administering the present credit program?
5. Would it be better for this firm at this time to discount all its receivables with a finance company or bank?
6. Are credit-card sales being collected efficiently? What is their cost?
7. Should the firm issue its own credit cards?
8. Does its credit policy reflect the fact that the company has both small and large credit sales?
9. Has an aging of accounts receivable been made lately? What does it show?
10. Has the write-off of bad debts been realistic, too low, or too high?
11. If the firm sells to business firms, has a sales discount been offered? Should it be?
12. Has the firm taken advantage of purchase discounts offered to it?

XV.   For Evaluating Protection Against Risks

1. Has the ownership truly analyzed all the major risks to which the firm is subject?
2. What protection has been provided against each of these risks?
3. Is the incidence of risk properly considered in the protective action taken?
4. Is self-insurance appropriate for this firm?
5. How many risks are being absorbed? Should they be?
6. Is coinsurance appropriate for this firm? How?
7. Are there any recommendations for reducing risks or getting protection more economically?

XVI.   For Evaluating Personnel Policies

1. What has been the turnover of desirable employees?
2. Are any outstanding reasons for resignations to be observed?
3. Does the company provide training for new employees?
4. Are company policies regarding personnel known to all new and old employees?
5. Are there incentives in the personnel policy for employees to seek advancement?
6. Does the policy reflect the generally agreed-upon objectives of all employees?
7. Do opportunities exist for employees to work at different types of positions?
8. Is the company image one that suggests this is a good firm to work with?
9. Are pay scales and/or other advantages consistent with larger firms in the area?
10. Is there any problem of employees being overtrained or undertrained?
11. Are there any recommendations for changes in the present policies?

MANAGEMENT—*Cost-Cutting*

Q: "*These days it seems that saving the pennies is the answer. We've cut all major overhead already. Do you have any examples of how other companies are saving money internally?*"

Finding little ways to cut big costs is often extremely difficult, though it can be extremely satisfying, Cutting small expenses often becomes a very personal matter. It requires thought, ingenuity, analysis—and sometimes self-sacrifice. The best way to illustrate the many ways of saving big on small overhead is to take the example of an Illinois distributor. Here is what the energetic president of this company achieved within a single year:

- Warehouse personnel was instructed to save and bundle all scrap cardboard. It was sold to a dealer for $7,200 during the first year.
- All exit and emergency signs were refitted with 12 watt fluorescent bulbs instead of 30 watt incandescent ones. First year savings: $1,800; second year savings: $3,000.
- The major carrier of products delivered to customers was called in to renegotiate a long-term contract based on established and proven annual volume. The annual savings to the distributor came to more than $30,000 a year.
- Each department was mandated to make supply requisitions once a month instead of as-needed. This consolidation was estimated to save at least $12,000 annually.
- The company got together with its health-care provider to explore ways of cutting paperwork and thus overhead and costs. The provider was able to save the company about $10,000 a year on labor and materials, cutting down considerable paperwork without reducing benefits.
- All department managers were called in for a brainstorming session to explore ways of working more closely together, without overlapping functions and supplies. It proved to be a cost-effective restructuring. When one of the managers left the company, his department was merged into a related one and a $20,000+ salary was saved.

No service reductions were effected, efficiency was maximized, and the company saved at least $80,000 the first year.

MANAGEMENT—*Discounts*

Q: *"So many of my customers want discounts, but I'm a one-price business. How do I handle this without insulting them—or losing them?"*

Every business person who buys goods and services, and of course each purchasing agent, tries to get the best deal for his or her company. Whether in manufacturing, wholesaling or retail transactions, seeking traditional discounts for cash purchases, quantity purchases, post-season buying or special promotions, for instance, is customary and expected. In some cases price reductions are made for members of certain organizations or senior citizens. These need to be recognized. But then there are the troublemakers. They might want to bargain down a price you find necessary, or nitpick some real or imagined shortcoming, or demand all kinds of service and extras, or refuse to pay after you have performed your end of the deal because of some fabricated error or failure. While it is often said that the customer is always right, you and I know that this isn't always so. Still, the customer is boss, even if he or she is difficult. Be pleasant for a short while, even going so far as to suggest that the customer will be happier with the competitor you name—who might be better equipped, larger, or cheaper. Most customers respond to reason. You might say, and even post a sign to this effect, that your annual or semi-annual or month-end sale is being held on such and such a date. You might ask for the customer's name and address so that you can let her or him know when a sale is coming up. You might even institute a quantity discount policy—a specific percentage off the price when a dozen are purchased, or total sales for the period exceed a gross amount. Especially in retailing, where you deal with large quantities of people, you are bound to run into boors and bargain-hunters who don't want you to make a living. Grit your teeth, grin, and send them to your competitor.

MANAGEMENT—*Electronic Mail*

Q: *"We send a lot of electronic mail to our reps and suppliers, but are concerned that some of that information, especially when it comes to quotes and bids, gets leaked out to outsiders. What can we do to protect ourselves?"*

Electronic mail, or E-Mail, is usually considered privileged information, like personal first-class letters. Others are not privy to read E-Mail if it is not addressed to them. However, since E-Mail goes through receivers and, like faxes becomes an open book, it is often difficult to maintain security. An employer who checks on E-mail sent by employees usually has the right to do so, because he furnishes the equipment and pays for its use. However, a policy should be established as to the privacy that an employee has, and such an explicit policy should be explained to the employee at the time of hiring or installation of the system. The best protection probably is to keep any snoops from having access to the messages in the first place on both the sending as well as the receiving stations. Every E-mail system should have a tight ID and password without which a transmission cannot be read. Users sometimes tend to be less than careful about keeping their passwords secret. You do not necessarily have to be a cryptologist to devise a password, but it should be clever enough not be too obvious. There is, however, no absolutely tight security system for electronic communications and existing laws (such as the Electronic Communications Privacy Act of 1986) do not provide complete assurance. Having good people working for you, keeping equipment out of unauthorized hands, and devising fairly foolproof passwords are your best protection.

MANAGEMENT—*Environmental Planning*

Q: *"How will the Clean Air Act and Clean Water Act affect starting and running a small business?"*

Federal acts designed to protect the environment and the global citizens who live on this earth affect every business. It is something every enterprise must learn and take into consideration. It is no longer enough to do business as usual and take for granted that our wasteful, polluting ways can continue. Landfill shortages, polluted water, and fouled air will result in many more laws and restrictions on municipal, state, and federal levels, and consequently higher costs to stop or even reverse the effects of pollution. These costs must be estimated in advance and factored into the costs of doing business. Every business today, existing or planned, must investigate possibilities of recycling its waste. Many companies have found that recycling can be an additional income producer. Businesses that produce pollutants that go into the air, hazardous wastes that go into water or ground, or that have storage tanks above or below ground, all need to consult with the EPA and with OSHA in many cases to make sure they do not run into costly violations. Even in buying or selling property, environmental clearance should be obtained in advance to make sure the next owner is not stuck with a backbreaking bill to effect corrections.

MANAGEMENT—*ESOPs*

Q: *"I've read about Employee Stock Ownership Plans as a way of increasing company morale and raising capital at the same time. How do they work?"*

ESOPs, as they are called, are generally advantageous to small businesses, but must be handled carefully and professionally through an attorney or CPA who understands them. Basically, an ESOP involves selling stock in your company to your employees in order to raise capital for your business without having to go outside of the company. It has the added benefit of boosting employees' morale, and possibly income, by making them shareholders. You can set the limits of the amount of stock that is made available to an ESOP and still retain management perogatives. There should be regulations regarding stock redemption if the employee leaves the company. In a way, an ESOP is like profit-sharing, but it puts additional working capital at the owner's disposal without a set amount of interest having to be paid, or without having to encumber collateral. One company of ten stores has all of its managers entered in an ESOP and deducts five percent from their weekly salary after the first six months. After setting up an ESOP, you must maintain good communications and hold occasional meetings with its partici-pants so that all company transactions appear above board. It is also advisable that an outside counsel, such as an attorney, handle the paper work, to remove any suspicion of internal manipulations. Having a committee of ESOP participants is also a good idea, because it provides an outlet for possibly valuable brainstorming, ideas, investment strat-egies, and morale building.

MANAGEMENT—*Family*

Q: "*I am really anxious to start a business that I think will have a real chance at success. I am worried, however, that I won't be able to handle the family responsibilities—two small kids and a wife at home. Any suggestions? They'd sure be welcome.*"

You have touched on a sensitive point that all entrepreneurs must consider. The business plan that a new business demands does not leave room for this point, but your family needs to be considered along with other concerns. An unsupportive family will ultimately undercut a venture and work against it; hence, it is wise to execute a plan of family survival along with the plan for business survival. Consider the following requirements before you start your new business:

- Make sure that everything in your family and your relations with your family are smooth. Stresses and conflicts within your family will directly affect your ability to launch a new business and can undo your best efforts or even you.
- Bring your spouse and children on board. Gain their approval. Let them in on what you're doing and even show them where you work, how and why, and how this benefits the family.

- A new business can easily overwhelm even the most ambitious and organized. Set up the amount of money as well as the amount of time you are willing to invest as well—ahead of time.
- Some changes in your family life might be necessary in which family responsibilities and work division needs to change. Set priorities for nonbusiness activities. Get the kids to pitch in. Farm out some chores.
- Your own physical and emotional needs have to be considered. If you are not in good health, do not sleep well, and eat poorly, then you will not be equal to the demands of running a new business. Like a car or airplane, a business requires more energy during take-off; less once momentum has been reached.
- Share your problems and concerns. Your spouse is your partner, if not in fact, then in spirit. Share victories and defeats. Agree that if you cannot solve problems from within, you can go outside to seek advice and counsel. (The SBA and its affiliate, SCORE, are available and at no charge!)
- Don't make commitments beyond your time, physical, and financial capabilities.
- Don't reinvent the wheel—perhaps the very problem for which you seek solutions has already been solved and you can either ask for it or purchase it much cheaaper.
- Create an environment, both at home and at work, in which you can be comfortable, be creative, do occasional "quiet work" and even be alone for a while.
- Last, but not least, schedule time, yes—schedule!—when you plan to do absolutely nothing related to business. Each entrepreneur has his or her own escape valve. Some like books, others music. Some escape to the movies or play cards, work out with the kids, or pursue a favorite hobby. This writer scheduled a trip to his favorite sunny island every three months. It's amazing how this will recharge one's battery. Awards work with animals and people —and, yes, even bosses.

MANAGEMENT—*Family Partnership*

Q: "My brother-in-law and I want to go into business together. What do you advise we should do to avoid any future conflict?"

In many cases when relatives join in a business partnership, they are walking a silken tightrope. They must prepare not only the legal groundwork for a partnership but also the emotional basis of a sensitive relationship. A frank discussion with the prospective partner before the start of business is the first step. Consider variances in personality, experience, money, working habits, spousal relationships and demands, and talents that each will bring to the relationship. In addition, there are the normal partnership details to be worked out, such as how much money will each one draw, how additional profits will be divided or shortfalls be made up, how loan papers will be signed and guaranteed, what is the role of the spouses and other family members, when and for how long will absences be taken, who will do what in the business without interfering with the other, and when do joint decisions and/or signatures become necessary. Sometimes, with the best of intentions, the emotional factors become so pronounced that an ombudsman, a third party like a lawyer who meets both parties approval, should be called in to adjudicate. Don't assume anything. Circumstances alter cases, and people outside the business, including spouses and older children, in-laws and friends, can influence future actions. A partnership, especially with a relative, is like a marriage. Frank and open communication, a total sharing of responsibilities and the ability to practice total empathy will make both succeed.

MANAGEMENT—*Financial Leaks*

Q: *"My business is doing well but I have a feeling that there are a lot of little leaks. An efficiency expert is too expensive for me—do you have any guidelines for better fiscal control?"*

It's "a penny earned is a dollar saved" or some variety of that adage. But in any operation that employs a number of people, inefficiencies and purposeful or negligent expenditures rob your bottom line of optimum profits. It is up to you as the manager of your business to analyze where these profit-robbing cracks might be, to set them down on paper, and transmit rules for their control to your employees. Here is a small list to start:

- Analyze and keep track of all transactions, especially routine transactions where controls are usually weakest, but for efficiency's sake, set a minimum of something like $10. Anything above that amount will require an OK from you or your manager, as well as a corroborating receipt.
- Any long-distance telephone call or fax transmission over $5.00 should have an explanation entered in a log book.
- Use charge cards for travel and other purchases instead of cash advances.

- Have all bills scrutinized by you or a manager before approving their payment. Check back whether item has been received, is satisfactory, or has been charged off against inventory or purchase.
- Outside charges in the name of the company should contain the purpose, person entertained, affiliation.
- Material or equipment taken off the premises should be logged properly, going out as well as coming back.
- Transportation expenses such as use of a company car can make profits disappear real fast. Milage use, gas purchases, and private utilization of vehicles need to be accurately controlled. (An exterminating company had a fleet of 36 trucks that cost in excess of $250,000 a year to operate. When they hired a dispatcher/controller, the cost dropped $50,000, which easily paid for the supervisor and the radio-remote system, and they reduced the insurance bill, too.)
- Internal shoplifting is a very serious profit leak. It has been known to put small businesses out of business. Inventory controls, checking of employees' packages, establishing a discount structure for employee purchases, and in-and-out cash controls are all necessary controlling devices. The greater the cash transactions, the greater the need for such controls. The deviousness and ingenuity of employees is positively amazing. If you have employees handling cash, try to get bonding for them. If they refuse, or are refused, don't hire them.

MANAGEMENT—*Food Delivery*

Q: *"I've read about a prepared-food delivery service. Do you have any information on that? How do they work?"*

These are delivery and promotion services rather than food operations. They work well in large cities that have a profusion of good restaurants and a sophisticated clientele that can afford to spend the money for home-delivered meals. In the Miami Beach area, for instance, food deliverers have long-term arrangements with elderly residents who do not want to or cannot cook themselves. They make advance choices of what they wish to eat, how many portions, and when they want to receive the delivery. They pay weekly or monthly for this "subscription service." In cities with high numbers of working couples and professionals with limited time and good incomes, like the Washington, DC, market, delivery services buy meals from a variety of restaurants. Their clients choose from a variety of menus, call one central number, and a complete meal of their choice—steaks, Chinese, seafood—is delivered within the hour, ready to eat or to be reheated in their microwave ovens. The delivery service buys the meals from participating restaurants at 20 percent off menu prices; the restaurants do additional business without having to provide space or service; the recipient does not have dress to go out or move from the television set. It appears to be a good symbiosis all around. One such delivery service in the Ft. Lauderdale suburbs is Room Service. They average about 60 orders each night at $26 each, netting 20 percent or about $312—and business is growing, especially to hotel guests in facilities without on-premise food service. Distribution of menus is one of the biggest expenses, but the young industry is increasing steadily.

MANAGEMENT—*Foodmarkets*

Q: *"We want to open a small foodmarket in an area that is under-served by major markets. We are greatly concerned about our chances to succeed especially when we read about the Mega Foods mess in Washington. Do you have any information on that failure?"*

We cannot comment on specifics of this case, but it proved that even when all elements for success are seemingly in place, other unforeseen factors can become serious stumbling blocks. It is often the unexpected problems in business that cause small enterprises to founder—and this underscores the need for adequate financing to meet the unexpected exigencies. In the case that you referred to, the supermarket was financed by a half-million dollar loan from the wholesaler and a $700,000 loan from a neighborhood economic development group. The latter loan removed the company from its minority status; an outside consultant declined to become involved when he realized all the various problems; a union threw up a picket line, pressuring management to permit workers to organize; and the neighborhood was not as supportive of the new venture as the developers thought. The owners were graduates of the Harvard Business School and themselves minorities, but they declined to make use of SBA-guaranteed loan facilities or other available counseling. Caught in a vise of unexpected problems and undercapitalization, the supermarket lasted two years before declaring bankruptcy. This case regrettably proves that an enterpreneur should 1) rely on every available source of assistance, preferably before he or she encounters problems, and 2) that his or her capitalization should be considerably more than his initial estimates.

MANAGEMENT—*Forecasting*

Q: *"How can we plan for the coming year when there is so much uncertainty and waffling coming out of Washington?"*

By *Washington* we suppose you mean government pronouncements. It's true that economists in the Bureau of Census, Labor Department, Commerce Department, the White House, and even at the SBA do not always talk as one voice. That is the nature of democracy. Often, of course, totally unforeseen events thousands of miles away from Washington affect circumstances and make previous prognostications sound uninformed. Such events as the Iraqi incursion into Kuwait and the subsequent oil price increases, and the cataclysmic events in Russia and Eastern Europe, were hardly predictable by even the best Washington economists. But to give you a private opinion from one of the capital's most respected oracles, the *Kiplinger Washington Letter* stated in one of their 1990 key forecasts:

> *"Expect the current slow-down to continue over the next few months, then a modest pick-up after midyear. Looking further ahead, there'll be solid economic growth in the '90s because of healthier exports, stronger productivity gains and a narrowing of the trade and budget deficits."*

MANAGEMENT—*Future Business Opportunities*

Q: *"I know that I want to go into business for myself when I graduate from college. Can you tell me what some of the hot businesses of the next decade will be?"*

As a collegian, you might want to contact an association named Association of Collegiate Entrepreneurs that was founded in 1983 at Wichita (KS) State University. It has about 5,000 members nationwide and can be contacted at Box 147, 1845 North Fairmount St., Wichita, KS 67208. Numerous magazines like *Entrepreneur, INC., Success,* and *Small Business Opportunities* report on a steady stream of new business innovations. In this writer's book *The Do-It-Yourself Business Book* (John Wiley & Sons Inc., 1989) are listed a number of future business opportunities or phenomena that will create opportunities:

- The continuing baby boom
- Crafts and arts

- Car customizing and detailing
- Recycling and waste disposal
- Any business working to improve the ecology
- More sophisticated and varied fast foods
- Frozen desserts, especially low-fat ones
- Home delivered foods, meals, services
- Religious merchandising
- Underground testing (gas tanks, etc.)

The innovative Japanese also have come up with hundreds of new products and services that are worth a second look.

MANAGEMENT—*Insurance*

Q: *"Risk insurance in my business is really getting out of hand. What can I do to minimize this profit drain?"*

To start, you can inquire about such insurance from a professional or trade association you belong to or can join. Group coverage is invariably more economical because the underwriter writes a fairly uniform policy for a large number of businesses. On the other side, you can do a great deal about reducing your insurance premiums by reducing risks in your business. Determine the real risks inherent in your business and ask the insurance agent to tailor a policy to match your needs. Consult your lawyer and accountant to determine the real and potential risk factors. Check your place of business, inside and out, to see if any safety hazards exist for employees and customers and correct them immediately. Institute a safety program for your employees; even consult your nearest OSHA office for guidelines. If customers have filed complaints, deal with them promptly to forestall possible suits in this litigous society. Pay particular attention to any vehicles used in your business and how they are operated. Your local chamber of commerce should have a booklet available entitled "Risk Management." Ask your insurance agent or carrier to get you a booklet published by the Insurance Information Institute (New York) called "Risk Management and Business Insurance." And finally, make a candid appraisal of your ability to absorb small claims and get a policy that is more affordable by taking this deductibility factor into consideration. You will find, too, that the carrier you choose, whether group or individual, will offer more favorable rates if you buy a "business-owner's package" (BOP) policy that includes your other insurance needs.

MANAGEMENT—*Meetings*

Q: *"Our association has monthly meetings plus special ones. It is always a struggle to get enough participation, even from members that attend. Do you have any guidelines on running more successful and productive meetings?"*

Sometimes it does seem that associations and corporations and government offices meet themselves to death—certainly into a state of inefficiency and inertia. It happens in any democratically run group in which the chief executive does not want to take full responsibility, or blame, for his decisions and actions. One meeting expert estimated that meetings cost American business as much as $37 billion a year in wasted wages alone. One-third of 903 managers asked about the effectiveness of their meetings replied that their presence or input had no impact on ultimate decision-making. Typical meetings allow two hours' notice and have no agenda, or if they have one, the agendas are not followed, are repetitive, or are interrupted by peripheral issues and ultimate boredom. Getting off-track, having no agenda, and being interrupted by nonessentials are the enemies of effective meetings. The basics of having productive meetings should include the following points:

- Prepare an agenda at least two days in advance
- Sharply define who should attend the meeting but don't skip any who might have pragmatic contributions or whose absence might step on sensitive toes
- If you are the meeting leader, prepare a short (3 to 5 minutes) orientation as an introduction to focus on the meeting's purpose and content
- Prepare for dissenting voices and opinions and give them space and time to be heard—but if they turn out to be troublemakers, challenge them to present solutions
- Let someone else run the meetings and discussions so that you can sit back and objectively evaluate the responses and reactions—and occasionally act as mediator
- Record what goes on at meetings; jot down who has promised to do what and who has been assigned to follow up on decisions— then be sure to follow up.

Lack of preparation and personality conflicts within the meeting group are the chief enemies of effective get-togethers. Ask yourself, too:

Are *all* the meetings necessary? Could the purpose be accomplished with a small, quick conference between pertinent persons? Were results of meetings circulated and comments invited so that the next meeting will be more effective? All this done, meetings should be more productive and less boring.

MANAGEMENT—*Operating Figures*

Q: "We want to start a general repair business. Do you have any operating figures that we can use as a guide?"

There are so many variables in using statistics for the operation of a business that we must warn that these are only averages. They *can* serve as guidelines as long as you use other factors in your final decision—such as competition, incomes and customs of your expected customers, location, reputation, amount of service you expect to render, credit policy, frills, quality level of your parts, and warranties offered. Here then are some sample figures for a small repair business that probably does a volume under $100,000:

Gross profit	**$52.49**
Cost of sales	**47.51**
Operating supplies	1.82
Gross wages	16.98
Repairs & maintenance	.38
Advertising	1.45
Car & delivery	1.52
Bad debts	.04
Administration & legal	.74
Outside labor	1.21
Miscellaneous expenses	.81
Total controllable expenses	**24.95**
Rent	3.35
Utilities	2.05
Insurance	.95
Taxes & licenses	.86
Interest	.12
Depreciation	1.25

Total fixed expenses	**8.58**
Total expenses	**33.53**
Net profit	**18.96**

MANAGEMENT—*Outside Professionals*

Q: *"We are expanding into another location or starting a new business. Do you advise that we use outside professionals to guide us and who should we pick?"*

There are basically four categories of outside advisors you can and should call upon to help you formulate and execute your company expansion plans, whether it will be in the direction of a branch operation or an entirely new business under your ownership. The four are: 1) attorneys, 2) accountants, 3) marketing specialists, or 4) counselors from SCORE or SBDC or other advisory group. Each category has its assets and here are some for you to consider:

Attorneys: Review proposed short- and long-term contracts and leases; check environmental concerns, product liabilities, and antitrust involvements; check all possible patent, trademark, and copyright properties; and go over all possible pitfalls with you to make sure all potential liabilities are covered.

Accountants: Help you in developing a viable and usable business plan and financial projections; determine best accounting methods if different from present ones; advise on internal bookkeeping methods, cost controls, inventory controls, and data collection that will include all foreseeable future contingencies; help train key financial personnel; advise on appropriate tax decisions that can affect your company financial health; and aid in liaison with capital sources.

Marketing specialists: Conduct market research you are unable to do; project growth potential for company and market; explore acceptance of new products and services; monitor competitive situations; guide research and development of new products; determine technical feasibilities; and suggest changes in design, packaging, and pricing.

Outside counselors: Advise on local feasibilities, market, demographics, labor market; help in location finding and layouts; analyze inventory turnover; monitor efficient production; and advise on local media and promotions.

In addition to commercial organizations like chambers of commerce, government-affiliated associations like SCORE are almost everywhere (4,500 chambers; 750 SCORE locations). If yours is a university town, professors and graduate students working through the SBA-affiliated SBDC or independently can often be of immense help in R&D and market research. Many universities also conduct incubator shops that help developing small businesses (see INCUBATORS—Getting Information). Business-based networking organizations like the Rotarians, local branches of trade and professional associations, and mature banking officials can also be named among outside counselors. Best of all, most of these cost nothing.

MANAGEMENT—*Record-Keeping*

Q: *"Record-keeping is one of those necessary evils, I know, and I tend to get sloppy about it. Is there any suggestion that you can give me to make the job easier?"*

"Recordkeeping in a Small Business" (publication FM-10) and "Analyze Your Records to Reduce Costs" (publication FM-7) are two useful SBA booklets you should obtain. The Code of Federal Regulations also goes into detail on what records you need in business and how long you should retain them. As a small business person, there are five general areas in which you should keep good personal records, in additional to such vital business papers as stock certificates, charters, property titles, partnership agreements, outside loan agreements, customer records and records of resources, as well as leases and titles to equipment. Each subject should have a separate folder in a filing cabinet, be clearly labeled and kept up-to-date at least monthly. On the personal side ask yourself:

- Is my will current and valid?
- What is my current net worth? Review it toward the end of each year.
- Are titles to family assets in the right names for best tax results? (This could change with tax laws.)
- Is my insurance coverage current and adequate?
- Are all of my vital papers in order so that they will not cause my survivors any problems?

You might prepare another item: a current list of all important contacts, such as your banker, lawyer, CPA, executor, doctor, burial plot location, and car titles.

MANAGEMENT—*Red Flags*

Q: *"You hear so much about sudden and unexpected bankruptcies. Aren't there any red flags that an owner can watch out for?"*

There are indeed many telltale signs of impending business doom. The SBA's affiliate agencies, SCORE and SBDC, often tell us that they get called in too late to save a business—even though this service is free. In many cases businesses can be saved and made fiscally viable again, especially in cases in which the SBA acts as a loan guarantor. Numerous books give warnings of such problems that often lead to the demise of a business. Among the major pitfalls that might be called the "red flags before the sunset" are the following:

- Your own sales results consistently lag well behind your forecasts. Who's fooling whom?
- If your traditional backlog of a manufacturer's supplies drops sharply, your salespeople are not producing as well as normally. Better look into it and be ready for adjustments.
- Cash shortfalls? Borrowing from payroll taxes? Playing catch-up ball with the IRS is a dangerous game.
- If your business is too dependent on one or a few large accounts, you could become vulnerable if that major customer cuts back sharply or finds a different resource.
- Your accounts payable suddenly become far larger than they used to be. Suppliers are often too lenient because they want your business—until the A/R become too burdensome to carry. When a major supplier lowers the boom, you are likely to go bust.
- Do major suppliers, and even minor ones, insist on talking to you about overdue accounts, instead of to your bookkeeper? It indicates that their ability to carry you or their patience is wearing thin. Look out, and look into it.
- If a supplier with whom you have enjoyed regular credits suddenly demands C.O.D. payments, don't get angry and look for other suppliers to add strain to your credit reputation. Find out what's happening and make amends. Corrective action can restore the needed faith between business partners.
- Angry creditors, impatient banks, and even personal lenders whom you cannot satisfy as promised, might gang up and force you to sign personal guarantees. It makes you vulnerable. This does not happen suddenly, but when it does, you need to examine the causes and take quick and positive action.
- Check your monthly "uncollectible" list. If there is a dramatic

increase from previous norms—one or two or three percent—you are either accepting too many high-risk accounts or whoever does your credit and collecting is too lax. One major accountant says "35 days is the beginning to pay attention and take action."

- When problems crop up in business, don't take a "mañana" attitude that somehow, miraculously, things will get better tomorrow. They rarely will. Work with professionals to get advice at the first sign of trouble. If you wait for the sunset, you can be sure old sol will go down. If you can catch the light while you can still see clearly, you have a chance. And as we said earlier—sometimes talking to an outside counselor at SCORE, SBDC, the Chamber of Commerce, the bank, and others, costs nothing except a little pride. And it surely doesn't have to precede a fall.

MANAGEMENT—*Regulations*

Q: *"There are so many government regulations, I'm afraid I might miss one and get myself into trouble. Do you have a list of them to check off?"*

There are so many on several levels that you are best off to check locally. The local SBA office or the SCORE office can help you, if you do not have an attorney. Here is a general checklist that will get you started:

- County or city tax collector's office to register as a business and get payroll report forms
- State employment office for forms on personal income tax, disability insurance, unemployment insurance, employee withholding taxes
- Workman's compensation insurance forms from your own insurance carrier or the State Compensation Insurance Fund
- Internal Revenue Service office for Federal Payroll Tax forms and to get an employers' identification number, as well as Forms W-4 and Circular E
- Information on occupational safety standards from the nearest OSHA office (federal)
- The U.S. Immigration and Naturalization Service requires documentation that each employee is registered if of foreign origin—get "Employment Elegibility Verification Form I-9" from the nearest INS office
- For exporting goods, contact nearest office of U.S. Department of Commerce regarding specific licensing requirements

- The county clerk's office will issue information on procedure if you are using a "fictitious name" other than you own
- If you plan to incorporate, contact the secretary of state of your state
- If you have business property, you need to contact the county assessor's office to register
- If you sell directly, sales taxes may have to be collected and your state sales tax office has to issue proper documentation as well as your municipality

The SBA office will be happy to send you a "Start-Up Kit," too.

MANAGEMENT—*Return-on-Investment (ROI)*

Q: *"What should my return-on-investment be in a retail business?"*

This question is too broad to answer with a single reply. How long do you cook a pound of meat? It depends on how you like it and on the quality of the meat and the eater's preferences. In retailing, each merchandise category has typical and traditional markups and profits. Of course you need to include your own income, or draw, in the overhead, as you need to be compensated for your work just as if you were working for someone else in the same capacity. What is left over after all expenses are satisfied and accounted for is the net profit—or the return-on-investment (ROI). If this were less than what you might get in a bank, you might question whether 1) you are conducting your business properly or 2) whether you wouldn't be better off working for somebody else. Of course there are other reasons for being in business—self-satisfaction, greater freedom of action and decision, and the hoped-for buildup of equity in the event you want to sell the business for a larger, lump-sum profit sometime in the future.

 Average returns on your investment can be determined by consulting a knowledgeable attorney or contacting your trade or professional association that might have such statistics available. The U.S. Department of Commerce and Dun & Bradstreet also compile averages in 45 categories from appliance stores to video stores. Net profits vary wildly, depending on the volume of total business done, on the category of merchandise, and on the type of operation. Obviously, stores that render much personal service, have an exclusive location and reputation, and sell highly selective merchandise will have a higher mark-up (profit) but make far fewer sales. These could include fine jewelry, designer fashions, gourmet foods, Rolls Royces, and high-powered law firms. On the other hand, mass marketers like supermarkets and discount variety stores operate on a high volume, low-mark-up basis. However, their smaller percentage profit is multiplied by a far higher unit count. All theory aside, ROI is often determined by sources outside your control such as competition. It will be helpful, however, to get some personal opinions from an experienced member of SCORE and to check out the following brochures published by the SBA:

> "Simple Breakeven Analysis for Small Stores" (publication FM-11)
> "A Pricing Checklist for Small Retailers" (publication FM-12)
> "Pricing Your Products and Services Profitably" (publication FM-13)

MANAGEMENT—*SBA Assistance*

Q: *"Sometimes it gets a bit lonely running one's own business. Occasionally, I'd like to get some outside opinions. Does the SBA provide any personal counseling?"*

The SBA, through more than a hundred field offices, has small business development officers. Usually small business inquiries by one-person businesses like yours are referred to the nearest SCORE office. This office will be staffed by volunteer executives, most of them retired, but some still actively engaged in business, who lend their time and expertise to counsel entrepreneurs like you. This service is not only free, but it is impartial and confidential. These SCORE volunteers come from all walks of business and it would be wise to be as specific as you can in your conseling application, so that the SCORE office to whom you apply can match up an executive with you who has had parallel or similar experience. He or she can be of truly pragmatic help and the price is right—it's free. SCORE counsels in three general areas: when you want to start a new business or expand the one you are running now; when you realize you are running into trouble and cannot solve the dilemma by yourself; and, of course, when you have a specific problem in management and are seeking a "second opinion." Look in the blue government section of your city phone book; under Small Business Administration, you will find a listing and phone number for the nearest office of the Service Corps of Retired Executives (SCORE). Call them for a Form 641, a detailed application form, and an appointment. The best time to do that is today.

MANAGEMENT—*Security*

Q: *"I think I'm being shoplifted to death . . . from the inside. How can I protect myself?"*

The number of cases that show how clever employees can be in syphoning off minor and major items and profits are legion. Especially in this age of electronic record-keeping and money transfers, it has become a very sophisticated cat-and-mouse game between employers and some less-than-honest employees. Internal theft does not have to be limited to the top-level employees. Anyone who handles money or finds lack of supervision can be tempted into petty thievery. We know of one case in which a bartender working the late shift by himself brought in his own cash register and siphoned off one-third of the gross intake. He was finally caught red-handed when a puzzled proprietor hired a private investigator whose report and subsequent eyewitness observance led to exposure of this clever scam. If at all possible, it is always best to have one trusted management or family member on hand at all times and to have the employees who handle money bonded by an insurance company. Here is a limited checklist of pointers:

- Keep constant inventory records and make spot comparisons against sales. This is especially true in restaurant and liquor businesses.
- Watch the back door even more than a front door. Too many products and profit leave by that route.
- Keep a sharp eye out for signals between customer and sales person, personal relationships, or customers clustering around one special clerk or sales person.
- Be alert to overrings (kiting), cash left on the counter by customers who don't wait for a receipt, by-passing an item when ringing up a sale.
- And do use a personal shopper occasionally to check on cash register procedures and violations.

MANAGEMENT—*Shifting Economy*

Q: *"The current recession has affected us, and cutbacks in government contracts are likely to increase this problem. Can you give us any help in surviving a possible slowdown?"*

Small businesses that rely on government purchasing departments (such as the Department of Defense) or have in past years benefitted from defense contracts will feel the pinch most acutely. If you haven't already, you should start immediately to diversify your sales. The same situation has occurred for generations when a very large company takes up too great a portion of a small company's production capacity—and then drops the small supplier because of shifts in consumer demand or price competition. It never pays to put too many eggs into one basket. Look into selling to other suppliers, becoming a subcontractor to major contractors, utilizing your personnel and space to produce other, related merchandise or services, testing whether existing customers can buy greater quantities from you, probing related new markets, or making related goods without increasing overhead. To maintain your head above the waters of economic turbulence, you can never be complacent. Complacency in a company is the death knell sounded prior to bankruptcy.

MANAGEMENT—*Starting a Business*

Q: *"I want to start a business of my own but am afraid I'd lose my family . . ."*

This "question" sounds more like a plea for help, but it is quite typical of many men and women who are already settled into a family relationship, have heard from other entrepreneurs how demanding it is to start a new business, and are frankly afraid of having their family and friends play second fiddle—and thus to risk losing them. All of these concerns are real. They must be weighed in relation to the potential gains. In an adjacent entry (see MANAGEMENT—Family), we have tried to outline the needs the entrepreneur must accomodate—how to get one's family involved, how to lay plans to create personal awards, to have both family and a business. No doubt youth and the enthusiasm, energy, and even naïveté that goes with comparative innocence, come in handy. One 26-year-old signmaker in San Francisco, who has become very successful in a decade of operation, stated ten years later, "you have to go into your own business with your eyes wide open. There is a high price to pay that is often too high." He was a bachelor when he started and life was admittedly simpler then. "I would do it all over again, but I am thankful I am established now," he said.

MANAGEMENT—*Taxes*

Q: *"Trying to plan for next year is almost impossible in my business what with all the new federal tax changes. And if Uncle Sam increases taxes, the states are never far behind. Does the SBA have any advance notice on next year's levies?"*

Congress often makes tax changes at the end of a year in order to make ends meet with proposed and enacted laws—all of which invariably call for the expenditure of money. The SBA has no special crystal balls that tell us what to do. However, there are some general areas in which tax adjustments are made, and it would be wise to pay particular attention to these areas and to go over them with your accountant, if you employ one, to anticipate and figure your tax program for the following year. These points include:

- Increased tax on fuel (affects transportation estimates)
- Special increases on selected products, like alcohol, cigarettes, etc.
- Changes in the Uniform Gift and Estate Tax in case you are planning to pass on lifetime gifts to others
- Capital gains tax changes
- Maximum tax rate on high incomes
- Estate tax burden and estate tax freeze
- Special taxes for ecological reasons—such as taxes on chlorofluorocarbons, large engine vehicles, great use of landfills or effluent run-offs
- Taxes on the transfer of securities or the sale of them
- Ceilings on deductions for interest, such as mortgages

MANAGEMENT—*Tax Deductions for Luxury Items*

Q: *"We have a cottage on a lake and a pontoon boat. Often we use these to entertain customers and prospects. Are such expenses still tax deductible?"*

According to recent IRS tax rulings for the 1990s, aside from operating expenses, the cost of facility, like a vacation home or a pleasure boat, cannot ordinarily be claimed as a deduction. The exception might be if such facilities were used by employees and the value thereof is included in the employees' income (and therefore taxed). If any recreational facility, or even a home, is used to entertain business clients, customers, or patients, the food and drink are tax deductible.

MANAGEMENT—*Unusual Businesses*

Q: *"Can you recommend any unusual small businesses that don't cost too much to start up?"*

See the entry under MANAGEMENT—Food Delivery for a typical new business that can be started up for less than $1,000, especially if you use contract drivers to deliver your products (a system pioneered by firms like Domino Pizza). Generally, any service business can be started with little capital. This is especially true if you can operate out of a home or garage; if you can do the work, like consulting, yourself; if you can network your business, your skills, your existence by yourself or within a limited territory or profession, without recourse to costly advertising. Some examples of low-cost start-up businesses are part-time employment service, for instance, placing nurses, domestic services, bookkeeping and budgeting services, reminder and shopping services; gift basket and package services; giving lessons (educational, dancing, music, remedial work) at your home or the home of clients; getting renovation contracts and farming them out; doing market research and surveys for larger firms; establishing newspaper delivery routes; computer repair and enhancement services; publicity and promotion for nonprofit organizations; meeting and dating services; and party-giving and hosting. There is no limit to small service businesses that have been tried and that are profitable and productive. Any one of these can be started within a $1,000 investment, but they all require a finely honed sense of the dramatic, of promoting, and an ability to sell. Most require good stationery, perhaps a box number at the post office, maybe an extra telephone. And all of them require a common ingredient: enough money to keep the entrepreneur going till the business becomes supportive.

MARKETING—*Definition*

Q: *"What actually is marketing? How does it apply to small business?"*

Marketing is a generic term for taking a product or service to the customer or client, including all the many-faceted activities that make such a transfer, and its assumed profit, possible. Some call this activity merchandising or simply selling. But marketing is more encompassing. It can even include the acquisition of the product, its processing and packaging, pricing, advertising and promotion, display and demonstration, selling processes, and training of the sales people involved, comparison shopping and other competitive activities, combination merchandising and markdowns, servicing and delivery, public relations and post-sale concerns—even market research. Just as real estate people say that the three most important ingredients in a property are location, location, location, so we can also say that the three most important phases in selling goods and services are marketing, marketing, marketing.

Because marketing involves so many facets and can be the source of sizable losses if erroneously executed, it becomes the most important, omnipotent, universal activity in small and large business. Entire college courses and ponderous books are written on marketing. The entrepreneur who is imaginative enough and sufficiently skilled in marketing knows that this is one major phase of business he or she must master in order to survive and succeed. Each of the facets mentioned above must be carefully planned, considered, weighed, tested, and related to results to see if the expenditure in effort and money was worthwhile and effective.

This one brief answer cannot substitute for a course, a focused book, or your pragmatic experience, but here is a 10-point checklist against which you can weigh your marketing plans and efforts:

1. Product or service—Is there a real need for this in the marketplace? Is the product or service *finished* as to quality, utility, value?
2. Location—Is your place of business suitable for it?
3. Market size—Is it large enough to make the marketing of the product or service profitable?
4. Customer/clients—Who are they? Does your product or service meet their demands and expectations?
5. Market mix—Is the product or service sufficiently specialized to be attractive to your planned audience?
6. Competition—Can it be overcome and still make a profit for you? How can you be different? What are the competitor's vulnerabilities?
7. Distribution—This two-sided facet includes purchasing (the adequacy and reliability of your sources or suppliers) and selling (responsible policies and personnel in place).
8. Price—Is it competitive as well as profitable to you? If not, can you find better resources? Can you shave your overhead and delivery cost?
9. Promotion—Is it adequate to reach enough of your actual and potential customers? Is it a comparatively good value? Does it return expected results? If not, what changes in method or medium should you make?
10. Financial—Have you projected the market size and price of your products or services in terms of total dollars? Do you have adequate financing to supply that market on a continuous basis?

A booklet published by the SBA will also be useful: "Marketing for Small Business: An Overview" (publication MT-2).

MARKETING—*Flea Markets*

Q: "Do you have any information on flea markets? I think that I can get into a part-time business of my own that way."

Flea markets can indeed be entered with very little capital. Because many of these markets are held outdoors, they tend to be seasonal in the North and more regular in the South where weather allows outdoor stands the year around. Outdoor space is also much cheaper to rent than indoor space. Flea markets are often held weekends only, which makes this form of marketing ideal for those holding fulltime jobs during the week. Considerable time must also be devoted to purchasing goods, processing, ticketing, and transportation to the site. If items are bulky, an appropriate vehicle will have to be acquired. Many outdoor flea market spaces will require that you have display tables, will proscribe certain sizes for fixtures, and place limitations on signs. Centralized services such as utilities, security, sanitation, and promotions are usually furnished as part of your rental. It takes relatively little "scratch" to become a flea market entrepreneur. The better and bigger ones are usually listed in the Yellow Pages or can be found in "The Great American Flea Market Directory" (P.O. Box 17131, Memphis, TN 38187), which lists state-by-state flea markets, swap meets, and antique and collectors' shows. Flea markets are good places to try out different types of merchandise, test-market, or sell discounted or discontinued goods that can usually be purchased at advantageous prices. Remember that, unless you have personal connections to merchandise resources, most flea market transactions are for cash.

MARKETING—*Mail Order*

Q: "I read that mail order is a growing segment of retailing. Do you have any corroboration of this trend?"

During the past few years, the mail order business has increased at least 10 percent each year. This is double the increase for more traditional forms of retailing. The reasons that customers are increasingly turning to ordering merchandise from mail order catalogs and offerings are the crowding of stores due to our burgeoning population, the entry of more and more traditional stores into mail order, and the fact that prices can be maintained in mail order merchandising better. Improvement in catalog design and copy, more competitive pricing, and better service than customers get in many large retail stores are some of the additional reasons for mail order growth. J.C. Penney, for instance, does about 20 percent of its $15 billion in nationwide business through mail order and expects to double this by the end of this decade. As retailing switches more to mail order marketing, such marketing must be conducted with greater sophistication. Each mailing piece is expensive and becoming more so. Constant testing is necessary to prevent major blunders and it takes experts—not merely wisdom and instinct—to arrive at the right formulae. Of course there are business patterns that we have learned, but they are neither infallible nor irrevocable. People change; regional likes and dislikes change. With the proper offerings, copy, and incentives, those merchandising peaks and valleys can be levelled off. No trend is 100 percent predictable. Constant, intelligent testing is needed to determine type of merchandise, headlines, copy approach, pricing, combinations, and focus. The surest rule in mail order is that there are no absolute rules.

MARKETING—*New Businesses*

Q: *"I want to go into a business of my own but have limited capital to invest. Which businesses have the best chances to make it in the nineties and beyond?"*

While the SBA and its affiliated agencies cannot tell you what business to go into, we can pass on information that might give you some inspiration and direction. As an example, an issue of *Entrepreneur* magazine described "21 Hottest Businesses for 1991." They listed the following:

1. Event planning—ways to jazz up meetings and conventions in this $50 billion business.
2. Cruise-only travel agencies—$4 billion in annual sales is this growing segment of the travel industry that annually attracts 3,700,000 travelers.
3. Gift baskets—Averaging $15 to $150 each, this phase of personal and corporate gift business is gaining in popularity. Many items are personalized or manufactured at home.
4. Chicken wings—Fast becoming eating-out favorites, these zesty snacks are the hot dorm-food alternative for pizza.
5. Specialty personnel—"Temps" have become a way life for companies, especially small ones or those with specialized and seasonal needs. It's a nearly $11 billion business.

6. Senior day care—A growing trend as our elderly population grows, the other end of the child day care center industry.

7. Mail order—As population expansion marches onward, more people prefer to shop the convenient by-mail way. In 1990 nonbusiness customers spent $81.7 billion, a figure almost doubled by business mail order sales.

8. Exercise wear—Growing in popularity as well as utility; now nearing $25 billion a year in volume. Add to that over $12 billion in athletic shoes.

9. Exporting—Encouraged by all levels of the federal and state governments, sales abroad amount to more than eight percent of GNP, and the figure is growing.

10. Food delivery—Restaurants sign up with the delivery service and customers can choose from virtually any type of food and have it delivered hot to their home or office. Restaurants do not need any expansion or additional help.

11. Desktop publishing—Nearly a million desktop computers are sold annually and the ready-for-the-printer business is flourishing.

12. Summer camps—Instructional and specialized culture camps are proliferating in this opulent society.

13. Child learning centers—Independent and franchise centers teach children with modern methods, after school and weekends, rather than having them stay at home, mesmerized by the boob tube.

14. Building doctors—Specialists who tie into the Environmental Protection Agency's warning about polluted *indoor* air and gases, chemical and water pollution, and help safeguard homeowners from the dangers of modern society.

15. Recycling consultants—Awareness that we are drowning ourselves in garbage and waste has created a new class of "environmentalists" who advise homeowners, offices, manufacturers, and institutions on how to reduce their refuse and perhaps even recoup money from the process.

16. Mexican food—$1.5 billion dollars worth of tacos, burritos, tamales, and enchilades are being swallowed up each year, all over the U.S. It's a trend that's continuing.

17. Gourmet take-out—Growing sophistication of the American palate has created a $57 billion takeout foods industry, and a growing percentage is in gourmet foods. It's a trend worth watching and sharing.

18. Educational products—Books and toys are becoming more and more education-oriented and specialized stores are doing well, especially when run by entrepreneurs with educational backgrounds.

19. Computer consulting—There are nearly 60 million computers of all types on the American market. Keeping those computers operating efficiently and the operators up-to-date with changes and software, is the business of a growing host of experts.
20. Healthful desserts—Calorie-conscious consumers and label-readers of nutritional information are making this food category a growth business of the decade.
21. Bicycle shops—More than $3 billion worth of bikes and accessories are sold annually. The resurgent popularity of bike transportation augurs well for the business.

MARKETING—*Newsletters*

Q: *"In my service business I think a periodical newsletter to clients and prospective clients would be the preferred public relations medium. Do you have any guidelines on how to put one together?"*

Newsletters, when well-done and not used as a chain letter or for the dissemination of internal gossip, can be a powerful advertising and public relations medium. They can last a long time if their content is of benefit to the recipient; they can make a favorable impression upon clients and prospects by their design and content; they can get lengthy messages across and capture the receiver's attention for a much longer period than ads and sales letters; they can penetrate spaces and times when the reader is at ease and receptive to the newsletter's messages; they can get several viewpoints, many bits of information, and many sales points across in one compact package; they might even be retained over a period of time and invite response. On the other hand, producing a newsletter requires considerable time, professionalism, effort, and money. The selection of the right subscriber list is even more critical because of its cost in production and probably postage. Today's computer capabilities make newsletter production more feasible and easier. To recap recommendations for an effective newsletter, consider these points:

- An effective nameplate or masthead.
- Use good, attention-getting headlines that lead the reader into each article.
- Use neat, easy-to-read body type, and proofread!
- Use photos and illustration, but be sure they reproduce clearly. If they are bad, eliminate them.
- Use graphic accents such as boxes, rules, and italics to highlight articles, features, and pages.

- Use consistency in elements that are repeated from one issue to the next—the masthead, column heads, features, logos. These build up familiarity and interest.

In addition you might consider a table of contents on the front page. Be sure, too, that the address is clear, straight, and correct. Use a title in the subscriber address, such as Mr., Mrs., Dr., or V.P. Be sure each newsletter is properly dated and paginated. Build in some device that might elicit a response, like a query, a quiz, an 800 number for inquiries, or a recommendation and contribution to the subsequent issue.

MARKETING—*Nose for News*

Q: *"What chances does a small business have when national issues create uncertainties and even recessions?"*

There is little the small, local businessperson can do about the larger national or even international economic situation. Yet it is important to keep yourself up-to-date on trends, preferences, layoffs, income and style shifts, etc. Small business is most frequently local in nature, hence what happens down at the diner, at the truck stop, at the Moose club or Legion hall, can and usually does affect your business in your own bailiwick. While you might be a small businessperson, you have a vote and you pay taxes. This entitles you to participate in the greatest organization in the world—the American taxpayers' league. Your local office of U.S. senator or representative, or your state and county and municipal representatives need not only your vote, but your opinion. In turn, they can keep you informed as to what's going on nationally and locally that affects your planning for the future. It seems that the small businessperson is helpless to effect changes in the larger context of our nation, but 90 million individuals in business and the many associations in which they hold memberships form the sounding board that makes up our national policy. If you sometimes feel a little alone and helpless, join the local chamber of commerce or a national trade or professional organization and become active, especially on the political action committee or communications medium. Tell yourself over and over again: "If it's to be, it's up to me!"

MARKETING—*Prospecting*

Q: *"How do I go about finding prospects? I am starting a personal service business."*

As with other marketing activities, candid analysis of your potential and real prospects, an honest assessment of your product or service, and a frank look in the mirror at the person who will be responsible for most of the contacts are the first steps. It takes personal honesty and courage to consider all the advantages and admit the disadvantages of your special talents and the products or services you will be trying to influence others to purchase. Put yourself into the place of your customer or prospect. Why would you want to buy your offering? What benefits do you hope to gain from it? How much is it worth to you? And would you be the one from whom you want to buy? If it is possible to be totally objective about these answers, then you will come close to becoming a successful entrepreneur and find prospects galore.

Using existing customers is probably one of the best ways of locating others, especially if you can build some sort of incentive into your presentation to your existing, satisfied customers. Talk to your suppliers and trade reps. They want you to do well because they depend on your success. Trade associations, professional groups, chambers of commerce, trade fairs and shows, even civic association luncheon meetings are all good sources for prospecting. Keep immaculate records on everyone; that is often half the battle. They can be a gold mine and you already own them.

MARKETING—*Publicity*

Q: "*I know that I must advertise my business to spread the word to my potential customers, but my expendable funds are so tight that I need to find other, less costly ways. What do you think of publicity? How do you handle that?*"

Publicity is a potent marketing medium that is used by virtually every major and medium firm—and is underused by small ones. It takes a little more effort than paid advertising, and it is never guaranteed, but if and when it does get into the local newspapers, magazine, radio or tv, it can be highly effective. Because publicity appears as a news story, it sounds more credible to the reader. There are three ingredients that you need for a publicity campaign:

1. A sound reason for sending out a publicity article—This could be a grand opening, relocation, acquisition of a new manager or other vital employee, a new product line, an anniversary, a particularly successful sale or application, a successful customer or client who used your product or service, a renovation or restyling, or a national award.

2. Professional-looking stationery and a professional style of writing
    the news story—It should be factual, concise, devoid of bombast
    and boasts, and not contain anything (like prices or price reduc-
    tions) that should be in a paid ad. Ask a pro for advice; ask a local
    SCORE counselor to help you; go to see the local editor or ad-
    vertising manager and ask for help.
3. Direct your publicity to the right source—Make sure the name of
    the editor or program manager is correct. Type the news story
    clearly on a typewriter or computer. Use white 8½ × 11 inch
    paper, and send the article with or without a picture via first class
    mail. Or deliver it in person.

    If you do not present your publicity release to the editor or
    station in person, write a little personal note and attach it to your
    news. It's just a little balm on the path to successful publicity.

    Don't overlook the small publications or stations (such as
    cable) or those specialized columnists and subeditors (like the
    business editor). It will be easier to get your article published if
    you aim it at a narrower audience. If there are society or gossip
    columns, you might be able to plant a juicy bit of humor or inside
    information, just so they spell your name right!

If you follow these general rules, you'll probably have a fifty-fifty
chance of getting a news story into the media. You need to create
publicity stories often and send them out regularly. The effort is great;
the cost is low; but when it works, it's great marketing. It can even be
used for post-publicity displays and mailings—and will look so good
in the scrapbook.

MARKETING—*Sales Promotion*

Q: *"How do I advertise and promote my business most effectively and
economically?"*

We cannot compress a four-year college course into one page, but there
are certain basic concepts to follow:

1. You need a goal: What do you wish to achieve by advertising? Set
    down your several goals for each purpose.
2. How can you reach your potential customers with your product,
    service, and corporate message? You need to study available me-
    dia, their circulation or audience, their cost (including production
    cost), the possible waste and overlap with other media.
3. How much do you want to invest in this activity? Is it a flat sum?

A percentage of known sales? Or of estimated sales? What are the traditional cost ratios in your industry? (Trade associations and journals as well as local newspapers can give you some answers.)

4. Who will prepare the advertising/promotion message professionally and at what cost? (Advertising agencies usually charge a 15 percent fee, though this is variable; most media, other than local newspapers and direct mail, have a 15 percent agency rebate built into their price structures or rates.)

5. Are you doing any testing before you invest the entire budget? Talking to trade reps and newspaper, radio and tv reps? Getting estimates from printers, including typesetting, artwork, addressing, stuffing and postage? Analyze critically the accuracy and age of your mailing list. The finest direct mail piece won't get results if it doesn't get to the right prospect. Ask around among other merchants and professionals, tradesmen and salesmen. Read your trade journals and the library's texts. Make an appointment with a SCORE counselor and ask pointed questions.

6. Keep records of results for each advertising effort. Make monthly comparisons and compare results.

7. Make long-range plans for marketing that include every facet of your business; never let up; marketing is a never-ending business. Customer loyalty usually lasts only as long as some competitor is absent.

8. Don't miss out on public relations, which is often free and even more effective than paid advertising. "PR" includes every single exposure to the public—newsworthy publicity stories, good signs, good stationery, neat vehicles and uniforms, utilization of all peripheral media, such as statements and bills; window displays; sales training of your employees; and relations with community organizations.

Some of the SBA's booklets can be useful. Get them now from the local SBA office, SCORE, or send for them:

"Marketing for Small Business," (publication MT 2)
"Marketing Checklist for Small Retailers," (publication MT 4)
"Researching Your Market," (publication MT 8)
"Selling by Mail Order," (publication MT 9)
"Advertising," (publication MT 11)

MARKETING—*Signs-to-Sell*

Q: "*We have a shop in a high-traffic, high-rent location. Because of that we limit our advertising expenditure, but want to take advantage of the high traffic with good signage. Do you have any information on how to use signs to best advantage?"*

Signs are a potent sales medium when handled judiciously. Their message (copy) needs to be as carefully developed as advertising copy and publicity releases. Their graphic execution should be professional and in keeping with the image that you want your shop to project. Unless you have the talent and time, you will do best to find a signmaker who is astute and artistic enough to create the appropriate signage. Signs provide identification; they are a medium for a direct message about your business; and they provide an image of your business. Although it seems elementary, make especially sure of correct spelling. It is surprising how many times a sign is misspelled and induces derision instead of producing dollars.

Your external sign and the proper zoning for it is no doubt already in place. So what we are talking about are signs that identify specific merchandising or promotional events, or that sell specific merchandise or services. Signs can also be subtle or direct sales tools. With personal salesmanship often lacking, signs can compensate by offering information, enticement, separation of suspects and prospects. They can carry permanent policy messages, give price and maker information, save the time of your personnel, bring lookers inside your shop and turn them into customers, and they are as unobtrusive or attention-getting as you want to make them. It's truly the medium that is the message.

MARKETING—*Test Marketing*

Q: *"How can I tell if my product will sell? Or how much I should stock in my inventory?"*

The determination of whether a product will sell and how much to keep on hand in your inventory is a combination of market know-how, research, and luck. Most products have cycles determined by fashions, styles, popularity, competition, seasons, and other factors. The fact that many marketers and manufacturers guess wrong is proved by the proliferation of discount stores, remainder piles in book stores, and warehouse and odd-lot sales across the country. Since keeping inventory on hand ties up money, adds to obsolescence, causes price reductions, and affects a company's liquidity, it requires some sharp guesstimating, knowledge of your particular market and supply-and-demand curves, and accurate record keeping and analysis. The SBA booklet "Inventory Management" (publication MP 22) can be a guide. Before manufacturing or buying any sizable quantity of merchandise, an astute businessperson will try to market-test the product with smaller quantities and in a confined market. Only if a product is proved by actual sales, market research and/or very obvious market trends, should it be stocked in depth. Unless you are dealing with a commodity that promises to be in scarce supply and thus increase in value, it is best to keep inventory lean. It is very rare that merchandising shortages occur, except during wartime, when goods are bought abroad, or are part of a liquidation sale.

MARKET RESEARCH—*Future Trends*

Q: *"It's difficult to expand a small business, so we'd like to minimize the risks by knowing what some of the national merchandising trends are in the nineties."*

Reading your trade journals, attending meetings of your trade or professional organizations, and networking with your peers is one good way to keep up with "what's ahead." Nobody has a crystal ball, but we know from reading and demographic studies as well as census data what some of the trends are. These are among the ones we perceive:

- Baby boomers (now in their forties) will spend more heavily in high-tech and computer items.
- Interest in nostalgia merchandise, as opposed to preoccupation with youthful things, will continue.
- First children will receive the lion's share of parents' expenditures.
- Unless a serious economic downturn occurs, upwardly mobile families will save more and accumulate assets for later years.
- In the big-spending area, dual-earning families and professionals (doctors, dentists, lawyers, CPAs, computer experts, major consultants) will invest much of the disposal income on major home improvements, larger homes, private schools, day care, home entertainment systems, and luxury station wagons. More expensive furniture and arty furnishings also will get a big boost.
- Education-related products will receive a goodly share of income—books, subscriptions, newsletters, video products; even seminars and accompanying learning products.
- Recreation will be regarded as a just reward for working hard or having saved money during peak productive years. Cruises will continue to be popular as will expensive trips within the U.S. and Canada.

- Population shifts will include numerical growth through immigration; growth of the over-65 segment (now greater than teenagers); and a concomitant growth of medical, health care, and elder-care products and services.

MARKET RESEARCH—*Getting Information*

Q: *"Where do I get general business information?"*

This is a very broad subject that will require much study. The more you can learn up front, the more secure you will be in your business afterwards. Many a business has foundered because of lack of information and knowledge—even more than businesses have gone bankrupt because of lack of money. If you know how to handle money properly, you will not get into financial binds that can lead to bankruptcy. Here is a checklist of 10 sources for business information:

1. SBA publications. These are available through the local SBA or SCORE office. Dozens of titles are 50 cents to $1.00 each. A free list is available by making a local phone call or the national toll-free number 800 368-5855 or ordering from SBA Publications, P.O. Box 15434, Ft. Worth, TX 76119.
2. SBA local office, SCORE or SBDC offices, your state's business development office (in the capital): Check for available workshops.
3. Local library: Some larger libraries have business reference sections and specialists available. *Books in Print, Readers Index, Standard Rate and Data Service, Literary Marketplace, Gale Directories, Thomas Directories,* as well as the *Business Information Sourcebook,* and *Small Business Information Handbook* by Gustav Berle (John Wiley & Sons, Inc.), are just some of the books that can be useful.
4. Chamber of Commerce: There are over 4,500 of them in the U.S. and they are a fount of information on local business. Membership in and identification with the local chamber of commerce can be valuable.
5. State Department of Economic Development: Virtually every state has, usually in the capital, one or more agencies that help businesses get started, progress, and even aid financing. Look in the blue government section of your capital's telephone book. A good resource: *The States and Small Business* published by the SBA and sold by the Superintendent of Documents, U.S. Government Printing Office, Washington, DC 20402.

6. Universities: Local universities might have departments in general business or specifically in your field, libraries, professors or graduate students available for professional consultations, or house an office of the SBDC (Small Business Development Center, affiliated with the SBA).

7. Trade Associations: Of the several thousand trade and professional associations, there must be one in your field. Membership in that group, a visit to their headquarters, reading their newsletter or magazine, and checking literature published by them are steps to gain specific knowledge. If you do not know where yours is located, ask the local reference librarian to check it out for you.

8. Suppliers: The manufacturers and distributors in your line of business might have much information available on merchandise and markets and even on your competititors. They will welcome you as a potential new customer.

9. Books: Each year 50,000 books are produced. *Books in Print*, to be found in your library, lists even more. *Gale's Directories in Print* lists over 9,700 directories on every conceivable subject. The U.S. Government Printing Office produces a stream of books and sells them by mail or in U.S. Government Book Stores. Many libraries have government books and business books in special sections. They are a gold mine of information and knowledge.

10. Periodicals: Every trade and profession, every form of business, has its plethora of periodicals issued on varying schedules. *Standard Rate and Data Service* is one directory that lists thousands of them, alphabetized by category—one in a consumer directory, the other in a business directory. Major libraries will have them on file. *Ulrich's Directory* and *Working Press of the Nation* as well as *Literary Market Place* (LMP) are other directories. Wiley's *Business Information Sourcebook* (1991) lists a good cross-section of all of them among its 2,000 entries.

MARKET RESEARCH—*Industry Information*

Q: "*Where do I get more specific information on my industry?*"

See MARKET RESEARCH—Getting Information, adjacent to this entry. Concentrate on trade associations and trade publications in your special field. Check suppliers. Check firms in the same field in your own area and in other areas further away. The latter especially can be sources of sound, pragmatic information, and because they will not feel that you will compete with them, will open up more readily. If there are trade shows or expositions that you can attend, talking to exhibitors, fellow tradesmen or professionals, and picking up literature that is invariably available, will be immensely helpful.

MARKET RESEARCH—*Out-of-State Research*

Q: "We are thinking of opening a branch operation in San Francisco. What are some ways we can do advance research to learn about this market?"

These suggestions apply not only to San Francisco, but to parallel situations almost anywhere in the U.S. There are certain basic resources that can be studied and that cost very little more than a few stamps and phone calls:

- The business editor or advertising manager of the major local newspaper: You can get the name, address, circulation, and costs from your library's files of the *Standard Rate and Data Service* (newspaper volume), *Literary Marketplace* (LMP), or *Working Press of the Nation* (newspaper section).
- Many major cities, and San Francisco is one of them, have city magazines, usually monthly. Their addresses are also in the above references (magazine section).
- Likewise, many large cities have business newspapers. In San Francisco you have the *S.F. Business Times*. Two valuable features in that publication are "On File," which lists more than 1,000 business contact leads each week, and the newspaper's "Top 25 List," a weekly listing of the top 25 companies in a particular industry. A collection of the year's pages makes for a good supplier and advisory list.
- You can contact local business organizations that are helpful, such as the local SBA office, SCORE, the Chamber of Commerce, and Better Business Bureau. The business office of the local telephone company and local banks are also good contacts, as is networking with clubs to which you might belong such as the Rotarians.

MARKET RESEARCH—*Product Forecast*

Q: "How can I tell if my product will sell and how much I might be able to sell?"

Since the amount of products you manufacture or purchase depends very much on your estimated sales, this is a highly critical problem.

The correct answers to this problem can mean the difference between profit and loss. Market research prior to manufacture or purchase is needed. There are three ways to go about it: 1) studying the market through research of published material; 2) making opinion surveys; and 3) testing the market through actual sales. A fourth test might be participation in a trade show. Let us explore the four methods.

1) Your library probably has books and trade references on your particular industry or profession. A good guidebook is *Do-It-Yourself Marketing Research* by A.B. Blankenship and George Breen (McGraw-Hill, Inc., 1989). Professional and trade publications and associations can reveal an astonishing amount of pertinent information, as will government studies available through the libraries or the U.S. Government Printing Office.

2) Opinion surveys can be made by asking a sufficient number of store, office, or manufacturers' buyers, or larger numbers of direct customers. One technique is to ask opinions on existing and established products vs. a "blind" item (unidentified) such as yours.

3) Sales testing is the real acid test. Ask people to buy a small quantity of your product or a limited amount of your service, offering either in person, by mail, or possibly on consignment in a few stores. Follow-ups are mandatory to obtain pragmatic test results.

4) Trade show participation is not always feasible, but it, too, is an acid test of your product or service. A dramatic sales booth display and attractive offer can result in hundreds of prospects or even sales, though the total cost of a trade show participation and the effort involved can be considerable. Be sure to use such trade show participation for an opinion survey.

MARKET RESEARCH—*Where to Locate*

Q: "I am retiring from the military [or from the federal civil service] and want to start a small business of my own in the field in which I am trained. I can go anywhere in the United States. Where do you think I have the best chance?"

The SBA has some statistics that might be helpful, but there are at least three other considerations in determining where to open or purchase a small business: 1) your family's preference and yours as to climate, recreational facilities, housing costs, need for your particular skill, proximity of friends and family, and a host of other criteria; 2) statistics of particular local communities that might be obtained from local chambers of commerce (i.e., Manchester, Vermont, Austin, Texas, and Orlando, Florida, are among the best growth communities); 3) cost-of-living index in a particular area that will determine the net cost of living well, and that would include property, rentals, taxes, food costs, health care, transportation, and more. Statistics can tell the general story, but visiting a location of your choice for an adequate period of time, talking to its inhabitants and business people and perhaps to the local SCORE counselors (which is a free service of this SBA-affiliated small business counseling association), will help you determine your next move. Meanwhile, here are some rounded-off figures from the 10 regions of the country into which the census, and the SBA, divides the U.S.

The following figures are rounded off and are typical for 1990. The ratios express the number of inhabitants for each known small business. Regions are identified as follows:

   I. Maine, New Hampshire, Vermont, Massachusetts, Rhode Island, Connecticut
  II. New York, New Jersey, Puerto Rico, Virgin Islands
 III. Pennsylvania, Delaware, Maryland, Virginia, West Virginia, Washington, DC
  IV. North Carolina, South Carolina, Georgia, Florida, Mississippi, Alabama, Tennessee, Kentucky
   V. Ohio, Indiana, Michigan, Illinois, Wisconsin, Minnesota
  VI. Louisiana, Arkansas, Texas, Oklahoma, New Mexico
 VII. Missouri, Kansas, Iowa, Nebraska
VIII. North Dakota, South Dakota, Colorado, Wyoming, Utah, Montana

Small Business vs. Population, U.S. 1990

Region	Population	Small Businesses	Ratio (number of people per business)
I	12,700,000	215,000	60.5
II	25,500,000	445,000	57.3
III	26,000,000	345,000	75.4
IV	44,000,000	595,000	73.9
V	46,000,000	700,000	65.7
VI	28,000,000	465,000	60.2
VII	12,000,000	205,000	58.5
VIII	7,700,000	145,000	53.1
IX	33,000,000	520,000	63.5
X	8,000,000	155,000	51.6

IX. California, Arizona, Nevada, Hawaii, Guam, American Samoa, Pacific Trust Territories

X. Oregon, Washington, Idaho, Alaska

MINORITY PROGRAMS

Q: *"What special minority programs does the SBA have available?"*

The principal minority assistance program is the 8(a) program, designed to help socially and economically disadvantaged small firms become government contractors. To be eligible for the 8(a) program, a small business concern must be at least 51 percent owned, controlled, and operated on a daily basis by one or more socially or economically disadvantaged persons. Socially disadvantaged individuals are those who have been subjected to racial or ethnic prejudice or cultural bias because of their identification with minority groups. Economically disadvantaged people are those socially disadvantaged individuals whose ability to compete in the free enterprise system has been impaired due to diminished capital and credit opportunities.

Black Americans, Native Americans, Hispanic Americans, Asian Pacific Americans, and Asian Indian Americans have been officially designated socially disadvantaged. Members of other groups must show proof of social disadvantage. Economic disadvantage must be established by all applicants. SBA establishes eligibility on a case-by-case basis.

The SBA cannot guarantee contract support, but will try its best to help. In the final analysis, contracts depend on approval of the 8(a) applicant, availability of Federal contracts in other agencies, and the viability of the applicant to produce the required products or services within a specified time.

Some valuable contacts exist outside of the SBA that are worth exploring. These include:

National Association of Black and Minority Chambers of Commerce, 654 13th St., Oakland, CA 94612-1241. Primarily in the tourist and convention field.

National Association of Investment Companies, 915 15th St. NW, Suite 700, Washington, DC 20005. A trade association that invests in small businesses owned by socially and economically disadvantaged companies.

National Association of Minority Contractors, 806 15th St. NW, Suite 340, Washington, DC 20005. Educational programs, networking opportunities.

National Business League, 4324 Georgia Ave. NW, Washington, DC 20011. Has 127 chapters countrywide; the voice of Black business on Capitol Hill since 1900.

U.S. Hispanic Chamber of Commerce, 4900 Main St., Suite 700, Kansas City, MO 64112. Represents over 400,000 enterprises through more than 200 chapters nationwide.

For more contacts within the Federal establishment, see OSDBU (Office of Small and Disadvantaged Business Utilization)—*Procurement Assistance/Contact Listings.*

MORTGAGE LOANS—*From the SBA*

Q: *"What are the present rules for mortgage financing through the SBA?"*

The SBA will guarantee mortgage loans up to $750,000 for buildings occupied by the business owner or commercial condominiums. Interest rates cannot exceed prime rate plus 2.75 percent, though they can be less. Another popular SBA mortgage loan program is the "504" plan. With this method, the borrower goes to a commercial lender like a bank and borrows 50 percent of the building's appraised value, while he puts up only 10 percent. The SBA will then become a second mortage lender and put up the remaining 40 percent.

MOVING A BUSINESS LOCATION

Q: *"We have to move our business location. It's a very complex and costly procedure and, frankly, I have some trepidations about it. Is there any information on how to handle such a situation?"*

"Locating or Relocating Your Business" is a booklet issued by the SBA (publication MP 2) that could be useful. You will also find that consulting with a local SCORE counselor can give you the advice and experience of others who have been through such a move. If you are already committed to a location, then you can follow these five general steps in making the announcements and getting optimum benefit from your move:

1. Employees—Notify them as soon as you have concluded all arrangements and legal work.
2. Suppliers—Let them know at least 60 days before moving day so that deliveries can be rescheduled properly.

3. Customers and prospects—Send an appropriate and attention-getting announcement about 30 days prior to M-Day. It is another good opportunity to make your business known.
4. Business community—These are the people with whom you network or have social, professional, and civic affiliations; let them know within two weeks before or after the move.
5. General public and the press—Announce it to them as it happens and for a period thereafter, until they get used to the new location.

Relocating your business might be a costly chore, but it can also be a major marketing event—an opportunity to attract customers and new prospects, community, and competitors.

NEW PRODUCT QUALIFICATION

Q: *"What is the procedure for getting a new product on the spec list of various government agencies?"*

A "qualified product" is an item that has been examined and tested for compliance with specification requirements and qualified for inclusion in a Qualified Products List. Such qualification is performed in advance, at the contractor's expense, and independent of any procurement action. The SBA suggests the following five steps be taken in order to have products included on the government's specification list:

1. Check the Commerce Business Daily publication for opportunities to qualify specific products.
2. Contact the procuring agency responsible for the product for specific information relative to qualification requirements.
3. Obtain the applicable specifications from the sources (GPO, GSA or NP&FC, see addresses below).
4. Perform, at your expense, the qualification tests required by the applicable specification.
5. Submit evidence of the qualification tests to the agency indentified in the specification.

Recommended publications, all available from the Superintendent of Documents, U.S. Government Printing Office, Washington, DC 20407, for study are the following:

Index of Federal Specifications and Standards (FPMR 101-29.1)
Department of Defense Index of Specifications and Standards

Federal Standardization Handbook (FMPR 101-29, chapter IV)
Defense Standardization Manual (4120.3-M, Chapter IV, as amended by Military Standards 961 and 962).

Specifications pertaining to civilian government agencies may be obtained from the General Services Administration, Specification Section, Washington, DC 20407.

Firms interested in obtaining specifications pertaining to Defense agencies may obtain the publications from the Naval Publications and Forms Center, 5801 Tabor Ave., Philadelphia, PA 19120.

OPENING A STORE

Q: "We are talking to a franchisor about opening a convenience store. Do you have any general operating figures that can give us some guidance?"

The convenience store industry does more than $60 billion of business a year. The major firm is the Southland Corportion, whose 8,000 "7-11" stores alone do about $8 billion business a year. The average net income is about $40,000 a year. Of that volume, 25 percent is in gasoline sales where pumps are part of the stores. There are around 67,500 stores in the U.S. and despite their sizable volume, as a group they do only a little over 7 percent of the nation's food business. According to the National Association of Convience Stores (NACS) customers patronize convenience stores, despite their 10 to 15 percent higher prices, because of a convenient location (84.4%), fast check-out (75.3%), easy parking (72.8%), long shopping hours (68.9%) and availability of gasoline (63%).

OSDBU (OFFICE OF SMALL AND DISADVANTAGED BUSINESS UTILIZATION)—*Procurement Assistance/ Contact Listings*

Q: "We are a small minority company and want to try and get federal contracts. Don't the various agencies have special sections to facilitate applications for contracts?"

Each of the federal agencies has special offices that offer procurement assistance, most through an Office of Small and Disadvantaged Business Utilization (OSDBU). Many also help in locating prime and subcontracting opportunities. Here is a complete list of their 49 locations:

ADMINISTRATIVE OFFICE OF
   THE U.S. COURTS
Office of Supply and Equipment
719 13th St., N.W.
Rm. 500
Washington, DC 20544
202 633-6299

AGENCY FOR INTERNATIONAL
   DEVELOPMENT
OSDBU
320 21st St., N.W.
Rm. 648
Washington, DC 20523
202 235-1840

BUSINESS SERVICE CENTER
7th & D Sts., S.W.
Rm. 1050
Washington, DC 20407
202 472-1804

COMMODITY FUTURES
   TRADING COMMISSION
Office of Administrative Services
2033 K St., N.W.
Rm. 205
Washington, DC 20581
202 254-9735

DEFENSE LOGISTICS AGENCY
OSDBU
Rm. 4B110. Cameron Station
Washington, DC 22314
703 274-6977

DEPARTMENT OF
   AGRICULTURE
OSDBU
14th St. & Independence Ave.,
   S.W.
Rm. 126-W
Washington, DC 20250
202 447-7117

DEPARTMENT OF THE AIR
   FORCE
OSDBU
Rm. 4C255. The Pentagon
Washington, DC 20330
202 697-5373

DEPARTMENT OF THE ARMY
OSDBU
Rm. 2A712. The Pentagon
Washington, DC 20310
202 697-2868 695-9800

DEPARTMENT OF COMMERCE
OSDBU
14th St. & Constitution Ave.,
   N.W.
Rm. H6411
Washington, DC 20230
202 377-3387

DEPARTMENT OF DEFENSE
OSDBU
Rm. 2A340, The Pentagon
Washington, DC 20301
202 697-1688

DEPARTMENT OF EDUCATION
OSDBU
400 Maryland Ave., S.W.
Rm. 2141
Washington, DC 20202
202 245-9582

DEPARTMENT OF ENERGY
OSDBU
100 Independence Ave., S.W.
Rm. 1E061
Washington, DC 20585
202 252-8214

DEPARTMENT OF HEALTH
AND HUMAN SERVICES
OSDBU
200 Independence Ave., S.W.
Rm. 513D
Washington, DC 20201
202 245-7300

DEPARTMENT OF HOUSING
AND URBAN DEVELOPMENT
OSDBU
7th & D Sts., S.W.
Rm. 10226
Washington, DC 20410
202 755-1428

DEPARTMENT OF THE
INTERIOR
OSDBU
18th & C Sts., N.W.
Rm. 2747
Washington, DC 20240
202 343-4907

DEPARTMENT OF JUSTICE
OSDBU
10th St. & Pennsylvania Ave.,
N.W.
Washington, DC 20530
202 724-6271

DEPARTMENT OF LABOR
OSDBU
200 Constitution Ave., N.W.
Rm. 5-1004
Washington, DC 20210
202 523-9151

DEPARTMENT OF THE NAVY
NICRAD Program
5001 Eisenhower Ave.
Alexandria, VA 22333
703 274-9315

DEPARTMENT OF STATE
OSDBU
Rm. 513 State Annex-6
Washington, DC 20520
703 235-9580

DEPARTMENT OF
TRANSPORTATION
OSDBU
400 7th St., S.W.
Rm. 9414
Washington, DC 20590
202 426-1902

DEPARTMENT OF THE
TREASURY
OSDBU
15th St. & Pennsylvania Ave.,
N.W.
Rm. 1320
Washington, DC 20220
202 566-9616

ENVIRONMENTAL
PROTECTION AGENCY
OSDBU
1921 Jefferson Davis Hwy.
Rm. 1108, Crystal Mall 2
Washington, DC 20460
703 557-7305

EXECUTIVE OFFICE OF THE
PRESIDENT
Office of Administration
17th St. & Pennsylvania Ave.,
N.W.
Rm. 494
Washington, DC 20500
202 395-3314

FARM CREDIT
ADMINISTRATION
Office of Administration
1501 Farm Credit Dr.
McLean, VA 22102-5090
703 883-4151

FEDERAL EMERGENCY
MANAGEMENT AGENCY
Office of Acquisition
Management
500 C St., S.W.
Rm. 728
Washington, DC 20472
202 646-3743

FEDERAL MARITIME
COMMISSION
Administrative Services Activity
1100 L St., N.W.
Rm. 10409
Washington, DC 20573
202 523-5900

FEDERAL MEDIATION AND
CONCILIATION SERVICE
Office of Administrative Services
2100 K St., N.W.
Rm. 100
Washington, DC 20427
202 653-5310

FEDERAL TRADE COMMISSION
Office of Procurement and
Contracts
6th St. & Pennsylvania Ave.,
N.W.
Rm. 705
Washington, DC 20580
202 523-5552

GENERAL SERVICES
ADMINISTRATION
OSDBU
18th & F St., N.W.
Rm. 6019
Washington, DC 20405
202 566-1021

INTERSTATE COMMERCE
COMMISSION
Office of Procurement and
Contracting
12th St., & Constitution Ave.,
N.W.
Rm. 1315
Washington, DC 20423
202 275-0893

NATIONAL AERONAUTICS
AND SPACE
ADMINISTRATION
OSDBU
600 Independence Ave., S.W.
Rm. 116
Washington, DC 20546
202 453-2088

NATIONAL ENDOWMENT FOR
THE HUMANITIES
Office of Administrative Services
1100 Pennsylvania Ave., N.W.
Rm. 202
Washington, DC 20506
202 786-0233

NATIONAL LABOR RELATIONS
BOARD
Office of Procurement
1717 Pennsylvania Ave., N.W.
Rm. 400
Washington, DC 20570

(Actual location)
SBA Hotline
1375 K St., N.W., 20205
Washington, DC
202 633-0623

NATIONAL SCIENCE
  FOUNDATION
OSDBU
1800 G St., N.W.
Rm. 1260
Washington, DC 20550
202 357-7464

NUCLEAR REGULATORY
  COMMISSION
OSDBU
Rm. 7217, Maryland Natl. Bank
  Bldg.
Washington, DC 20555
202 492-4665

OFFICE OF CIVIL RIGHTS
Urban Mass Transit Authority
Procurement Program (UMTA)
400 7th St., S.E.
Rm. 7412
Washington, DC 20590
202 426-2285

OFFICE OF PERSONNEL
  MANAGEMENT
OSDBU
1900 E St., N.W.
Rm. 1308
Washington, DC 20415
202 653-6300

OFFICE OF PROCUREMENT
  AND GRANTS
  MANAGEMENT
409 Third St., S.W.
Washington, DC 20416
202 205-6622

PEACE CORPS
Office of Contracts
806 Connecticut Ave., N.W.
Rm. 300-P
Washington, DC 20526
202 254-3513

PENNSYLVANIA AVENUE
  DEVELOPMENT
  CORPORATION
Office of Real Estate
1331 Pennsylvania Ave., N.W.
Rm. 1220-N
Washington, DC 20004-1703
202 724-9091

SMALL BUSINESS
  ADMINISTRATION
SBA District Office
1111 18th St., N.W.
Rm. 625
Washington, DC 20036
202 634-1805

SMITHSONIAN INSTITUTION
Office of Supply Services
955 L'Enfant Plaza, S.W.
Rm. 3120
Washington, DC 20024
202 287-3343

TENNESSEE VALLEY
  AUTHORITY
c/o Natural Resources and
  Economic Development
Rm. 2J107, Old City Hall
Knoxville, TN 37902
615 632-6030

UNITED STATES
  INFORMATION AGENCY
Office of Contracts
300 C St., S.W.
Rm. 1619
Washington, DC 20547
202 485-6404

U.S. CONSUMER PRODUCT
SAFETY COMMISSION
EEO and Minority Enterprise
5401 Westbard Ave.
Washington, DC 20207
202 492-6570

U.S. GOVERNMENT PRINTING
OFFICE
Office of General Procurement
North Capitol and H Sts., N.W.
Rm. A332
Washington, DC 20401
202 275-2470

Office of Printing Procurement
North Capitol & H Sts., N.W.
Rm. C899
Washington, DC 20401
202 275-2265

U.S. POSTAL SERVICE
Office of Material Management
475 L'Enfant Plaza, S.W.
Rm. 1340
Washington, DC 20260-6201
202 268-4633

VETERANS ADMINISTRATION
OSDBU
c/o Natural Resources and
Economic Development
Rm. 2J107, Old City Hall
Knoxville, TN 37902
615 632-6030

PATENTS AND INVENTIONS

Q: *"I have an invention that I want to protect and have manufactured or sell to a manufacturer. How can I go about it and still feel safe?"*

The easiest and best way, of course, is to consult a local patent lawyer and use his experience and expertise—as long as you know up front what the possible costs will be. There are a number of steps you can take yourself that will help to give you some security and even reduce the cost of getting the product or process to market.

Among the many pertinent booklets published by the SBA, two are basic and should be obtained right away: "Can You Make Money with Your Idea or Invention?" (publication PI 1) and "Introduction to Patents" (publication PI 2). Also useful will be "General Information Concerning Patents" from the Superintendent of Documents, Government Printing Office, Washington, DC 20202. Another is "Basic Facts About Patents" from the Patent and Trademark Office, Department of Commerce, Washington, DC 20231. If you do not have access to a patent attorney, the GPO sells a booklet listing all "Patent Attorneys and Agents Registered to Practice Before the U.S. Patent Office" in alphabetical and geographical order (see address above or go to the nearest Government Bookstore). A book that treats this subject in greater detail and lists all state offices that can be helpful in patent and new product development is *Planning and Forming Your Own Company* by Gustav Berle (John Wiley & Sons, Inc., 1990).

The basic questions that only you can answer include:

- Do you want to produce the item yourself and market it? What equipment and space and people will you need? How much investment? (Single products are rarely successful, financially; it takes a line of products to really make money!)
- Do you want someone else to make it? That also will take much financing, selling in considerable quantity, and still being concerned with marketing it after the item is produced.
- Do you plan to sell it yourself? Perhaps by mail order? Agents? Distributors? Can you be in two places at the same time—producing it or supervising its production *and* marketing it?
- Should you perhaps try to sell the patent rights to another manufacturer in return for a lump-sum payment or royalty or percentage payments?

All methods involve different kinds of risks. To begin with, you want to consider a patent application, which includes a patent search to make sure that your product or service is indeed unique. You can get interim protection with a *patent pending* application. To file a Disclosure Documents Program form with the Patent Office, good for two years at a nominal cost, write to the U.S. Patent Office, Department of Commerce, 14th St. and Constitution Ave. NW, Washington, DC 20231. If you have the time to go to Washington, you can conduct your own patent search at the Search Room, Scientific Library, Patent and Trademark Office, 2021 Jefferson Davis Highway (Crystal Plaza), Arlington, VA.

PERSONNEL—*Hiring the First Employee*

Q: *"I am about to hire my first employee and I am frankly concerned. It's easy to hire, but hard to fire. Do you have any guidelines?"*

Because of the importance of hiring the right employees and providing training and motivation, the SBA has available three booklets: "Employees: How to Find and Pay Them" (PM 2), "Checklist for Developing a Training Program" (PM 1), and "Managing Employee Benefits" (publication PM 3). There are a couple of precautions to bear in mind: You are right, it is easier to hire than to fire, but unfortunately, discharging an unsatisfactory employee is part of running an operation. It is best to make sure *before* the employee starts to work. Get references, and check them out, especially those of supervisors, coworkers, and managers (not the personnel department); stay away from hiring on the basis of appearance or friendship, unless you set the rules for employment and performance in objective and unequivocal terms; put all agreements in writing and have the employee sign a copy of your proposal and acceptance; and stay away from making grandiose statements about the employee's prospects, even in passing, that you cannot later on fulfill. Be sure you provide continued motivation to the employee. He or she does not usually have the same get-up-and-go as you or he or she would be the boss. Have some form of ongoing training that will make the employee more valuable. And determine a remuneration plan that will keep a good employee on your payroll and that your business can afford. And watch the laws pertaining to employees. Consult a lawyer if you have any doubts.

PERSONNEL—*On-the-Job Training*

Q: *"Can you offer any encouragement on training of people vs. automation?"*

Automation seems to go only so far—then you still need human beings to supervise and even instruct machinery to perform its functions. The trend, of course, is toward robotization and automation in production. It is a matter of evaluating costs and efficiency. American industry has been shifting toward automation for two reasons: The first is a general lack of interest in training because the cost of training has to be treated as an expense rather than as an investment; and second, parents are not too keen to have their children enter vocational training or an apprenticeship system in an industry. These dual attitudes, compounded by the lack of stability of our workers as compared to others—the Japanese, for example, who often make a lifetime career out of their first job—makes training production workers often too costly and disappointing. Current accounting system demands assign training to costs and that affects a company's short-term profitability. Again, compared to Japanese and many European industries, we take a short-range views of investing in training, while our foreign competitors assume the long-range risk of investing in training. Many manufacturers have been conditioned to invest in technology rather than in people. Our Accelerated Cost Recovery System (ACRS) tax law only helped to encourage manufacturers to shift from man to machines. There are some signs that this is changing. Training employees not only technologically, but also attitudinally (e.g., motivation) can help reduce unemployment and increase productivity. The National Bureau of Standards and Technology and other government agencies offer transfer of government-developed and -paid high-tech methods and machinery, such as robotics. This might make technology available to small and medium industries at lower cost, freeing more money for on-the-job training. A discussion with the local SBA or SCORE counselors can be productive and is cost-free. Ask also for the SBA booklet "Checklist for Developing a Training Program" (publication PM-1) and "Employees: How to Find and Pay them" (publication MP-2).

PRICING PRODUCTS AND SERVICES

Q: *"I've checked out prices on a number of products we want to handle, but can't seem to price them without becoming uncompetitive—or even losing money. I wonder what we may be doing wrong?"*

Often, buying is as important as selling. If you need to reduce your prices in order to meet competition, look first at your own overhead, then at the way you are buying merchandise, and third, at how you are promoting your products. Here is a checklist that might help you pinpoint areas where you can shave your costs:

- Shop around to obtain the best prices from suppliers—sometimes by increasing the quantity to gain a price break, sometimes a little later in the season when prices are more favorable.
- Closely control your inventory. Tying up cash on goods that do not turn over sufficiently is loosing money, especially if you had to borrow money to pay for inventory or had to forego a supplier's discount because of delayed payment. Higher turnover is often the way to higher profits.
- Analyze turnover and eliminate slow-moving merchandise. Concentrate your money and space on fast-moving items.
- Focus your advertising and promotion on high-traffic merchandise; use displays and no-cost promotions to expose slower-moving goods.
- Analyze your service and peripherals, such as repairs, packaging, deliveries, installation—and see if you cannot add reasonable service charges for these "extras."
- Do some spot-checking on employees' charge-outs to see if errors are made; check and analyze exchanges.
- Train employees to use suggestions for tie-in sales, upgraded sales, coordinated items (i.e., a tie with a shirt; ribbons with a PC; a matching lipstick with rouge; a new wine to go with the other liquor purchase).
- Check each of your internal costs, fixed and especially optional

(utilization of personnel, waste of utilities, abuse of vehicles, wasted merchandise used in displays, security measures that nip internal and external shoplifting in the bud; cost of permanent vs. temp personnel; comparison-shopping costs like insurance, gas purchases, office supplies, and the like).

- In pricing services, pay particular attention to unaccounted for time. You will find that about 50 percent of your time is spent in travel, research, telephoning, shopping for supplies, bookkeeping, and solicitations. If you have to charge $15 an hour to cover the obvious overhead costs, better make it $30 to cover unaccounted-for time. Cost accounting and accuracy increases profits!

Ask the SBA or SCORE office nearest you for it's free information sheet FF6 on this subject.

PRODUCTION—*Quality Control Problems/Returns*

Q: *"As a small manufacturer, I feel that each product returned is a loss. How can I stem the number of returns and keep my customers happy and healthy?"*

Merchandise returns, or service rejections, are a double-edged sword. They cost you money and reduce your net; and they can directly influence your company image. Immediately investigating and fixing such problems is the cheapest way to avoid repetition. Returned goods or rejected service should be returned to the person who was responsible for whatever the problem is, so that corrective action can be taken. Evaluation of all possibilities must then be undertaken. Here is a checklist that will help you come to grips with the problem and work out corrections:

- Examine and analyze specifications of all products and parts used in a given situation to make sure you are not passing on substandard parts.
- Check production line procedures for state of equipment used and adequacy of tools.
- Check parts handling, it's critical, especially if parts are fragile or sensitive, or if their packaging is damaged.
- Examine and analyze shipping procedures and packaging quality.
- Evaluate quality control procedures measured against customers' requirements.
- Evaluate customer service candidly and honestly. The customer

is not always right, but if you you think you are, better have an airtight explanation ready. Twenty-five to 30 percent of customer returns are unjustified. Check your own warranty to make sure where you stand. Acknowledge all complaints in a logical and helpful manner immediately. Some people are best left alone, but most of them deserve your best efforts.

PUBLICATIONS

Q: *"Can you tell me about the 'Commerce Business Daily' newspaper that lists all small invitations to bid?"*

"Commerce Business Daily" (CBD) is a newspaper published each work day by the International Trade Administration of the Department of Commerce (See also GOVERNMENT—Publications). It is available by subscription (about $160 a year) from the Superintendent of Documents, U.S. Government Printing Office, Washington, DC 20402. All ITA and SBA field offices maintain a file on the publication also. For the $160 fee the newspaper is delivered to you via first-class. To keep up with what federal government departments are buying, this is the surest way to keep current. The following information is reported daily in CBD:

- Requests for bids and proposals for planned military and civilian purchases over $10,000
- Procurements for small businesses under $10,000
- Contractors seeking subcontractors on government bids
- Sales of surplus property, including supplies, equipment, machinery, and real estate
- Research and development leads
- Foreign governments' procurement in the U.S.

PUBLIC RELATIONS—*Customer Loyalty*

Q: *"Loyal customers seem to be a vanishing breed these days. It costs so much to get one. How do I keep them?"*

Tom Peters, the author of *In Search of Excellence* and other business training books, has an interesting formula when it comes to evaluating a customer. He figures what a customer can spend in a business and multiplies it by 10 to arrive at the potential purchases the customer can make over a decade. It is estimated, for instance, that the average American family might spend $150,000 during a lifetime for automobiles. Given the lack of loyalty, especially in the automotive field, a dealership proprietor or even a salesperson might look at a customer quite differently if that customer is regarded as a $150,000 nestegg. The same formula can be applied even more credibly to more frequent repeat customers—like grocery buyers. If a food shopper spends $50 a week in a market, that's $2,500 a year or $25,000 over the 10-year loyalty-cycle that Peters envisions as a criterion. The same thinking can be applied to valued employees. A sales representative, a beauty shop stylist, or a clerk in an exclusive clothing shop is in control of an enormous amount of gross income. Wouldn't it be worthwhile to 1) pay that person adequately in order to keep him or her producing for you? and 2) would that employee not be worth some time and investment to be trained properly? Quality of goods and services sold is important, but the personal one-on-one relationship between the sales or service person and the customer is of primary importance in developing customer loyalty.

QUALITY CONTROL

Q: "What are the government's quality requirements for selling to a federal agency?"

Quality, price, and timely delivery are the three most important elements in a successful government contract. An acceptable quality program for your product or service should be available, as the government contracting officer might request this. Such a program—which is also a valid guide for your own control—should include:

- Organization chart showing the place of quality control in your company
- Persons performing quality control, responsibility, and authority as they pertain to the government contract
- A production flow chart
- Inspection procedures, test methods, sampling method, corrective action, recording results
- Accuracy of equipment, procedures, and standards used in quality control
- Samples of quality control forms, charts, and other written materials

A government representative will evaluate the contractor's quality assurance program. Standards are available from any General Services Administration office for civilian products. Military quality standards are obtainable from the Commanding Officer, Naval Supply Depot, 5801 Tabor Avenue, Philadelphia PA 19120. Scientific standards are available from the American National Standard Institute, 1430 Broadway, New York, NY 10018.

REGULATIONS—*License to Buy Liquor*

Q: *"Do I need a special license to be able to buy alcoholic beverages from a wholesaler or distributor?"*

No, no special license is required. You do, however, need a valid liquor license and a tax number to *sell* alcoholic beverages. The license comes from the state liquor board, the tax number from the local tax and IRS office. Copies of these will most likely be requested by the wholesaler or distributor. They will be delighted to work with you in getting licenses, keeping adequate inventory, and merchandising help—as long as you have the money to pay for the goods, usually on delivery. The high mortality rate of bars and taverns makes the liquor business principally a cash business—based on the adage that "cash makes no enemies."

REGULATIONS—*Licenses and Permits*

Q: *"Do I need a license to open a business of my own?"*

You will need a license from a local authority if you plan to sell any of the following products:

> drugs
> foods
> guns
> health services
> liquor/alcoholic beverages
> items or services sold door-to-door

To be sure, check with the license bureau of your local jurisdiction. If you have problems in obtaining a license or in finding the right office, check with the nearest state Small Business Assistance office listed in the "State" section of your telephone book's blue pages. Be especially careful that you also have insurance to cover the products you sell to consumers and that your employees are properly licensed and, if necessary, bonded. Getting a license to sell alcoholic beverages is usually fraught with special problems. See the question REGULATIONS—Liquor License.

REGULATIONS—*Liquor License*

Q: "*I want to buy a package liquor store and perhaps open an adjacent lounge to go with it. What special permits will I need?*"

Liquor licenses are not a federal matter, but come under each state's jurisdiction. Liquor licenses are usually transferable and a hearing is held by the local liquor board to determine the qualifications of the new prospective owner. First, contact your local liquor commission or state liquor Control Board. If you run into any problems or questions, check with the nearest SCORE office for counseling and the local chamber of commerce, licensed beverage association, or other community associations for guidance and information. Second, pay a call on one or several of the local liquor wholesale suppliers, who usually know everything that is going on in this business. Third, say hello to the local banker who has dealt with the present owner. You will usually pick up some valuable but guarded opinions. Fourth, visit some competitive establishments and scan the ads in the local papers to get a feel of the business in general. Once the transaction is complete, the only other "permit" you will need is some form of bonding on any employee who handles cash. If you or your family do not handle cash, then an outside, hired employee must be bondable, or if that is not feasible, look for another one who can be bonded.

REGULATIONS—*Taxes*

Q: "*What about city, state, and federal taxes?*"

All jurisdictions usually collect taxes in some form and the local telephone book (the blue section listing all government offices) will give you the locations and phone numbers. When filling out a license application, you will automatically receive a tax form. If you buy an existing business, have been in business before, or employ an accountant or attorney, this information will be obvious to you. If you are searching a location in the U.S. where you will buy or establish a business, you will want to know that there are eight states that have no personal income tax; five states that have no corporate income tax; 34 states that have no inventory tax; four states that have no real property tax; and 13 states that have both a manufacturing sales and use tax. Ask your local SBA office for copies of "Steps in Meeting Your

Tax Obligations" (publication MA 13) and "Getting the Facts for Income Tax Reporting" (publication MA 144).

RESPONSIVENESS—*In Bidding*

Q: *"I see the words 'responsiveness' and 'responsibility' in government contracts and government agency services. Can you explain the difference?"*

Responsiveness means replying to an advertised government bid in the exact manner of the request. Such compliance or responsiveness assures that the government gets exactly what it needs and that all bidders stand an equal chance. It tells bidders as precisely as possible what they may offer. If there is any deviation, the bid will be rejected as being "unresponsive."

Responsibility means that the contractor has the obligation to fulfill the contract in a satisfactory manner and that low price is not the sole criterion. Before making an award to a bidder, the contracting officer must have information that indicates clearly that the winning contractor meets all applicable standards of responsibility.

The minimum standards that a contractor must prove include 1) adequate financial resources or the ability to obtain them promptly; 2) ability to meet the delivery or performance schedule; 3) a satisfactory record of integrity; and 4) qualifications and elegibility for award under the Walsh-Healy Public Contract Act (see entry WALSH-HEALY ACT).

SBIR PROGRAM

Q: *"We're a minority business involved in considerable research and development. We've heard about an SBIR program and want to find out more about it."*

The SBIR Program is the Small Business Innovation Research program. Its purpose is to stimulate small business, especially disadvantaged businesses, to participate in technological innovation with the government. One important aspect is that the program offers small businesses some of the research and development created by federal agencies. This program is conducted in three phases:

Phase I: Submittal of the results the private firm wishes to accomplish.

Phase II: Funding is approved by the SBIR program to develop the proposed ideas that have been chosen.

Phase III: The SBA, together with the R&D partnership, pursues commercial applications of the research and development described in Phases I and II.

Eleven different federal agencies participate in this SBIR program. You may want to discuss your eligibility with an SBIR representative located at any SBA district office or ask for a Form 1386 in person or by mail. The 18-page booklet that accompanies the application explains the procedure. It is titled "Proposal Preparation for Small Business Innovation Research."

SECURITY CLEARANCE

Q: *"Do we need security clearance in order to get a federal government contract?"*

The contracting officer of the federal agency with whom you deal has the responsibility to determine and disseminate security requirements. Most of the time security clearance is required. The SBA can give you information about this procedure but cannot itself issue security clearances for other agencies. Each agency and each contract will be handled differently. The contracting officer of whatever federal agency is required to

- Review the proposed solicitation to determine whether access to classified information may be required.
- Include the appropriate security requirements clauses in the contract.
- Inform contractors and subcontractors of the security classifications and requirements.

It is logical that probably the strictest security regulations will be encountered when dealing with the Department of Defense (DoD). The DoD Industrial Security Manual can be obtained from The Defense Investigation Service, 1900 Half St., SW, Washington, DC 20324. Frank discussion with the contracting officer of whatever agency you choose to do business with will probably resolve any problems. However, if you need more help, the Program Assistance Division in each SBA regional office is recommended.

SELLING A BUSINESS—*Appraisal*

Q: *"We are thinking of selling a business and want to get an official appraisal. What information must we prepare for an appraiser? What intangibles must we consider?"*

Your own lawyer and accountant will be helpful in determining information required. Business brokers, if you use one, will have a checklist of requirements. Intangibles are difficult to determine, as they are so often subjective. Your reputation, the number of regular or repeat customers, the length of your establishment's business life, the location, special relationships you might enjoy with suppliers and even with key employees, the favorable residual effect of advertising and public relations investments, the perceived loyalty of your customers, the nature of a good lease—all these are hard to determine in dollars and cents, but they are assets nonetheless. You need to be cognizant of these items and their value, so that you can present them convincingly to your prospective purchaser. For the appraiser, whom you can locate through your professional association or through the listing in the Yellow Book of licensed practitioners, you will need to prepare statements on the following:

- Complete sales records
- Three years of financial records, including income tax statements, state and federal returns, and state sales tax reports
- Personal or nonbusiness expenses, especially in the case of an individual or closely held business
- Tangible assets such as furniture, equipment, ages and replacement cost
- Intangible assets, including leases, contracts, licenses, patents and formulas for which a fair market value can be determined
- Contractual obligations such as employee contracts, bonus and profit-sharing arrangements, pension plans, insurance commitments
- Leases and/or deeds of trust involving real property; using the latest available appraisals.

All of these factors together make for an appraisal and a solid basis for negotiating a sale price. The SBA has a booklet entitled "How to Buy or Sell a Business" (publication MP-16) that will also be helpful. In your own appraisal of your business, leave out all demands for the moon—there haven't been any lunar flights scheduled for quite some time.

SELLING A BUSINESS—*General Information*

Q: "With the economy slowing down, we want to explore selling our business. Can you give us some general advice?"

The principal item you sell in a business is cash flow. When that slows down or stops, it would take a world-class optimist to make a satisfying offer. Even business brokers have to be selective, because they cannot waste their time peddling unproductive products. Entrepreneurs who wish to sell their business need to make many, many contacts—and yet be discrete about it. If too many people in the trade and customers get wind of your desire to sell out, they will quickly become curious, if not suspicious, and the price will go down. A good way to look for potential buyers is through personal inquiries among out-of-town competitors who might want to expand into your location, or absorb your market and customers; suppliers, accountants, lawyers, and sales representatives also represent sources of potential buyers. If you belong to a trade or professional association, you might make worthwhile contacts there. Another way to attract buyers is through creative financing, such as taking back some of the debt to be paid out over a period of time. Unless an out-and-out cash sale is involved, retention of some equity in the business will give you a continuing pulse on how well the business is doing under new management. In any event, if money is still owed to you, it is basic to have a recapture clause in the sales contract that allows you to take back the business under spelled-out circumstances.

"Goodwill" is one of the toughest and most subjective assets to sell at a price that the seller thinks is fair. Goodwill can include such intangibles, but very real assets, as a customer list, good relationships with suppliers, favorable contracts, low prices on supplies and services, and a unique but successful marketing strategy. Recognizable brand names, trademarks, and patents are also assets to be evaluated separately. Age of inventory is vital and often subject to negotiations, as much as accounts receivables. In most sales the seller is invariably owed some money and this debt becomes almost like a hostage against fulfillment of seller's claims and promises. Bearing this in mind, the buyer's success will directly impact on whether the seller gets paid or not. Even if a sale is consummated directly, it is usually thought to be best if a professional is involved in the final negotiations.

SELLING A BUSINESS—*Retirement*

Q: "We are planning to retire in a couple of years and want to plan ahead to sell our business at its optimum value. Is there anything I should do early to prepare for that?"

If you are an average small business, your assets in your company represent 75 percent of your worth. Just as you would spruce up your home before putting it on the market, or fix up your car before selling it, you need to look at every angle to make your business's value as high as possible. Here are seven facets of your business to check out, all of which can help maximize your returns from a sale:

1. Environmental concerns and conformance with EPA regulations: Check this early in your planning, especially if you have underground storage, hazardous materials, energy-saving appliances and construction, a profitable recycling process, and pollution-control devices on air and liquid exhausts.

2. Efficient operation: Look at your trade magazines and associations; find out who the most efficient, most profitable operators in your business are, and how you can borrow some of their expertise to enhance yours.

3. Cash flow: This is, after all, the key to running (and selling) a business. Smooth out the peaks and valleys in your monthly business cycles by diversifying product lines, adding new territories, or eliminating products and areas that are unprofitable.

4. Borrowing capacity: Try to increase your capacity by stablizing cash flow performance and let your banker and other financial resources know about it. It will in turn give your potential buyer greater leverage in making the acquisition.

5. Working capital: Examine every phase of it and determine whether you are making extra capital work for you, without jeopardizing it in dubious investments. Keep money in an interest-bearing account; shop around for best rates in insurance, best prices in supplies and equipment, and best lease terms.

6. Market expansion: Analyze your products and services to see whether related or other industries can also use them. Such new opportunities might help even out seasonal peaks and valleys.

7. Improve customer sales: Your own customers might need other, related products and services that you could supply, perhaps even with the same sales call and delivery. One's own customers are always the best market and can be used advantageously to network add-on sales.

SELLING TO THE GOVERNMENT

Q: *"I understand that the General Services Administration is the one that can tell you how to sell products to the federal government. How do you go about getting in on that?"*

The General Services Administration (GSA) processes primarily new products that have not been solicited by a specific federal agency. GSA has what is called the New Item Introductory Schedule (NIIS), which is used to introduce new or improved products into the federal supply system. The form on which you submit your proposal is called GSA Form 1171. It can be obtained from and be returned to any of the 13 GSA Service Centers listed here:

General Services Administration
300 North Los Angeles Street
Los Angeles, CA 90012
213 688-3210

General Services Administration
525 Market Street
San Francisco, CA 94105
415 974-9000

General Services Administration
Denver Federal Center, Bldg. 41
Denver, CO 80225
303 234-2216

General Services Administration
7th and D Streets, S.W.
Washington, DC 20407
202 472-1804

General Services Administration
Richard B. Russel Federal
   Building & Courthouse
75 Spring Street S.W.
Atlanta, GA 30303
404 221-5103

General Services Administration
230 South Dearborn Street
Chicago, IL 60604
312 353-5383

General Services Administration
John W. McCormack Post Office
   & Courthouse Bldg.
Boston, MA 02109
617 223-2868

General Services Administration
1500 East Bannister Road
Kansas City, MO 64131
816 926-7203

General Services Administration
26 Federal Plaza
New York, NY 10279
212 264-1234

General Services Administration
9th & Market Streets, Rm. 5142
Philadelphia, PA 19107
215 597-9613

General Services Administration
515 Rusk Street
Houston, TX 77002
713 226-5787

General Services Administration
819 Taylor Street
Fort Worth, TX 76102
817 334-3284

General Services Administration
440 Federal Building
915 Second Avenue
Seattle, WA 98174
206 442-5556

SERVICE BUSINESSES

Q: *"How do I plan a service business that has virtually no inventory?"*

A good start would be to obtain the SBA booklet "Business Plan for Small Service Firms" (publication MP 11) from the nearest SBA or SCORE office. Like starting up any new business, it is good to start by consulting one or all of the following: SCORE, SBA, State Development Office, and Chamber of Commerce. All consultations are free. Their competency depends on the individual you find within the organizations and often his or her specific experience in or with your service business. See also the entry BUSINESS START-UPS in this book. Just because you will not need any or very little inventory does not mean that you won't have overhead. Your biggest overhead will be your own expenses—your living expenses while your service business gets off the ground. Figure that it will take longer than anticipated, unless you are fortunate enough to line up clients and customers in advance on whom you can count (and not just on promises!). You will need a place out of which to work; utilities and deposits; stationery; reference books or tools; memberships; licenses; transport; office supplies; samples; advertising. A meticulous list of anticipated expenses for the first year will give you an approximate idea of expenses. Joining these with estimated income will enable you to make up a cash flow table and a business plan. To be safe, add 25 percent to your estimated expenses and timetable.

SMALL BUSINESS—*Definition*

Q: *"What actually is a "small business"? My store does close to $800,000 a year. Am I still eligible to get advice from the SBA and its affiliated agencies?"*

Most retailers who do less than a million dollars a year in business are considered "small businesses" under SBA regulations. The only exceptions are automobile dealers selling new cars. Wholesalers can do up to $5,000,000, with a few exceptions. Likewise, manufacturers who employ fewer than 250 people are still considered "small businesses" under SBA guidelines. Detailed definitions and exceptions are listed in legal tracts available at all SBA offices. SBA offices also have a booklet that defines size standards, titled "The SBA—What It Is and What It Does." (See also the Introduction to this volume.)

SBA—*Buying from the SBA*

Q: *"I understand that the SBA owns property that it sells from time-to-time, sometimes at bargain prices. How do I find out about that?"*

Check with the local regional SBA office about any sales or auctions coming up. Sales are often made by means of sealed bids. Most of the SBA sales involve real estate properties, although occasionally equipment and inventory will be caught in the net of such a transaction. How does the SBA get involved in such sales? When a borrower defaults on a SBA direct or guaranteed loan, the SBA will protect the taxpayers by foreclosing on the equity it holds, get it appraised, and sell it at the most favorable terms. At a public auction in which the SBA holds an interest in property being sold, the SBA may enter a protective bid and get the property back for resale. During a past year, SBA owned-and-sold properties included a horse ranch, a retail shop, a part ownership in a T-shirt company, and interests in a cable TV company and an electronics manufacturing firm. Usually the SBA sells its real estate collateral for 10 to 20 percent down with 10 years to pay off the balance. Traditional sources of information do not normally reveal such buying opportunities, hence it is necessary to contact your local regional SBA office or the Operations Assistance Branch, Office of Portfolio Management, SBA, 409 Third St., S.W., Washington, DC 20416.

SBA—*Counseling*

Q: *"Can the SBA make any suggestions as to acceptable lawyers, accountants, business brokers, franchises, and such?"*

Neither the SBA nor its allied organizations like SCORE or SBDC can furnish you with any "approved" lists of professionals or advisory firms. The SBA, SCORE, and SBDC are mandated only to offer advice and usually only in person, after you are duly registered with one of the counseling offices. SBA cannot try to "solve" business situations, but can act only as an advisor. When the problems go beyond the capabilities and legal mandates of the federal government or government-affiliated organizations, you will be referred to other government agencies, trade associations, chambers of commerce, or other pertinent private professionals and counselors. For instance, if you wish to consult a counselor from SCORE, the Service Corps of Retired Executives, you will be given Form 641 to fill out before any counseling can begin. The latter, however, is free, confidential, and often very valuable.

SBA—*Direct Loans*

Q: *"Can I get a direct loan from the SBA? What can I do if the local office turns me down?"*

The SBA makes direct loans only as a last resort and then under regulated conditions very similar to those employed by banks. First of all, you need to make formal loan applications to two banks that are recognized as SBA loan correspondents. If they turn you down, then you are eligible to apply to the local SBA office for loan consideration. The SBA district office handles the loan. If it, too, turns you down, you have the right to contact the nearest SBA regional office for reconsideration. In applying for a loan, whether from a bank or the SBA district office directly, you will need credible evidence that you need the money, have a thorough business plan to back up your application, and show proof of your ability to repay the loan within a stipulated time.

SBA—*Dispelling Loan Myths*

Q: *"There continues to be a lot of confusion about getting loans from the SBA. Can you straighten me out and give me the current facts on getting an SBA loan?"*

Since old stories and hopes die hard, it is quite understandable that the rumors persist about the SBA handing out millions of dollars in easy money to start-up businesses. Here are some of the *myths* and the real answers:

- Bank turn-downs: When applying for a loan directly to the SBA, you need first be turned down by two commercial, SBA-approved lender banks. The SBA-guaranteed loan makes up for some of the shortfall in your collateral, management ability, or proven track record in your business.
- Need for collateral: Some applicants believe that when you apply for a SBA loan, you don't need collateral. That is false. The SBA requires the same amount of collateral that regular banks would need. Among collateral considered is real estate, inventory, accounts receivable, machinery and equipment, and even investments. That is why the SBA, and some other government lending agencies, occasionally have property and businesses for sale at auctions, designed to reimburse the government lender for loans that went flat.
- The SBA will not touch your home: If you put up your home as

collateral, the SBA will not refuse that. The SBA's feeling, just like the bank's, is that if you are not willing to risk all of your assets, why should they? A refusal to list one's home as collateral indicates that the borrower does not think his businesses will really make it and he or she won't exert all possible efforts to make it successful.

• Any bank can offer a SBA-guaranteed loan: That is also in error. To get a bank loan backed by the SBA guarantee, that bank must usually be certified by the SBA before it can accept an SBA loan application. If you have in mind that you might need a SBA guarantee, find out from your bank, before you go to a lot of trouble, whether they have been certified by the SBA. This condition has been eased in recent months and non-certified banks can now also submit guaranteed loan applications. However, SBA approval for applications from non-certified banks will take longer.

SBA—*Loans*

Q: "*How do I borrow money from the SBA?*"

This is probably the single most-asked question of the million questions asked by callers to the SBA's Answer Desk hotline. It is also the question most fraught with wrong impressions and possible disappointment. The reality of getting a loan is that the SBA guarantees to private banks 90 percent of the principal loaned under its auspices. Usually the borrower has to come up with the first 10 percent, a detailed business plan, and a squeaky-clean record. Executing a detailed and professional-looking business plan is a prerequisite for making a loan application (see LOANS). Finding one or two banks who are approved SBA lenders is the next step. Neither the bank's loan nor the SBA's guarantee of it will be automatic. It all depends on what your business plan reveals, what collateral you have available, what your sales and profit projections look like, how your management ability impresses the loan officers, what you own, and what you owe. There are a number of SBA brochures that are helpful and that you can send for or obtain through a local SBA or SCORE office:

"ABCs of Borrowing" (publication FM 1)
"Understanding Cash Flow" (publication FM 4)
"Sound Cash Management and Borrowing" (publication FM 9)

Several booklets are also listed under BUSINESS PLAN.

SBA—*Loan Guarantees*

Q: "Is it true that the SBA has tightened up on loan guarantees?"

Not at all. In 1990 a bill was passed in Congress that was good news for all small businesses. It was the annual appropriation for the Small Business Administration, and it included $3.2 billion for small-business loan guarantees—$800 million more than in 1989. What made this liberalization move especially noteworthy is that only a few years ago the preceding administration was campaigning to put the SBA out of business. There are other indications, which you can find in adjacent entries, that the SBA loan programs are healthy indeed.

SBA—*Loan Interest*

Q: "What is the interest rate of an SBA guaranteed loan and how long is its maturity?"

The interest rate of an SBA guaranteed loan varies with the prime money rate established in New York. On loans under seven years' duration, the rate is 2.25 percent over the existing New York prime rate. On loans over seven years maturity and with a maximum maturity of 25 years, the rate can be 2.75 percent above existing New York prime rate.

SBA—*Loans out of State*

Q: "I want to borrow funds for a business in another state. Can the SBA help me?"

The location in which you plan to open a business is immaterial, except that banks generally prefer to do business in their own area where they can investigate the location, property, and references. The steps in applying for a loan in another city are the same as those explained in the answer to the previous question, "How do I borrow money from the SBA." You need a detailed business plan, though a plan submitted to an out-of-town financial institution needs to be even more thorough—proving that you know the market, have reliable management in that location, and know the demographics there. Since it is likely that you do not know the bankers in the new city as well as you do in your own hometown, the first step would be to get acquainted with them and assure them of your sincerity, capability, and fiscal liquidity. Opening an account in the out-of-town bank might be a good first step. Others could be ownership of property, belonging to the chamber of commerce, Better Business Bureau, and other service and civic associations. Knowing prominent local citizens in the town who can introduce you to the bank or even vouch for you should be very helpful. If there is an SBA office and/or SCORE office in the town, you will want to explore their assistance and advice.

SBA—*Loan Policy*

Q: "*I think the SBA is unduly hard on small entrepreneurs who are applying for loan guarantees. Aren't you people just the custodians of the taxpayers' money?*"

You are absolutely right. The SBA, as every other federal agency, is the custodian of the taxpayers' money and thus responsible to the people, through the U.S. Congress, for every dollar spent. As an example, during a typical recent year, the SBA guaranteed about 17,500 loans through thousands of banks. This action resulted in the necessity to have $580 million in assets to provide for losses, plus an additional $49 million to pay for losses and expenses on collateral put up by defaulting businesspeople. In addition, half a million dollars had to be paid out in rentals on defaulted properties. Fortunately, the SBA also collected fees on the sound loans and guarantees, which helped to offset some of the losses incurred by those unable to make their agreed payments. If anything, the banks' and the SBA's best scrutiny cannot always foresee the results of economic downturns, mismanagement on the part of borrowers, and other causes that result in bankruptcies. For the borrowers' own protection, the SBA tries hard to advise, manage, scrutinize, and, if necessary, to warn and even reject those who are not yet ready to enter the risky world of entrepreneurship. The SBA's business development programs, which include numerous affiliated agencies like SCORE, SBDC, and SBI, are available to safeguard your and every other taxpayer's dreams of business independence.

SBA—*Opportunities for the Visually Impaired*

Q: "*I am visually impaired but have an opportunity to go into a business. Are there any special programs made for the blind or visually impaired entrepreneur?*"

We are just getting into methods of helping the visually impaired. Despite economic downturns on occasion, opportunities for the visually handicapped are always available. One reason is that of the 600,000 Americans between the ages of 18 and 69 who have visual disabilities to limit their work, only one-third are employed in some capacity, even if underemployed in most cases. This leaves more than 400,000 Americans who could work but cannot find meaningful employment because of their handicap. Once the Americans with Disabilities Act becomes effective, some federal assistance will become available. In the meanwhile, some local Lighthouse for the Blind organizations have developed computers that operate on the Braille system or have screens that display extra-large letters—usually 13 across the screen and only three to four lines from top to bottom—and are thus able to train visually impaired on their premises. An example is the Columbia Lighthouse for the Blind on P Street, NW, in Washington, DC. The center received a $100,000 private grant to acquire the kind of computers that can be used by many trainable visually impaired clients. The center advises that, for as little as $500, a computer can be adapted to this use, and that magnifying software, voice synthesizers, Braille translators and printers, and document scanners are all now available.

At a seminar in Washington DC, the Americans with Disabilities Act of 1990 was discussed in great detail for human resource and corporate executives. This Littler Task Force Report is available from Littler, Mendelson, Fastiff & Tichy, Attorneys, 650 California St., 20th Floor, San Francisco, CA 94108.

SBA PUBLICATIONS

Q: *"Does SBA have special publications for new businesses?"*

Check your local SBA office or call the toll free Answer Desk hotline (800 827-5722) and ask for a Starter Kit. It contains much useful information at no charge to you. Form 115A is a two-page list of several dozen business development publications. Many of these are specifically designed for start-up businesses. Also check with the nearest SCORE or SBDC office or visit them to see how they can help you and when they will have the next business start-up workshop. Here is a list of SBA publications available from regional and field offices or directly from SBA Publications, P.O. BOX 30, Denver, CO 80201-0030:

FINANCIAL MANAGEMENT AND ANALYSIS

FM 1 *ABC's of Borrowing*

Some small business people cannot understand why a lending institution refused to lend them money. Others have no trouble getting funds but are surprised to find strings attached to their loans. Learn the fundamentals of borrowing.

FM 2 Profit Costing and Pricing for Manufacturers

Uncover the latest techniques for pricing your products profitably.

FM 3 Basic Budgets for Profit Planning

This publication takes the worry out of putting together a comprehensive budgeting system to monitor your profits and assess your financial operations.

FM 4 Understanding Cash Flow

In order to survive, a business must have enough cash to meet its obligations. The owner/manager is shown how to plan for the movement of cash through the business and thus plan for future requirements.

FM 5 A Venture Capital Primer for Small Business*

This best-seller highlights the venture capital resources available and how to develop a proposal for obtaining these funds.

FM 6 Accounting Services for Small Service Firms

Sample profit/loss statements are used to illustrate how accounting services can help expose and correct trouble spots in a business' financial records.

FM 7 Analyze Your Records to Reduce Costs

Cost reduction is not simply slashing any and all expenses. Understand the nature of expenses and how they interrelate with sales, inventories, and profits. Achieve greater profits through more efficient use of the dollar.

FM 8 Budgeting in a Small Business Firm

Learn how to set up and keep sound financial records. Study how to effectively use journals, ledgers, and charts to increase profits.

FM 9 Sound Cash Management and Borrowing

Avoid a "cash crisis" through proper use of cash budgets, cash flow projections, and planned borrowing concepts.

FM 10 Recordkeeping in a Small Business*

Need some basic advice on setting up a useful record keeping system? This publication describes how.

FM 11 Breakeven Analysis: A Decision Making Tool

Learn how "breakeven analysis" enables the manager/owner to make better decisions concerning sales, profits, and costs.

FM 12 A Pricing Checklist for Small Retailers

The owner/manager of a small retail business can use this checklist to apply proven pricing strategies that can lead to profits.

FM 13 Pricing Your Products and Services Profitably

Discusses how to price your products profitably, how to use the various techniques of pricing and when to use these techniques to your advantage.

GENERAL MANAGEMENT AND PLANNING

MP 1 Effective Business Communications

Explains the importance of business communications and how they play a valuable role in business success.

MP 2 Locating or Relocating Your Business

Learn how a company's market, available labor force, transportation, and raw materials are affected when selecting a business location.

MP 3 Problems in Managing a Family-owned Business

Specific problems exist when attempting to make a family-owned business successful. This publication offers suggestions on how to overcome these difficulties.

MP 4 Business Plan for Small Manufacturers

Designed to help an owner/manager of a small manufacturing firm. This publication covers all the basic information necessary to develop an effective business plan.

MP 5 Business Plan for Small Construction Firms

This publication is designed to help an owner/manager of a small construction company pull together the resources to develop a business plan.

MP 6 Planning and Goal Setting for Small Business

Learn how to plan for success.

MP 7 Fixing Production Mistakes

Structured as a checklist, this publication emphasizes the steps that should be taken by a manufacturer when a production mistake has been found.

MP 8 Should You Lease or Buy Equipment?

Describes various aspects of the lease/buy decision. It lists advantages and disadvantages of leasing and provides a format for comparing the costs of the two.

MP 9 Business Plan for Retailers

Learn how to develop a business plan for a retail business.

MP 10 Choosing a Retail Location

Learn about current retail site selection techniques such as demographic and traffic analysis. This publication addresses the hard questions the retailer must answer before making the choice of a store location.

MP 11 Business Plan for Small Service Firms

Outlines the key points to be included in the business plan of a small service firm.

MP 12 Going into Business

This best-seller highlights important considerations you should know in reaching a decision to start your own business. It also includes a checklist for going into business.

MP 14 How to Get Started with a Small Business Computer

Helps you forecast your computer needs, evaluate the alternative choices, and select the right computer system for your business.

MP 15 The Business Plan for Homebased Business

Provides a comprehensive approach to developing a business plan for a homebased business. If you are convinced that a profitable home business is attainable, this publication will provide a step-by-step guide to develop a plan for your business.

MP 16 How to Buy or Sell a Business

Learn several techniques used in determining the best price to buy or sell a small business.

MP 17 Purchasing for Owners of Small Plants

Present an outline of an effective purchasing program. Also includes a bibliography for further research into industrial purchasing.

MP 18 Buying for Retail Stores

Discusses the latest trends in retail buying. Includes a bibliography that references a wide variety of private and public sources of information on most aspects of retail buying.

MP 19 Small Business Decision Making

Acquaint yourself with the wealth of information available on management approaches to identify, analyze, and solve business problems.

MP 20 Business Continuation Planning

Provides an overview of business owner's life insurance needs that are not typically considered until after the death of one of the business' principal owners.

MP 21 Developing a Strategic Business Plan

Helps you develop a strategic action plan for your small business.

MP 22 Inventory Management

Discusses the purpose of inventory management, types of inventories, record keeping, and forecasting inventory levels.

MP 23 Techniques for Problem Solving

Instructs the small business person on the key techniques of problem solving and problem identification, as well as designing and implementing a plan to correct these problems.

MP 24 Techniques for Productivity Improvement

Learn to increase worker output through motivating "quality of work life" concepts and tailoring benefits to meet the needs of the employees.

MP 25 Selecting the Legal Structure for Your Business

Discusses the various legal structures that a small business can use in setting up its operations. It briefly identifies the types of legal structures and lists the advantages and disadvantages of each.

MP 26 Evaluating Franchise Opportunities

Although the success rate for franchise-owned businesses is significantly better than start-up businesses, success is not guaranteed. Evaluate franchise opportunities and select the business that's right for you.

MP 27 Starting a Retail Travel Agency

Travel agencies are a rewarding yet challenging business. Learn how to start your own agency.

MP 28 Small Business Risk Management Guide

Strengthen your insurance program by identifying, minimizing and eliminating business risks. This guide can help you secure adequate insurance protection for your company.

CRIME PREVENTION

CP 1 Reducing Shoplifting Losses

Learn the latest techniques on how to spot, deter, apprehend, and prosecute shoplifters.

CP 2 Curtailing Crime—Inside and Out

Positive steps can be taken to curb crime. They include safeguards against employee dishonesty and ways to control shoplifting. In addition, this publication includes measures to outwit bad check passing and ways to prevent burglary and robbery.

CP 3 A Small Business Guide to Computer Security

The computer is a valuable and essential part of many small businesses and your computer related assets need protection. This publication helps you understand the nature of computer security risks and offers timely advice on how to control them.

MARKETING

MT 1 Creative Selling: The Competitive Edge

Explains how to use creative selling techniques to increase profits.

MT 2 Marketing for Small Business: An Overview

Provides an overview of "marketing" concepts and contains an extensive bibliography of sources covering the subject of marketing.

MT 3 Is the Independent Sales Agent for You?

Provides guidelines that help the owner of a small company determine if a sales agent is needed and pointers on how to choose one.

MT 4 Marketing Checklist for Small Retailers

This checklist is for the owner/ manager of a small retail business. The questions outlined cover customer analysis, buying, pricing, and promotion and other factors in the retail marketing process.

MT 8 Research Your Market

Learn what market research is and how you can benefit from it. Introduces inexpensive techniques that small business owners can apply to gather facts about their customer base and how to expand it.

MT 9 Selling by Mail Order

Provides basic information on how to run a successful mail order business. Includes information on product selection, pricing, testing, and writing effective advertisements.

MT 10 Market Overseas with U.S. Government Help

Entering the overseas marketplace offers exciting opportunities to increase company sales and profits. Learn about the programs available to help small businesses break into the world of exporting.

MT 11 Advertising

Advertising is critical to the success of any small business. Learn how you can effectively

market your products and services.

PERSONNEL MANAGEMENT

PM 1 Checklist for Developing a Training Program

Describes a step-by-step process of setting up an effective employee training program.

PM 2 Employees: How to Find and Pay Them

A business is only as good as the people in it. Learn how to find and hire the right employees.

PM 3 Managing Employee Benefits

Describes employee benefits as one part of the total compensation package and discusses proper management of benefits.

NEW PRODUCTS/IDEAS/INVENTIONS

PI 1 Can You Make Money with Your Idea or Invention?

This publication is a step-by-step guide that shows how you can make money by turning your creative ideas into marketable products. It is a resource for entrepreneurs attempting to establish themselves in the marketplace.

PI 2 Introduction to Patents

Offers some basic facts about patents to help clarify your rights. It discusses the relationships among a business, an inventor and the Patent and Trademark Office to ensure protection of your product and to avoid or win infringement suits.

SBA—SBDC (Small Business Development Center)

Q: *"Can you tell me what the SBDCs do at the universities? I understand that they run workshops and do individual counseling."*

SBDCs are university-affiliated advisory centers located in more than 500 cities. There are about 54 universities that have SBDCs in 42 states and each has satellite offices to serve outlying area. SBDCs are a partnership of the SBA, the local university, and the local state government. Senior and graduate students and paid professionals offer high-quality, low-cost assistance to local businesses and often conduct moderately priced workshops on such topics as start-ups and taxation. When a small business requires technical help, research studies, or other types of specialized assistance, these centers, located in academic institutions, are prime resources for the alert and growth-oriented entrepreneur.

SBA—SBI (Small Business Institute)

Q: "Don't some universities have SBA assistance available?"

The SBA operates Small Business Institutes on almost 500 college campuses in every state of the union. These are staffed by instructors and students trained to give in-depth counseling to select small business clients. The nearest SBA office will have a list of the SBIs nearest you, or you can call, toll free, the SBA's Answer Desk at 800 827-5722.

SBA—SBIC (Small Business Investment Company)

Q: "The banks rejected my application for an expansion loan. One mentioned that the SBIC might consider our proposal. Can you tell me how SBICs work?"

SBICs are Small Business Investment Companies. Formed in 1958, they are private investment companies licensed by the SBA to provide loans to small businesses. SBICs can be limited partnerships, corporations, or even bank subsidiaries. They are required to have a minimum of one million dollars in capital. An SBIC can borrow up to four dollars for every dollar of private capital it has available directly from the SBA. The SBIC then can make loans to or equity investments in small businesses that meet pre-established investment criteria. It earns money on the borrower's earnings, on future stock sales, or on leveraged buyouts. An amendment to the act that created SBICs allows them to do smaller debt financing in the $100,000 to $200,000 range, usually to minority enterprises, including those owned by Blacks, Hispanics, Asians, native Americans, and Vietnam veterans. Generally SBICs work fast and can get a deal going in a comparatively uncomplicated manner. You will need a sound business plan in any event, just as you would when approaching any other investment company. Contact your nearest SBA office for addresses or write to the National Association of SBICs, 1156 15th St., NW, Suite 1101, Washington, DC 20005.

SBA—SCORE (Service Corps Of Retired Executives)

Q: "I'd like to get some advice on setting up a new business, but I'd prefer to work with somebody who's going to be available in the future when I need him. Is SCORE the one I should go to?"

SCORE is indeed the world's largest volunteer small business counseling organization. It has been affiliated with the SBA since 1964 and consists of about 385 offices and an equal number of satellite or branch offices. The more than 12,000 men and women who are SCORE members are all volunteers and their services are free and confidential as long as you need them. Most counseling is done on a one-on-one basis, though with larger firms, or "cases," local SCORE chapters will sometimes get a team together in which each volunteer represents a different specialty. SCORE also conducts popular workshops in many chapters that cost between $5 and $25. Since the men and women who volunteer for SCORE counseling are retired, they work at mutual convenience and complement each other rather than staying on one case indefinitely. Each SCORE counselor has an average of 35 years of experience and many of them have had vast experience in virtually every phase of business. It is important that SCORE clients give their prospective counselors complete and detailed information on their needs so that a productive "matchmaking" can be arranged between the client and the counselor. All counseling is free and confidential. Local SCORE offices can be found in the blue government section of major phone books, under Small Business Administration, or by calling 800 827-5722 (toll free).

SBA—Services

Q: *"I'm a small business operator—can the SBA actually do anything for me?"*

The U.S. Small Business Administration's services to the American business community is in two major areas: management assistance and financial assistance.

This 4,000-person government agency has more than one hundred offices all around the country. In addition it supports affiliated associations like the Small Business Development Corporation (SBDC), Service Corps of Retired Executives (SCORE), and Small Business Investment Companies (SBICs). SBA has an internal division called the Office of Advocacy which is the watchdog for small business within the federal government, ensuring that small business will continue to be the cornerstone of our free enterprise system. While SBA has a variety of loan programs for small enterprises, most loans are made by private lenders and then guaranteed by the SBA. Guaranteed loans carry a maximum of $750,000. The average size loan during the past years has been $175,000 and the average maturity is about eight years. In addition to traditional bank loan guarantees, the SBA has licensed about 700 companies as Certified Lenders. The SBA encourages job creation and retention through Development Company Loans (the 504 Program and the longer-range 502 Program), Small General Contractor Loans, Seasonal Line of Credit Guarantees, Energy Loans, Handicapped Assistance Loans, Export Revolving Line of Credit guarantees, International Trade Loans, Pollution Control Financing, and Physical and Economic Disaster Loans. Where bonding becomes a necessity—such as with small contractors and minorities who have a hard time obtaining adequate bonding—the SBA guarantees a qualified surety up to 90 percent or performance bonds valued up to $1.25 million. In the area of sales to the U.S. government, the SBA makes sure a fair share of government contract awards go to small businesses with its Procurement Assistance Program that includes prime and subcontracts, certificates of competency, and maintenance of the Procurement Automated Source System (PASS). To obtain help from any SBA office or from one of the SBA's affiliated agencies like SCORE, SBDC, or SBIs, small business people can call the national toll free hotline, 800 827-5722, or look in the blue section of any city telephone book under Small Business Administration. A booklet titled "Your Business and the SBA" is available from any SBA office (publication OPC-2).

SBA—*Small Loans from SBICs (Small Business Investment Companies)*

Q: "Does the SBA make small loans that don't have to go through the banks?"

The SBA arranges indirectly for some specialized loans through Small Business Investment Companies (SBICs). These are private firms licensed and regulated by the SBA to supply equity capital, to extend unsecured loans and partially collateralized loans to small enterprises that meet certain predetermined investment criteria. They are profit-making ventures and as such prefer to make major rather than very small, unprofitable loans. Usually such loans are backed by equipment collateral, title to which is retained by the SBIC that makes the loan. Loans to minority and disadvantaged entrepreneurs are often made under a special 301(d) SBIC program.

SBA—*Troubled Businesses*

Q: "Does the SBA have any information on small businesses that are in trouble?"

The first thing you should do is immediately contact your nearest SBA office or a SCORE office directly. It is possible that a counselor is available who can guide you to a feasible solution of your problems—unless you have waited too long to get help. The SBA has a publication entitled "Techniques for Problem Solving" (publication MP 23) that might be helpful. If you are a manufacturer, obtain "Fixing Production Mistakes" (publication MP 7). Also useful might be "Analyze Your Records to Reduce Costs" (publication FM 7) and "Sound Cash Management and Borrowing" (publication FM 9). Have a candid talk with your banker, accountant, and lawyer, as well as with your principal suppliers. Perhaps you can work out a staggered payment plan, factor your receivables, or put pressure on your customers or clients to collect overdue accounts. Consider whether you might be able to attract new investors or even a partner.

SBA—*Using Your Own Bank*

Q: *"My small town bank is not an SBA-certified lender, but they know me best. Isn't there a way the SBA can cooperate with a bank like mine?"*

Your problem is not unique and the SBA has done something about it. While most of the more than 17,000 loans approved last year came from SBA-certified lending institutions, the SBA now will also consider loans from noncertified banks, though approval of applications from such banks might take a little longer. Here is a statement that was made by the SBA loan department in Washington, DC:

> Any bank or savings and loan is eligible to submit applications for guaranty to the SBA. Of course, some lenders are more frequent users of the program and understand it better. These are often granted certified or preferred status, which enables faster handling. Other banks/lenders seldom use the SBA loan program and may have limited knowledge of how it works.

You might want to advise your bank to contact the SBA Loan Department, 409 Third St., SW, Washington, DC. 20416, or phone 202 205 6490.

START-UP—*Checklist*

Q: *"Can you give me a quick checklist of the steps I need to go through in opening a new business? I want to make sure I don't skip any of the important ones."*

The Arthur Andersen Organization, a worldwide accounting firm, lists the following nine steps for starting a new company:

1. Consult an attorney regarding the legal requirements of setting up and operating your business.
2. Consult an accountant regarding the financial and tax requirements of setting up and operating your business.
3. Register the name of the business with the state.
4. Make appropriate applications for licenses to operate in desired states.
5. Obtain federal employer identification number (Form SS-4).
6. Apply for state workers' compensation and unemployment insurance.
7. Determine applicable job safety and health regulations (OSHA).
8. Determine applicable environmental regulations (EPA or state environmental protection agency).
9. Apply for local business license.

The SBA publishes a small booklet entitled "Checklist for Going Into Business" (publication MP-12) and various booklets on how to develop a business plan for various kinds of enterprises. Also ask if a booklet called "What Is Needed to Operate a Good Small Business" is still available. It lists in some detail the following steps and others we have added:

- Type of business or service
- Capital
- Location
- Product or service
- Bookkeeping
- Records
- Management
- Personnel
- Inventory
- Advertising
- Tax payments
- Attorney
- License and registration requirements
- Outside assistance (SCORE, SBDC, etc.)

Your library is also a rich resource for start-up businesses.

Look for a looseleaf binder titled "How to Start a Business in (Your State)"—there is one published for each of the 50 states.

START-UP—*Cost Estimates*

Q: *"Do you have a checklist of expenses that can be expected for the start-up of a small business?"*

The SBA has a booklet that will be a good starting point for your entry into business—"Checklist for Going Into Business" (publication MP-12). There are many others that will be useful, all listed in the free SBA Directory of Business Development Publications (Form 115A-M), which you can send for or obtain at any SBA or SCORE office. There are 12 general categories of start-up expenses that you need to consider:

- Decorating and remodeling
- Fixtures, equipment
- Installation costs
- Services, supplies
- Opening inventory costs
- Legal and professional fees
- Licenses and permits
- Telephone and utility deposits
- Insurance premiums
- Signs
- Advertising for opening
- Unplanned expenses

There are of course other expenses, depending on the type of business you plan to open. Transportation (vehicles), if any; outside help, if needed; rental for current period and security deposit, if required; and most important of all—money to pay your personal expenses until money starts coming in from sales. These items are covered in the next question.

START-UP—*Financing*

Q: *"How much money does it really take to start a new business?"*

Surprisingly, about 89 percent of all business beginnings are financed with less than $100,000. Businesses in the largest single start-up category, 25 percent of all recorded start-ups, are capitalized at between $20,000 and $49,000. In fact, more than 17 percent of all new businesses begin with less than $5,000 in cash. Perhaps adequate financing is important, and, in fact, lack of it is often a source of business failure, but management is even more important. Here is a breakdown of percentages of businesses started with various sums:

Amount in Dollars	Percent of Firms Starting
Less than $5,000	17.5
$5,000–$9,000	14.0
$10,000–$19,000	15.5
$20,000–$49,000	25.0
$50,000–$99,000	15.0
$100,000–$249,000	8.0
$250,000–$499,000	2.0
$500,000–and up	1.0
(figures rounded off)	

START-UP—*The First Months*

Q: *"We have figured that it will take about $20,000 to open our new shop. We are opening at the peak season but still would like to know what expenses we can expect?"*

There are so many variables built into your question that it would be best to call the nearest SCORE office and set up an appointment with a knowledgeable SCORE counselor. He will be able to guide you in determining a safe cash flow projection. If you have and can afford an accountant, he will be able to steer you also in the right direction. You will probably need sufficient cash or available resources to carry you for three months. Unless yours is an all-cash business, a financial cushion of three months is a safe estimate. The 10 items for which you need to make expense projections are the following:

- Your living costs
- Employee wages
- Rent
- Advertising
- Supplies
- Utilities
- Insurance
- Taxes
- Maintenance
- Delivery/transportation

To the total, multiplied by three to cover three months, you need to add one very important item: miscellaneous. In every business some unforeseen items crop up that no Solomon can divine—25 percent is usually a safe figure for miscellaneous expenditure. See also the entry **START-UP—*Cost Estimates.***

START-UP—*Pitfalls*

Q: *"After the excitement of a grand opening, I am told, there are always problems that are not anticipated. What are some of the pitfalls I should watch out for?"*

The pitfalls in continuing a new business are many. Even with the best of education and experience, one cannot anticipate all these problems. One of the best ways to insure yourself against unforeseen pitfalls is to have enough cash reserves or access to fiscal resources, to be flexible in your operation and in your mind, and to consult outside counsel when needed—people like SCORE, who are available across the country and whose counsel is free. The four major areas of post-opening problems can be grouped as follows:

- More cash taken from the business for personal needs than the business can afford
- Failure to recognize seasonal trends
- Slow collection of accounts if credit is extended to customers
- Expanding too rapidly, buying too much inventory, hiring more employees than you really need, making business expenditures that cannot be covered by real income

STATE ASSISTANCE—*Business Development Offices in 50 States*

Q: *"Do the states have business development offices that help small start-up businesses?"*

Yes, indeed, all states have business development offices, usually in the state capitals. Their services vary, but they are worth checking out. As when you go to the SBA or SCORE or the SBDC, the clearer and more complete your question, the better they will be able to tell whether they can be of help to you. Here are the 52 addresses (including Washington, DC, and Puerto Rico):

Alabama:

Development Office,
State Capitol, Montgomery, AL
   36130,
800 248-0033
or 205 263-0048

Alaska:

Division of Business
   Development,
P.O. Box D, Juneau, AK 99811
907 465-2017

Arizona:

Department of Commerce,
1700 W. Washington St., 4th Fl.,
   Phoenix, AZ 85007,
602 255-5705

Arkansas:

Small Business Information
   Center,
One State Capitol Mall, Rm.
   4C300, Little Rock, AR 77201,
501 682-3358

California:

Office of Small Business,
1121 L St., Suite 600,
Sacramento, CA 95814,
916 445-6545

Colorado:

Business Information Center,
1525 Sherman St., Rm. 110,
   Denver, CO 80203,
303 866-3933

Connecticut:

Small Business Services,
210 Washington St., Hartford, CT
   06106,
203 566-4051

Delaware:

Development Office,
99 King's Highway, P.O. Box
   1401, Dover, DE 19903,
302 736-4271

District of Columbia:

Office of Business and Economic
   Development,
7th Fl., 1111 E St., NW,
Washington, DC 20004,
202 727-6600

Florida:

Bureau of Business Assistance,
107 Gaines St., Tallahassee, FL
   32339-2000,
800 342-0771
or 904 488-9357

Georgia:

Department of Industry and
   Trade,
230 Peachtree Rd. NW, Atlanta,
   GA 30303,
404 656-3584

Hawaii:

Small Business Information
   Service,
250 S. King St., Rm. 727,
Honolulu, HI 96813,
808 548-7645

Idaho:

Economic Development Division,
   Department of Commerce,
State Capitol, Rm. 108,
Boise, ID 83720,
208 334-3416

Illinois:

Small Business Assistance
  Bureau,
620 E. Adams St., Springfield, IL
  62701,
800 252-2923
or 217 785-6282

Indiana:

Division of Business Expansion,
  Department of Commerce,
One North Capital, Suite 700,
  Indianapolis, IN 46204-2288,
800 824-2476
or 317 232-3527

Iowa:

Bureau of Small Business
  Development,
200 E. Grand Ave., Des Moines,
  IA 50309,
800 532-1216
or 515 281-8310

Kansas:

Division of Existing Industry
  Development,
400 S.W. Eighth St., 5th Fl.,
  Topeka, KS 66603,
913 296-5298

Kentucky:

Small Business Division,
Capitol Plaza, 22nd Fl.,
Frankfort, KY 40601,
800 626-2250
or 502 564-4252

Louisiana:

Development Division,
Office of Commerce and
  Industry,
P.O. Box 94185, Baton Rouge,
  LA 70804-9185,
504 342-5365

Maine:

Business Development Division,
State Development Office, State
  House,
Augusta, ME 04333,
800 872-3838
or 207 289-2659

Maryland:

Office of Business and Industrial
  Development,
45 Calvert St., Annapolis, MD
  21401,
800 654-7336
or 301 974-2946

Massachusetts:

Small Business Assistance
  Division,
100 Cambridge St., 13th Fl.,
Boston, MA 02202,
617 727-4005

Michigan:

Business Ombudsman,
  Department of Commerce,
P.O. Box 30107, Lansing, MI
  48909,
800 232-2727
or 517 373-6241

Minnesota:

Small Business Assistance Office
  American Center,
150 E. Kellogg Street, St. Paul,
  MN 55101,
800 652-9747
or 612 296-6949

Mississippi:

Small Business Bureau,
3825 Ridge Rd., Jackson, MS
  39211-6453,
601 982-6231

Missouri:

Small Business Development
  Office
Box 118, Jefferson City, MO
  65102,
314 751-4982

Montana:

Business Assistance Center,
1424 Ave., Helena, MT 59620,
800 221-8015
or 406 444-3923

Nebraska:

Small Business Division,
P.O. Box 94666,
301 Centennial Mall S., Lincoln,
  NE 68509, 402 471-4167

Nevada:

Office of Community Service,
1100 East William, Suite 116,
Carson City, NV 89710,
702 885-4602

New Hampshire:

Office of Industrial Development,
105 Loudon Rd., Prescott Park,
  Bldg. 2, Concord, NH 03301
603 271-2591

New Jersey:

Office of Small Business
  Assistance,
IW State St. (CN-835), Trenton,
  NJ 08625,
609 984-4442

New Mexico:

Economic Development Division,
1100 St. Francis Dr., Santa Fe,
  NM 87503,
800 545-2040
or 505 827-0300

New York:

Division for Small Business,
230 Park Ave., Rm. 834, New
  York, NY 10169,
212 309-0400

North Carolina:

Small Business Development
  Division,
Dobbs Bldg., Rm. 2019, 430 N.
  Salisbury St., Raleigh, NC
  27611,
919 733-7980

North Dakota:

Small Business Coordinator,
Economic Development
    Commission,
Liberty Memorial Bldg.,
    Bismarck, ND 58505,
800 472-2100
or 701 224-2810

Ohio:

Small and Developing Business
    Division,
P.O. Box 1001, Columbus, OH
    43266-0101,
800 282-1085
or 614 466-1876

Oklahoma:

Oklahoma Department of
    Commerce,
6601 Broadway Ext., Oklahoma,
    OK 73116,
405 521-2401

Oregon:

Economic Development
    Department,
595 Cottage St. NE, Salem, OR
    97310,
800 233-3306
or 547-7842; or 503 373-1200

Pennsylvania:

Small Business Action Center,
Department of Commerce,
404 Forum Bldg., Harrisburg, PA
    17120,
717 783-5700

Puerto Rico:

Commonwealth, Department of
    Commerce,
Box S, 4275 Old San Juan
    Station, San Juan, PR 00905,
809 758-4747

Rhode Island:

Small Business Development
    Division,
7 Jackson Walkway, Providence,
    RI 02903,
401 277-2601

South Carolina:

Business Development M
    Assistance Division,
P.O.Box 927, Columbia, SC
    29202,
800 922-6684
or 803 737-0400

South Dakota:

Governor's Office of Economic
    Development,
Capital Lake Plaza, Pierre, SD
    57501,
800 952-3625
or 605 773-5032

Tennessee:

Small Business Office,
320 Sixth Ave. N., 7th Fl.,
    Rachel Jackson Bldg.,
Nashville, TN 37219,
800 922-6684
or 803 737-0400

Texas:

Small Business Division,
P.O. Box 12728 Capitol Station,
410 E. Fifth St., Austin, TX
78711,
512 472-5059

Utah:

Small Business Development
Center,
660 S. Second St., Rm. 418, Salt
Lake City, UT 84111,
801 581-7905

Vermont:

Agency of Development and
Community Affairs,
The Pavillion, Montpelier, VT
05602,
800 622-4553
or 802 828-3221

Virginia:

Small Business and Financial
Services,
1000 Washington Bldg.,
Richmond, VA 23219,
804 786-3791

Washington:

Small Business Development
Center,
441 Todd Hall, Washington State
University, Pullman, WA
99164,
509 335-1576

West Virginia:

Small Business Development
Center Division,
Governor's Office, Capital
Complex, Charleston, WV
25305,
304 348-2960

Wisconsin:

Small Business Ombudsman,
Department of Development,
123 W. Washington Ave., P.O.
Box 7970, Madison, WI 53707,
800 435-7287
or 608 266-0562

Wyoming:

Economic Development and
Stabilization Board,
Herschler Bldg., 3rd Fl. E.,
Cheyenne, WY 82002,
307 777-7287

STUDENT ENTERPRISES

Q: "I am a senior at a university and want to get started, while I am still here, on developing a software service and consulting business, possibly with a student-partner. Where can I get some assistance?"

SCORE chapters all over the country and SBDC offices located at many universities offer free counseling to start-up businesses. In obtaining help from one of the SBA-affiliated small business counseling agencies, or in applying for a loan from a bank, you need to prepare and present a detailed business plan. In a typical scenario, 18 students at a college in Lubbock, Texas, formed a company to produce and sell T-shirts on campus. With an instructor's help and evaluation of members of the local SCORE group, the student company obtained an interview with the Lubbock State Bank. One spokesman was selected by his peers to make the presentation of a 52-page business plan. The bank officers were so impressed that they not only granted the loan, but also obtained a contribution from their bank for the college's Young Entrepreneurs' Program.

A good contact for student entrepreneurial groups is the Association of Collegiate Entrepreneurs, Center for Entrepreneurship, Box 48, Wichita State University, Wichita, KS 67208; 316 689-3000. ACE is represented in more than 300 universities located in all 50 states.

TECHNOLOGY—*Assistance Centers*

Q: *"Can you tell me whom I can contact in the federal government regarding high-tech assistance on new innovations?"*

For any entrepreneur whose business includes the manufacture, sale, research, and servicing of high-tech products, there are two valuable resources, one federal, one private:

> National Institute of Standards and Technology (formerly the National Bureau of Standards), Room A-617, Gaithersburg, MD 20899; 301 975-4009.
> Manufacturing Productivity Center, IIT Research Institute, 10 W. 35th St., Chicago, IL 60616; 312 567-4800.

The NIST has a model workshop where the latest high-tech innovations, such as robots, are tested. Information on innovations and procedures are passed on to private individuals and companies in order to make them more efficient and competitive in the international marketplace.

The MPC in Chicago provides information on new manufacturing techniques and acts as a liaison between other technological companies. It acts as conduit for at least 33 other manufacturing technology centers located in 16 different states. You may contact any of them for information.

TRADEMARKS—*Protection*

Q: *"How can I protect my company name or trademark?"*

Your name or trademark is important because it facilitates recognition of your business. It has considerable residual value in the event of a sale of the business. The safest name, of course, is your own, because it is least likely to be contested. Like filing for a patent, getting trademark or brand name protection is quite complicated and a good lawyer familiar with this specific field should be employed. However, there some steps you can take if you have the time and inclination:

1. Obtain a booklet called "Basic Facts About Trademarks" from Trademark Information, Patent and Trademark Office, Department of Commerce, Washington, DC 20231, 703 557-4636. It will contain an application that must be filed by the trademark owner.
2. As of 1989 the United States Trademark Law has been amended to make it no longer mandatory for a product to be in commercial use before being registered.
3. A trademark should not have a commonly used or generic name, but could be a person, a company, word, phrase, letter, number, picture, or design, or a combination of any of them. Kodak, Kotex, Kleenex and Xerox are just some examples of artificial names that have become generic with time and infinite exposure.
4. Be mindful of the fact that a trademark on a product has psychological impact as well as legal protection and it should be exposed on every medium—trucks, letterheads, uniforms, buildings, trade show booths, ads, direct mail, etc.

TRADEMARKS—*Small Business Protection*

Q: *"I read about a small company trademarking a product and when a large company used it, the small guy sued and won a couple of million dollars. Is it expensive to trademark a name?"*

Winning a couple of million dollars in a trademark infringement suit against a large company is like winning the jackpot in a state lottery. It can happen, but the primary purpose of filing a trademark with the federal or state governments is to prevent unfriendly competition. The U.S. Patent and Trademark Office charges $175 application fee for each class of goods or services. The federal registration is applicable only if you sell in several states. It will be checked for possible duplication by a government attorney, published four times in the Official Gazette, and then entered in the active, federally registered trademark register. If you just plan to do business within your state, trademark registration with this state will afford you comparable protection. You may send for a number of useful publications from the U.S. Trademark Association, 6 E. 46th St., NY, NY 10017. Enclose a stamped, self-addressed envelope for a list of publications available for purchase. To work through a knowledgeable attorney will probably cost you less than $1,000 but save you potential grief. Remember that names as well as logos and other graphic designs can also be protected.

VETERANS

Q: *"I am a veteran and plan to go into my own business. Are there any special programs or advantages?"*

SBA offers a special loan program for disabled and Vietnam era veterans. All veterans are entitled to special considerations under the SBA's regular 7(a) loan program. Each SBA office and many major SCORE chapters have veterans' officers who will be glad to discuss your needs with you or send you pertinent literature.

WALSH-HEALY ACT

Q: *"I am planning to bid on a government contract and am told that I must adhere to the provisions of the Walsh-Healy Act. What is that all about?"*

The Walsh-Healy Public Contracts Act was enacted in 1936. It is a federal law setting basic labor standards for work on all government contracts if they exceed $10,000 in value. Employees must be paid at least the prevailing wage rates, and they must be paid time-and-one-half for hours worked in excess of eight hours a day or 40 hours a week, whichever is greater. The act is administered by the Department of Labor. There is another act that applies to work on government contracts, and that is the Davis-Bacon Act originally formulated in 1931 and revised in 1964. This act applies to all contracts amounting to $2,000 or more for work performed on government-owned public buildings. Wages for these contracts are usually based on rates paid in a particular geographic area—the going rate. This rate may be lower or higher than the union rate.

WOMEN'S BUSINESS—*Minority Programs*

Q: *"I am a woman and want to go into business. Do I qualify for the minority programs?"*

Women as a class are not a minority. To be classified as eligible for minority assistance, a woman must prove that she is socially and economically disadvantaged. Each of the more than 100 SBA offices across the country has a women's business opportunity representative who will be happy to discuss your opportunities with you. One of the illuminating and encouraging trends is that more women are entering the small business arena than men. Magazines like *INC., Success, Entrepreneur, In Business, New Business Opportunities,* and *Working Woman* are full of case histories. Two useful books on the subject, among the many available, are

> On Your Own: A Women's Guide to Building a Business by Laurie Zuckerman (Upstart Publishing, 1990)
> The Woman Entrepreneur: Starting, Financing and Managing a Successful New Business by Robert D. Hisrich and Candida G. Brush (Lexington Books, 1990)

WOMEN'S BUSINESS—*Opportunities*

Q: *"Much is being written about helping women get into business. What do you think of the chances of women making it?"*

The SBA's Women's Business Opportunities (WBO) division focuses on working with women entrepreneurs all across the country. Affiliate organizations like SCORE also have many WBO volunteer executives who counsel women, hold seminars, and assist the increasing number of women who are entering the world of business independence. Some businesses are already dominated by women—child care centers, gift shop and fashion store management, agencies for personnel placements, travel agencies, and more. There are numerous government programs that help women get a share of federal procurement.

Regarding barriers, female entrepreneurs, through their many business and professional associations, report their own barriers much like those of men—a fear of the risks involved; the difficulty of balancing work demands with needed family time; a lack of support from family and colleagues; and a lack of business background that sometimes translates into difficulty in establishing credit independently or raising capital (see MANAGEMENT—Family). Some peripheral difficulties women have encountered are lack of accounting skills and lack of experience in hiring and firing of employees.

WOMEN'S BUSINESS—*Opportunities/SBA Programs*

Q: *"Women in business have not exactly been part of our business or social culture. Does the SBA have any programs that especially help women get started?"*

Of the more than 260,000 fledgeling and established business people who sought help from the SBA or its affiliated SCORE and SBDC organizations, about one-third were women. This figure is apparently increasing each year. The SBA has women's business coordinators in each of the ten regions. SCORE counselors, too, will help women entrepreneurs with targeted workshops that focus on procurement, business, and credit assistance to women-owned businesses. These initiatives will gather momentum as SBA gains experience in the special needs of women entrepreneurs and as more and more women enter the ranks of independent entrepreneurial activities. Woman-oriented workshops are also held at many libraries, local schools, universities and banks. One thing women entrepreneurs must remember is that the rules of the marketplace are the same for men and women, and that they are unrelentingly tough. While some consumers will prefer women because of special requirements and needs, it is generally the type and quality of their products and services that determine success and survival.

WORKSHOPS

Q: *"Does the SBA provide any workshops for people who want to go into business?"*

The SBA provides many workshops throughout the country through its affiliated SCORE and SBDC organizations. The Service Corps of Retired Executives alone holds between 3,000 and 4,000 workshops each year at many of its 385 principal locations. You can find out the dates and topics by calling the nearest SCORE office. Each is usually attended by 20 to 40 persons and costs $5 to $25, which includes materials and sometimes even lunch. These workshops are run by experienced retired executives and allow considerable question-and-answer sessions. If you want more information after the workshop, you can make an appointment for individual one-on-one counseling right after the workshop. The counseling is always free and confidential. The typical start-up business workshop might include such topics as

- analysis of your own motivation
- need for experience
- financial requirements and various ways of capitalizing a new business
- forms of business organizations
- marketing your business, products or services
- requirements for permits, licenses, insurance, taxes
- how to keep needed business records
- reason for a business plan and how to prepare one

A major advantage to attending these workshops is the opportunity you have to network with the other entrepreneurs who attend them—and you are encouraged to ask questions and make suggestions of benefit to others.

Appendix A

ANTITRUST DIVISION OFFICES

Main Office

U.S. Department of Justice
Antitrust Division
Office of Operations
10th St. & Pennsylvania Avenue,
  N.W.
Washington, DC 20530
202 633-3544

Field Offices

Atlanta
Suite 420
1776 Peachtree Street N.W.
Atlanta, GA 30309
404 881-3828

Chicago
John C. Kluczynski Building
Room 3820
230 S. Dearborn Street
Chicago, IL 60604
312 353-7530

Cleveland
995 Celebreeze Federal Bldg.
1240 East 9th Street
Cleveland, OH 44199-2089
216 522-4070

Dallas
Earle Cabell Federal Bldg.
Room 8C6
1100 Commerce Street
Dallas, TX 75242
214 767-9051

New York
Room 3630
26 Federal Plaza
New York, NY 10278
212 264-0390

Philadelphia
11400 U.S. Courthouse
601 Market Street
Philadelphia, PA 19106
215 597-7405

San Francisco
450 Golden Gate Avenue
Box 36046
San Francisco, CA 94102
415 556-6300

Appendix B

FEDERAL INFORMATION CENTER PROGRAM

The Federal Information Center Program (FIC) is a focal point for information about the federal government. The FIC assists people who have questions about federal services, programs, and regulations, but do not know where to turn for an answer. FIC information specialists either answer an inquirer's questions directly, or perform the research necessary to locate and refer the inquirer to the expert best able to help. Residents of 72 key metropolitan areas reach the FIC through locally listed, toll-free telephone numbers; statewide toll-free 800 service is available to the residents of four states: Iowa, Kansas, Missouri, and Nebraska. The FIC telephone numbers are listed below. If you are not in one of the metropolitan areas listed below, you may call the FIC at 301 722-9098 or write to Federal Information Center, P.O. Box 600, Cumberland, MD 21502. TTY/TDD users may reach the FIC by dialing a toll-free number, 800 326-2996.

Alabama
Birmingham—800 366-2998
Mobile—800 366-2998

Alaska
Anchorage—800 729-8003

Arizona
Phoenix—800 359-3997

Arkansas
Little Rock—800 366-2998

California
Los Angeles—800 726-4995
Sacramento—916 973-1695
San Diego—800 726-4995
San Francisco—800 726-4995
Santa Ana—800 726-4995

Colorado
Colorado Springs—800 359-3997
Denver—800 359-3997
Pueblo—800 359-3997

Connecticut

Hartford—800 347-1997
New Haven—800 347-1997

Florida

Fort Lauderdale—800 347-1997
Jacksonville—800 347-1997
Miami—800 347-1997
Orlando—800 347-1997
St. Petersburg—800 347-1997
Tampa—800 347-1997
West Palm Beach—800 347-1997

Georgia

Atlanta—800 347-1997

Hawaii

Honolulu—800 733-5996

Illinois

Chicago—800 366-2998

Indiana

Gary—800 366-2998
Indianapolis—800 347-1997

Iowa

From all points in Iowa—800 735-8004

Kansas

From all points in Kansas—800 735-8004

Kentucky

Louisville—800 347-1997

Louisiana

New Orleans—800 366-2998

Maryland

Baltimore—800 347-1997

Massachusetts

Boston—800 347-1997

Michigan

Detroit—800 347-1997
Grand Rapids—800 347-1997

Minnesota

Minneapolis—800 366-2998

Missouri

St. Louis—800 366-2998
From elsewhere in Missouri—800 735-8004

Nebraska

Omaha—800 366-2998
From elsewhere in Nebraska—800 735-8004

New Jersey

Newark—800 347-1997
Trenton—800 347-1997

New Mexico

Albuquerque—800 359-3997

New York

Albany—800 347-1997
Buffalo—800 347-1997
New York—800 347-1997
Rochester—800 347-1997
Syracuse—800 347-1997

North Carolina

Charlotte—800 347-1997

Ohio

Akron—800 347-1997
Cincinnati—800 347-1997
Cleveland—800 347-1997
Columbus—800 347-1997
Dayton—800 347-1997
Toledo—800 347-1997

Oklahoma

Oklahoma City—800 366-2998
Tulsa—800 366-2998

Oregon

Portland—800 726-4995

Pennsylvania

Philadelphia—800 347-1997
Pittsburgh—800 347-1997

Rhode Island

Providence—800 347-1997

Tennessee

Chattanooga—800 347-1997
Memphis—800 366-2998
Nashville—800 366-2998

Texas

Austin—800 366-2998
Dallas—800 366-2998
Fort Worth—800 366-2998
Houston—800 366-2998
San Antonio—800 366-2998

Utah

Salt Lake City—800 359-3997

Virginia

Norfolk—800 347-1997
Richmond—800 347-1997
Roanoke—800 347-1997

Washington

Seattle—800 726-4995
Tacoma—800 726-4995

Wisconsin

Milwaukee—800 366-2998

Appendix C

FEDERAL TRADE COMMISSION OFFICES

Headquarters

Federal Trade Commission
Bureau of Competition
Washington, DC 20580
202 523-3404

Regional Offices

Atlanta
(Serves AL, FL, GA, MS, NC, SC,
TN, VA)
Room 1000
1718 Peachtree Street N.W.
Atlanta, GA 30367
404 881-4836

Boston
(Serves CT, ME, MA, NH, RI,
VT)
Room 1301
150 Causeway Street
Boston, MA 02114
617 223-6621

Chicago
(Serves IL, IN, IA, MN, MO, WI,
KY)
Suite 1437
55 East Monroe Street
Chicago, IL 60603
312 353-4423

Cleveland
(Serves MI, OH, PA, WV, DE,
MD)
Suite 500—Mall Building
118 St. Clair Avenue
Cleveland, OH 44114
216 522-4207

Dallas
(Serves AR, LA, NM, OK, TX)
8303 Elmbrook Drive
Dallas, TX 75247
214 767-7050

Denver
(Serves CO, KS, MT, NE, ND,
SD, UT, WY)
Suite 2900
1405 Curtis Street
Denver, CO 80202
303 844-2271

Hawaii
Room 6324
300 Ala Moana
Honolulu, HI 96850
808 546-5685

Los Angeles
(Serves AZ, S. CA)
11000 Wilshire Boulevard
Los Angeles, CA 90024
213 209-7575

New York
(Serves NJ, NY)
2243-EB Federal Building
26 Federal Plaza
New York, NY 10278
212 264-1207

San Francisco
(Serves N.CA, HI, NV)
450 Golden Gate Avenue
San Francisco, CA 94102
415 556-1270

Seattle
(Serves AK, ID, OR, WA)
28th Floor, Federal Bldg.
915 Second Avenue
Seattle, WA 98174
206 442-4655

Appendix D

SERVICE CORPS OF RETIRED EXECUTIVES (SCORE)
Offices In The 50 United States and Territories

SCORE is an affiliate of the U.S. Small Business Administration (SBA) with approximately 385 offices or chapters that are staffed by over 12,000 men and women volunteers. In addition, many SCORE chapters maintain satellite offices in nearby population centers that are staffed either occasionally or by appointment, especially in the less heavily populated jurisdictions. Most SCORE offices are located in federal buildings, especially where SBA offices already exist, or within chambers of commerce and colleges. Consulting services, either on a one-on-one basis or by teams of SCORE consultants, are free and confidential. Workshops are held by many chapters—nearly 4,000 a year—that charge a moderate fee of $5.00 to $20.00 for materials and, at times, refreshments. To obtain the exact address and or telephone number of the SCORE office nearest you, check the blue (government listing) section of your nearest city telephone book. SCORE is listed under Small Business Administration. Ask for a counselor who has experience and expertise in the field of your interest, and every effort will be made to match you up with someone to suit your particular need.

The cities in which SCORE chapters and their satellite offices operate are listed below.

Alabama
Birmingham

Foley

Mobile
Florence

Tuscaloosa

Alaska
Soldotna

Arizona
Phoenix
   Phoenix-Bell

Tucson
   Kino Park (Nogales)

Willcox
Casa Grande
Payson
Saint Johns
Snowflake

Prescott
Flagstaff
Glendale
Yuma
Green Valley
Sierra Vista

Mesa
Holbrook
Pinetop
Snow Low
Springerville
Cottonwood
Sedona

Lake Havasu
Kingman

Arkansas
Little Rock

Bella Vista

Fort Smith

Hot Springs

formation *California*
Los Angeles
Hollywood
Lakewood
Los Alamitos
North Hollywood
Pasadena
Pico Rivera
Torrance
Burbank
Culver City

El Monte
Agoura
Inglewood
Long Beach
Monterey Park
Northridge
Bellflower
Santa Monica
Van Nuy
Canoga Park
Downey
Gardena
Hawthorne
Concord
Pleasanton
Richmond
San Leandro
S. San Francisco
Danville
Fremont
Pottsburg
Novato

Santa Ana

San Francisco
Pacifica
Redwood City
San Carlos
San Mateo
Walnut Creek
Foster City
Hayward
Menlo Park
Oakland

San Diego
Brawley
Chula Vista
El Centro
Escondido
Vista

Redlands
  Fontana
  San Bernardino
  Yucca Valley
  Camarillo
  Ojai
  Calexico
  El Cajon
  Encinitas
  Oceanside

Santa Barbara
  Colton
  Hesperia
  29 Palms

Ventura
  Conejo Valley
  Oxnard
  Port Hueneme
  Simi Valley
  Chino
  Claremont
  La Puente
  Montclair
  Cucamonga

Palm Springs
  La Quinta

Fresno
  Oakhurst
  Santa Paula

Pomona
  West Covina
  Covina
  La Verne
  Ontario
  Upland
  Indio
  Palm Desert
  Monterey

Salinas
Visalia
Milpitas
Sunnyvale
Trukee

Santa Rosa
Vallejo
Lakeport
Petaluma
Sonoma
Vacaville
Angels Camp

San Jose
  Mountain View
  Tahoe City

Sacramento
  Clearlake
  Fairfiel
  Napa
  Sebastopol
  Ukiah

Stockton

Santa Maria
  Arroyo Grande
  Grover City
  San Luis Obispo
  Solvang
  Riverside

Aptos

Modesto

Bakersfield
  Ridgecrest
  Atascadero
  Morro Bay
  Lompoc

Hemet
  Moreno

Redding
  Merced
  Sonora
  Tehachapi

Colorado

Denver

Grand Junction

Loveland
  Lamar

Durango

Pueblo
  Glenwood Spring
  Fort Morgan

Colorado Springs

Boulder

Connecticut

Norwalk
  South Woodstock
  Bristol

New Haven

Norwich
  Danbury

Hartford
  Manchester
  Old Saybrook

Bridgeport

Torrington

Delaware

Wilmington
  Dover

Lewes
  Milford
  Milton

Florida

Fort Lauderdale
  Homestead
  Orange Park

Largo

Lakeland

Tampa

West Palm Beach

Ft Pierce

Cocoa
  Merritt Island
  Melbourne

Miami

Jacksonville

Daytona Beach

Sarasota

Orlando

Fort Myers

Hollywood

Charlotte Harbor
  Titusville

Gainesville

Delray Beach
  Lake Sumpter

Ocala

Leesburg

Port Richey

Georgia

Atlanta
  Columbus
  Gainesville
  St. Simons Is.

Dalton
  Albany
  Macon

Savannah
  Augusta

Guam

Agana
  Saipan

Hawaii

Honolulu
  Kahului

Lihue, Kauai
  Kailua-Kona
  Hilo

Idaho

Boise

Twin Falls

Pocatello

Illinois

Chicago
  Northbrook
  Freeport
  Rockford
  Belvidere
  Galesburg
  Downers Grove
  Glen Ellyn
  Sycamore
  Danville

Sterling
University
Palatine
Joliet
Kankakee

Peoria

Aurora
  Elgin
  St. Charles

Decatur
  Champaign
  Mattoon

Marion
  Godfrey

Moline

Bloomington
  Springfield

Alton
  Edwinsville

Quincy

Indiana

Indianapolis

South Bend
  Jasper

Gary
  Laporte
  Merrillville
  Valparaiso

Columbus
  Portland

Jeffersonville
  Madison

Fort Wayne

Evansville
  Vincennes
  Crown Point
  Hammond
  Michigan City

Terre Haute

Muncie

Anderson
  Salem
  Marengo
  Paoli

Kokomo

Marion

Bloomington
  Logansport
  Wabash

Iowa
Des Moines

Davenport

Cedar Rapids

Waterloo
  Waverly

Dubuque

Fort Dodge

Ottumwa

Marshalltown

Clinton

Sioux City

Council Bluffs

Mason City
  Independence

Burlington
  Decorah

Spencer

Iowa City

Shenandoah

West Union

Kansas
Wichita

Emporia

Topeka

Hays

Liberal

Manhattan

Pittsburg

Salina

Winfield
  Sabetha

Hutchinson

Great Bend

Dodge City

McPherson

Kentucky
Louisville
  Glascow

Lexington
  Bowling Green

Paducah

Ashland

Louisiana

New Orleans

Lake Charles

Lafayette

Baton Rouge

Shreveport

Maine

Portland

Caribou

Auburn

Norway

Augusta

Bangor

Ellsworth

Maryland

Baltimore
  Dundalk
  Pikesville

Salisbury

Annapolis

Hagerstown
  Glen Burnie
  Towson
  Bel Air
  Cambridge

Columbia

Massachusetts

Boston

Hyannis
  Pittsfield
  North Adams

Salem
  Lawrence
  Newburyport
  Taunton

Fall River

Worcester

Springfield
  Greenfield

New Bedford
  Haverhill
  Lowell

Brockton
  Carver

Michigan

Detroit
  Jackson
  Ann Arbor

Kalamazoo
  Battle Creek
  Muskegon
  Traverse City
  Flint
  Lansing

Saute Ste. Marie
  Allegan
  Grand Rapids
  Holland

Minnesota
Minneapolis

Mankato

Rochester

Duluth
  Redwing
  Winona

St. Paul
  Owatonna
  Austin

St. Cloud

Mississippi
Biloxi

Meridian

Greenville

Jackson

Columbus

Missouri
Kansas City

Springfield

Cape Girardeau

Columbia

Cuba

Poplar Bluff

Camdenton

St. Louis

Branson

Mexico

St. Joseph

St. Peters

Hannibal

Montana
Great Falls

Butte

Helena

Kalispell

Missoula

Bozeman

Billings

Glasgow

Nebraska
Lincoln
  Omaha

Columbus

Norfolk

North Platte

Chadron

Omaha

Hastings

Fremont

Nevada
Las Vegas
  Incline Village

Stateline
Elko

Reno
  Carson City
  Minden

New Hampshire
Laconia

Rye

Manchester

Concord

Lebanon
  Dover

Keene

Berlin

New Jersey
Sommerville

Newark
  Madison
  Clifton

Lincroft
  Shrewsbury
  Manalpan

Paramus

Camden
  New Brunswick
  Jersey City
  Randolph
  Wayne
  Newton
  Brookdale
  Freehold

Pleasantville

Toms River

New Mexico
Albuquerque

Roswell

Las Cruces
  Farmington

Santa Fe

New York
Rochester
  Canandaigua
  Lockport
  Batavia

Syracuse
  Cobleskill

Watertown
  Norwich

Binghamton

Jamestown

Elmira
  Geneva

Buffalo
  N. Tonawanda

Poughkeepsie

Albany
  Saranac Lake

Utica

Auburn

Ronkonkoma

Mount Vernon

Huntington

Ithaca
  Newberg

Stone Ridge

Mineola

Middletown

Staten Island

New York
North Carolina
Charlotte
  Kinston
  Marion

Greensboro
  Jacksonville

Hickory
  Henderson
  Sanford
  Greenville

Raleigh

Asheville

Hendersonville

Wilmington

High Point

Durham

Southern Pines

Chapel Hill

Kitty Hawk

North Dakota
Fargo

Grand Forks

Dickinson

Minot

Bismarck

Ohio
Columbus
  Lima

Cleveland

Toledo

Akron
  Centerville
  Huber Hts.

Springfield

Marietta

Newark

Marion
  Chillicothe
  Piqua

Cincinnati
  Fostoria

Dayton
  Middleton

Youngstown

Mansfield

Zanesville

Oklahoma
Tulsa
  Stillwater

Lawton
  Anadarko
  Frederick

Oklahoma City
  Altus
  Duncan

Oregon
Portland

Eugene

Bend

Talent

Salem

Pennsylvania
Pittsburgh
  Altoona

Lancaster
  Lewiston
  Media

  Philadelphia

Bethlehem

Williamsport
  Sunbury
  Wellsboro

Wilkes-Barre
  Indiana

Reading

Harrisburg

Bala Cynwyd
  Willow Grove
  Fairless Hills

Erie
  Shamokin
  Lock Haven

Scranton

York
  Hanover

Uniontown

Huntington Valley
  Shippensburg

Stroudsburg

Latrobe
  Gettysburg

Monessen

Chambersburg
  Waynesboro

West Chester

Puerto Rico
Hato Rey

Mayaguez

Ponce

Rhode Island
Providence
  Warwick
  North Kingstown
  Warren
  Westerly
  Woonsocket

South Carolina

Columbia
  Greenwood
  Spartanburg

Myrtle Beach

Greenville
  Anderson

Charleston

South Dakota

Sioux Falls

Rapid City

Aberdeen

Tennessee

Memphis
  Cookeville

Knoxville

Jackson
  Johnson City

Nashville

Chattanooga
Morristown

Kingsport
  Greeneville

Texas

Dallas
  Richardson

Fort Worth
  Bedford
  Granbury
  Stephenville

San Antonio

Corpus Christi
  Alpine

Abilene

Austin
  Denton

Houston
  Arlington
  Cleburne
  Haltom City
  Brownwood

Harlingen

El Paso

Lubbock

Amarillo

Odessa

Tyler

Waco

College Station

Temple

Beaumont

Midland

Clute

Longview

Brownsville

Wichita Falls

SW Houston

Victoria

Denison

Utah
Salt Lake City

St George

Ogden

Provo

Vermont
Montpelier

Rutland

Johnson

Burlington
  Bennington

Virgin Islands
St. Thomas

St. Croix

Virginia
Richmond
  Blacksburg
  Pulaski

Hampton

Winchester

Danville

Fredericksburg

Woodbridge

Williamsburg

Roanoke
  Radford

Norfolk

Bristol

Waynesboro

Charlottesville

Lynchburg

Martinsville

Hopewell

Washington
Seattle
  Pullman
  Lewiston
  Moses Lake

Everett
  Gig Harbor
  Lakewood
  Pierce
  Shelton

Vancouver

Spokane
  Walla Walla
  Kennewick
  Moscow

Takoma
  Gray's Harbor
  Olympia
  Puyallup
  Chehalis

Washington, DC

West Virginia
Clarksburg

Charleston

Athens

Huntington

Elkins

Wheeling

Fairmont

Wisconsin

Milwaukee
  Waukeshaw
  Beloit

Eau Claire

Lacrosse

Wausau

Stevens Point

Superior
  Fond du Lac

Madison

Rhinelander

Appleton
  Prairie du Chien

Green Bay

Wyoming

Casper

Cheyenne

Appendix E

U.S. GOVERNMENT BOOKSTORES

The U.S. Government Printing Office operates 24 bookstores all around the country. You can obtain any publication there, browse to your heart's content, and purchase whatever you like without paying any tax. The GPO has printed in excess of 20,000 books—although not all of them are inventoried in each branch, any may be ordered and shipped for your pick-up or to your home or business at no additional cost to you. All of the stores accept VISA, MasterCard, and charges against a previously arranged Superintendent of Documents deposit account. All stores, except the one in Kansas, are open Monday through Friday; the one in Kansas is open seven days a week.

Atlanta, GA
Room 100, Federal Building
275 Peachtree Street, NE
P.O. Box 56445
Atlanta, GA 30343
404 331-6947

Birmingham, AL
O'Neil Building
2021 Third Ave., North
Birmingham, AL 35203
205 731-1056

Boston, MA
Thomas P. O'Neill Building
10 Causeway Street
Room 179
Boston, MA 02222
617 565-6680

Chicago, IL
Room 1365, Federal Building
219 S. Dearborn Street
Chicago, IL 60604
312 353-5133

Cleveland, OH
Room 1653, Federal Building
1240 E. 9th Street
Cleveland, OH 44199
216 522-4922

Columbus, OH
Room 207, Federal Building
200 N. High Street
Columbus, OH 43215
614 469-6956

Dallas, TX
Room 1C46, Federal Building
1100 Commerce Street
Dallas, TX 75242
214 767-0076

Denver, CO
Room 117, Federal Building
1961 Stout Street
Denver, CO 80294
303 844-3964

Detroit, MI
Suite 160, Federal Building
477 Michigan Avenue
Detroit, MI 48226
313 226-7816

Houston, TX
Texas Crude Building
801 Travis Street
Suite 120
Houston, TX 77002
713 653-3100

Jacksonville, FL
Room 158, Federal Building
400 W. Bay Street
Jacksonville, FL 32202
904 791-3801

Kansas City, MO
120 Bannister Mall
5600 E. Bannister Road
Kansas City, MO 64137
816 765-2256

Laurel, MD
Warehouse Sales Outlet
8660 Cherry Lane
Laurel, MD 20707
301 953-7974
792-0262

Los Angeles, CA
ARCO Plaza, C-Level
505 South Flower Street
Los Angeles, CA 90071
213 894-5841

Milwaukee, WI
Room 190, Federal Building
517 E. Wisconsin Avenue
Milwaukee, WI 53202
414 297-1304

New York, NY
Room 110
26 Federal Plaza
New York, NY 10278
212 264-3825

Philadelphia, PA
Robert Morris Building
100 North 17th Street
Philadelphia, PA 19103
215 597-0677

Pittsburgh, PA
Room 118, Federal Building
1000 Liberty Avenue
Pittsburgh, PA 15222
412 644-2721

Portland, OR
1305 S.W. First Avenue
Portland, OR 97201-5801
503 221-6217

Pueblo, CO
World Savings Building
720 North Main Street
Pueblo, CO 81003
719 544-3142

San Francisco, CA
Room 1023, Federal Building
450 Golden Gate Avenue
San Francisco, CA 94102
415 556-0643

Seattle, WA
Room 194 Federal Building
915 Second Avenue
Seattle, WA 98174
206 442-4270

Washington, DC
U.S. Government Printing Office
710 North Capitol Street, NW
Washington, DC 20401
202 275-2091

1510 H Street, NW
Washington, DC 20005
202 653-5075

Appendix F

IMPORTANT OFFICES AND PROGRAMS FOR SMALL BUSINESSES IN ALL 50 STATES

SBA Management Assistance

SBA Financial Assistance

SBA Veterans Affairs

SBA Women in Business

Small Business Development Centers

SCORE (see separate listing of 380 offices)

Internal Revenue Service (IRS)

Farmer's Home Administration (FHA)

Department of Commerce

Department of Energy

Department of Labor

OSHA

International Trade Administration (ITA)

Federal Information Centers

State Small Business Program

State Loan Information

State Procurement Office

State Minority Business

State Department of Revenue

State Export Agency

State Consumer Complaints

State Ombudsman

APPENDIX G

SBA AND OTHER FEDERAL AND STATE ASSISTANCE OFFICES IN THE 50 STATES AND TERRITORIES

On the following pages you will find information about:

- Small Business Administration (SBA) offices for Management Assistance, Financial Assistance, Veterans Affairs, and Women in Business
- Small Business Development Centers (SBDCs) operating under the auspices of the SBA (usually located in universities)
- Other federal offices, including Internal Revenue Service, Farmer's Home Administration, Department of Commerce, Department of Energy, Department of Labor, Occupational Safety and Health Administration, International Trade Administration, and Federal Information Centers
- State Business Development Assistance offices, usually located in state capitals unless otherwise indicated, including offices for Small Business Programs, Loan Information, Procurement, Minority Business, Department of Revenue, State Export, Consumer Complaints, and, if available, Ombudsman or Public Liaison Advocate.

ALABAMA   Region IV

Small Business Administration

Management Assistance
Birmingham   205 254-1338

Financial Assistance
Birmingham   205 254-1344

---

*   None identified
**   Number may be used only within this city

Veterans' Affairs Officer
Birmingham   205 254-1338

Women in Business Representative
Birmingham   205 254-1338

Small Business Development Centers
Auburn   205 826-4030
Florence   205 766-4100, ext. 420
Huntsville   205 895-6407
Huntsville   205 895-6303
Jacksonville   205 435-9820, ext. 342
Livingston   205 652-9661, ext. 439
Mobile   205 460-6130
Montgomery   205 293-4137
Normal   205 859-7481
Troy   205 566-3000, ext. 342
Tuscaloosa   205 348-7011
Tuskegee   205 727-8710
University   205 348-7011

State Offices

Small Business Program   205 832-6980
Loan Information   205 832-3889
Procurement Information   205 832-3580
Minority Business   205 832-5633
Department of Revenue   205 269-6861 (Montgomery)
State Export   205 284-8722
Consumer Complaints   800 392-5658
Ombudsman   *

Other U.S. Government Offices

Internal Revenue Service   800 292-6300; 205 254-0403
                                               (Birmingham)
Farmer's Home Administration   205 832-7077 (Montgomery)
Department of Commerce   205 254-1331 (Birmingham)
Department of Energy   205 826-4718 (Auburn)
Department of Labor,
   Wage/Hour Division   205 254-1305 (Birmingham)
                                            205 832-7450 (Montgomery)

Occupational Safety and
   Health Administration   205 822-7100 (Birmingham)
                                            205 690-2131 (Mobile)
International Trade Administration   205 254-1331 (Birmingham)
Federal Information Centers   **322-8591 (Birmingham)
                                            **438-1421 (Mobile)

ALASKA   *Region X*
Small Business Administration
Management Assistance
Anchorage	907 271-4028
Fairbanks	907 452-1951

Financial Assistance
Anchorage	907 271-4022
Fairbanks	907 452-1951

Veterans' Affairs Officer
Anchorage	907 271-4022

Women in Business Representative
Anchorage	907 271-4022

State Offices

Small Business Program	907 465-2018

Loan Information:
Alaska Resources Corporation	907 561-2210
	(Loan must be secured; limit $500,000 for small businesses with sales of less than $10 million. No service businesses.)
Procurement Information	*
Department of Revenue	907 586-5265
State Export	907 465-2500
Consumer Complaints	*
Ombudsman	*

Other U.S. Government Offices

Internal Revenue Service	907 276-1040
Farmer's Home Administration	907 745-2176 (Palmer)
Department of Commerce	907 271-5041 (Anchorage)
Department of Energy	907 276-0512 (Anchorage)
Department of Labor,	
*Wage/Hour Division	206 442-4482 (Seattle, WA)
Occupational Safety and	
*Health Administration	907 271-5152 (Anchorage)
International Trade Administration	907 271-5041 (Anchorage)
Federal Information Center	907 271-3650 (Anchorage)

ARIZONA   *Region IX*
Small Business Administration

Management Assistance
Phoenix	602 241-2205
Tucson (POD)	602 629-6715

Financial Assistance
Phoenix	602 241-2217
Tucson (POD)	602 629-6715

Veterans' Affairs Officer
Phoenix	602 241-2203

Women in Business Representative
Phoenix	602 241-2237

State Offices

Small Business Program	602 225-5705
Loan Information	*
Procurement Information	*
Department of Revenue	602 271-5537 (Phoenix)
State Export	602 255-5374
Consumer Complaints	800 352-8431
Ombudsman	*

Other U.S. Government Offices

Internal Revenue Service	800 352-6911; 602 261-3861 (Phoenix)
Farmer's Home Administration	602 261-6701 (Phoenix)
Department of Commerce	602 261-3285 (Phoenix)
Department of Energy	*
Department of Labor, Wage/Hour Division	602 261-4224 (Phoenix)
Occupational Safety and Health Administration	602 261-4858 (Phoenix)
International Trade Administration	602 261-3285
Federal Information Centers	602 261-3313 (Phoenix) 602 622-1511 (Tucson)

ARKANSAS   *Region VI*
Small Business Administration

Management Assistance
Little Rock	501 378-5813

Financial Assistance
Little Rock	501 378-5871

Veterans' Affairs Officer
Little Rock   501 378-5871

Women in Business Representative
Little Rock   501 378-5871

Small Business Development Centers

Arkadelphia	501 246-5511
Conway	501 450-3190
Fayetteville	501 575-5148
Little Rock	501 371-5381
Monticello	501 268-6161
Searcy	501 268-6161
State University	501 972-3517

State Offices

Small Business Program	501 371-1121
Loan Information	501 374-9247
Procurement Information	*
Minority Business	501 371-1121
Department of Revenue	501 371-1476 (Little Rock)
State Export	501 371-7781
Consumer Complaints	800 482-8982
Ombudsman	*

Other U.S. Government Offices

Internal Revenue Service	800 482-9350; 501 378-5685 (Little Rock)
Farmer's Home Administration	501 378-6281 (Little Rock)
Department of Commerce	501 378-5794 (Little Rock)
Department of Energy	501 371-1370 (Little Rock)
Department of Labor, Wage/Hour Division	501 378-5292 (Little Rock)
Occupational Safety and Health Administration	501 378-6291 (Little Rock)
International Trade Administration	501 378-5794 (Little Rock)
Federal Information Center	**378-6177 (Little Rock)

CALIFORNIA   *Region IX*

Small Business Administration

Management Assistance

Fresno	209 487-5605
Los Angeles	213 688-7173
Sacramento	916 440-2956
San Diego	619 293-5444
San Francisco	415 974-0590

San Jose (POD)   408 275-7584
Santa Ana   714 836-2494

Financial Assistance
Fresno   209 487-5605
Los Angeles   213 688-5543
Sacramento   916 440-2956
San Diego   619 293-5440
San Francisco   415 974-0617
San Jose   408 291-7584
Santa Ana   714 836-2494

Veterans' Affairs Officers
Fresno   209 487-5790
Los Angeles   213 688-2991
San Diego   619 293-6307
San Francisco   415 974-0590

Women in Business Representatives
Fresno   209 487-5789
Los Angeles   213 688-4894
Sacramento   916 440-2956
San Diego   619 293-6514
San Francisco   415 974-0590

State Offices

Small Business Program   916 445-6545

Loan Information:
California Office of Small Business
    Development   916 445-6545 (Sacramento)
Business and Industrial
    Development Corporations   415 557-3232
Alternative Energy Source
    Financing   916 445-9597
Procurement Information   *
Minority Business   916 322-5060
Department of Revenue   916 355-0370 (Sacramento)
State Export   916 324-5511
Consumer Complaints   800 952-5225
Ombudsman   *

Other U.S. Government Offices

Internal Revenue Service   800 242-4585; 213 572-7814 (Los
                                          Angeles)
                                        415 556-0880 (San Francisco)
Farmer's Home Administration   916 666-3382 (Woodland)

Department of Commerce	213 824-7591 (Los Angeles)
	714 293-5395 (San Diego)
	415 556-5860 (San Francisco)
Department of Energy	916 323-4388 (Sacramento)
Department of Labor, Wage/Hour	
Division	213 240-5274 (Glendale)
	916 484-4447 (Sacramento)
	714 863-2156 (Santa Ana)
	415 974-0535 (San Francisco)
	213 688-4957 (Los Angeles)
Occupational Safety and Health	
Administration	213 432-3434 (Long Beach)
	415 556-7260 (San Francisco)
International Trade Administration	213 209-6707 (Los Angeles)
	415 556-5860 (San Francisco)
Federal Information Centers	213 688-3800 (Los Angeles)
	916 440-3344 (Sacramento)
	619 293-6030 (San Diego)
	415 556-6600 (San Francisco)
	**275-7422 (San Jose)
	**836-2386 (Santa Ana)

COLORADO *Region VIII*

Small Business Administration

Management Assistance
Denver   303 844-2607

Financial Assistance
Denver   303 844-2607

Veterans' Affairs Officer
Denver   303 844-6531

Women in Business Representative
Denver   303 844-6526

State Offices

Small Business Program	303 492-5611 (University of Colorado)
Loan Information	*
Procurement Information	303 757-9011; 303 886-2077
Minority Business	303 866-2077
Department of Revenue	303 825-9061 (Denver)
State Export	303 866-2205
Consumer Complaints	*
Ombudsman	*

Other U.S. Government Offices

Internal Revenue Service	800 332-2060; 303 825-7041 (Denver)
Farmer's Home Administration	303 837-4347 (Denver)
Department of Commerce	303 837-3246 (Denver)
Department of Energy	303 839-2186 (Denver)
Department of Labor, Wage/Hour Division	303 837-4405 (Denver)
Occupational Safety and Health Administration	303 245-2502 (Lakewood)
International Trade Administration	303 837-3246 (Denver)
Federal Information Centers	303 234-7181 (Denver)
	**471-9491 (Colorado Springs)
	**544-9523 (Pueblo)

CONNECTICUT   *Region I*

Small Business Administration

Management Assistance
Hartford	203 722-2544

Financial Assistance
Hartford	203 722-3600

Veterans' Affairs Officer
Hartford	203 722-3603

Women in Business Representative
Hartford	203 722-2544

Small Business Development Centers
Bridgeport	203 335-3800
Hartford	203 525-4451
New Haven	203 787-6735
New London	203 443-8332
Stamford	203 323-1883
Storrs	203 486-4135
Waterbury	203 757-0701

State Offices

Small Business Program	203 566-4051

Loan Information:
Connecticut Product Development Corporation	203 566-2920
	(Risk capital to established manufacturing firms with a primary focus on job creation)

Department of Economic	
Development	203 566-4051
	(Enterprise zone business start-ups)
Procurement Information	203 566-4051
Department of Revenue	203 566-8520 (Hartford)
State Export	203 566-3071
Consumer Complaints	800 842-2649
Ombudsman	203 566-7035
Department of Energy	203 566-5803
Product Development Corporation	203 566-2920

Other U.S. Government Offices

Internal Revenue Service	800 343-9000; 203 722-3064
	(Hartford)
Farmer's Home Administration	413 253-3471 (Amherst, MA)
Department of Commerce	203 722-3530 (Hartford)
Department of Energy	800 424-0246 (Hartford)
Department of Labor,	
Wage/Hour Division	203 722-2660 (Hartford)
Occupational Safety and	
Health Administration	203 722-2294 (Hartford)
International Trade Administration	203 244-3530 (Hartford)
Federal Information Centers	**527-2617 (Hartford)
	**624-4720 (New Haven)

DELAWARE   *Region III*

Small Business Administration

Management Assistance
Wilmington	302 573-6294

Financial Assistance
Wilmington	302 573-6294

Veterans' Affairs Officer
Wilmington	302 573-6294

Women in Business Representative

Small Business Development Center
Newark, Delaware	302 451-2747

State Offices

Small Business Program	302 736-4271
Loan Information	302 736-4271
Procurement Information	*

Department of Revenue	302 654-5111 (Wilmington)
State Export	302 736-4271
Consumer Complaints	*
Ombudsman	*

Other U.S. Government Offices

Internal Revenue Service	800 292-9575; 302/573-6083 (Wilmington)
Farmer's Home Administration	302 573-6694 (Newark)
Department of Commerce	215 597-2866 (Philadelphia, PA)
Department of Energy	302 736-5647 (Dover)
Department of Labor, Wage/Hour Division	301 962-2265 (Baltimore, MD)
Occupational Safety and Health Administration	*
International Trade Administration	215 597-2866 (Philadelphia, PA)
Federal Information Centers	*

DISTRICT OF COLUMBIA *Region III (for national SBA* offices, see following list)

Small Business Administration

Management Assistance
Washington, D.C.	202 634-6200

Financial Assistance
Washington, D.C.	202 634-6200

Veterans' Affairs Officer
Washington, D.C.	202 634-6061

Women in Business Representative
Washington, D.C.	202 634-1818

Small Business Development Center
Washington, D.C.	202 636-7187
	202 727-1051

State Offices

Small Business Program	*
Loan Information	202 727-6600
Procurement Information	202 727-0171
Internal Revenue Service	202 488-3100, ext. 2222
Department of Revenue	202 629-4665
State Export	*
Consumer Complaints	202 727-7000

Telephone Consumer Hotline, Inc.	202 483-4100
Ombudsman	*
Licensing	202 727-3645

Other U.S. Government Offices

Internal Revenue Service	202 488-3100
Farmer's Home Administration	202 447-4323
Department of Commerce	202 377-2000
Department of Energy	202 727-1830
Department of Labor, Wage/Hour Division	202 576-6942
Occupational Safety and Health Administration	202 523-5224
International Trade Administration	202 377-3181
Federal Information Center	202 655-4000

National SBA Offices at 409 Third St., SW, Washington DC 20416

Advocacy	202 205 6533
Answer Desk	800 827 5722
Business Development	202 205 6665
Certification & Elegibility	202 205 6416
Economic Research	202 205 6530
Eight A (8a) Appeals	202 205 7732
Financial Institutions	202 205 6497
Five-O-Four (504) Loans	202 205 6485
Hi-Tech	202 205 6450
Incubator Programs	202 205 6665
Information-Public Relations	202 205 6531
Inter-Agency Affairs	202 205 6532
International Trade	202 205 6720
Loans	202 205 6490
Minority Enterprises	202 205 6410
Portfolio Management	202 205 6481
Procurement	202 205 6460
Contract Size Standards	202 205 6618
Industrial Contracts	202 205 6475
Natural Resources	202 205 6470
PASS	202 205 6469
Prime Contracts	202 205 6471
Program Development	202 205 6423
Rural Development	202 205 6730
Rural Information	800 633 7701
SBDC	202 205 6766
SBIC	202 205 6510
SCORE (national office)	202 205 6200

Surety Bonds	202 205 6540
Veterans' Affairs	202 205 6773
Women's Business Opportunity	202 205 6673

FLORIDA   *Region IV*
Small Business Administration

Management Assistance
Jacksonville	904 791-3105
Miami	305 350-5521
Tampa (POD)	813 228-2594
West Palm Beach (POD)	305 689-2223

Financial Assistance
Jacksonville	904 791-3782
Miami	305 350-5521
Tampa (POD)	813 228-2594
West Palm Beach (POD)	305 689-2223

Veterans' Affairs Officers
Jacksonville	904 791-3107
Miami	305 350-5833

Women in Business Representatives
Jacksonville	904 791-3782
Miami	305 350-5521

Small Business Development Centers
Boca Raton	305 393-3174
Deland	904 734-1066
Elgin AFB	904 678-1143
Fort Lauderdale	305 467-4238
Gainesville	904 377-5621
Jacksonville	904 646-2476
Key West	305 294-8481
Miami	305 554-2272
North Miami	305 940-5790
Orlando	305 275-2796
Panama City	904 769-3556
Pensacola	904 474-2908
St. Petersburg	813 893-9529
Tallahassee	904 644-6524
Tallahassee	904 599-3407
Tampa	813 974-4264

State Offices

Small Business Program	800 342-0771; 904 488-9357
Loan Information	*
Procurement Information	904 243-7624
Minority Business	904 488-9575
Department of Revenue	904 488-2574 (Tallahassee)
Consumer Complaints	800 342-2176
State Export	904 488-5280; 904 488-6124
Ombudsman	*
High Tech	904 457-1880

Other U.S. Government Offices

Internal Revenue Service	800 342-8300; 904 791-2514 (Jacksonville)
Farmer's Home Administration	904 376-3218 (Gainesville)
Department of Commerce	305 350-5267 (Miami)
	813 461-0011 (Clearwater)
	904 791-2796 (Jacksonville)
	904 488-6469 (Tallahassee)
Department of Energy	904 488-2475 (Tallahassee)
Department of Labor, Wage/Hour Division	904 791-2489 (Jacksonville)
	305 527-7262 (Fort Lauderdale)
	305 350-5767 (Miami)
	813 228-2154 (Tampa)
Occupational Safety and Health Administration	305 527-7292 (Fort Lauderdale)
	813 228-2821 (Tampa)
	904 791-2895 (Jacksonville)
International Trade Administration	305 350-5267 (Miami)
Federal Information Centers	**522-8531 (Fort Lauderdale)
	**354-4756 (Jacksonville)
	305 350-4155 (Miami)
	**422-1800 (Orlando)
	813 893-3495 (St. Petersburg)
	**229-7911 (Tampa)
	**833-7566 (West Palm Beach)
	800 282-8556 (North Florida)
	800 432-6668 (South Florida)

GEORGIA   *Region IV*

Small Business Administration

Management Assistance
Atlanta   404 881-2441
Statesboro (POD)   912 489-8719

Financial Assistance
Atlanta   404 881-4325
Statesboro (POD)   912 489-8719

Veterans' Affairs Officer
Atlanta   404 881-2441

Women in Business Representative
Atlanta   404 881-4325

Small Business Development Centers
Albany   912 439-7232
Athens   404 542-7436
Atlanta   404 658-3550
Augusta   404 828-4993
Columbus   404 571-7433
Macon   912 746-7601
Morrow   404 961-3414
Rome   404 295-6327
Savannah   912 233-3067
Statesboro   912 681-5194
Valdosta   912 247-3262

State Offices

Small Business Program   *
Loan Information   *
Procurement Information   404 656-4291
Minority Business   404 656-1794
Department of Revenue   404 656-4291 (Atlanta)
State Export   404 656-4504
Consumer Complaints   800 282-4900
Ombudsman   *
High Tech   404 894-3575

Other U.S. Government Offices

Internal Revenue Service   800 222-1040
Farmer's Home Administration   404 546-2162 (Athens)
Department of Commerce   912 944-4205 (Savannah)
                                      404 881-7000 (Atlanta)
Department of Energy   *

Department of Labor, Wage/Hour Division	404 221-6401 (Atlanta) 912 944-4222 (Savannah)
Occupational Safety and Health Administration	404 221-4767 (Tucker) 912 746-5143 (Macon) 912 354-0733 (Savannah)
International Trade Administration	404 881-7000 (Atlanta) 912 944-4204 (Savannah)
Federal Information Center	404 221-6891 (Atlanta)

HAWAII *Region IX*

Small Business Administration

Management Assistance
Honolulu	808 546-3119

Financial Assistance
Honolulu	808 546-3151

Veterans' Affairs Officer
Honolulu	808 546-7336

Women in Business Representative
Honolulu	808 546-3119

State Offices

Small Business Program	808 548-4172
Loan Information	800 367-5218; 808 548-4616
Procurement Information	*
Department of Revenue	808 548-2211 (Honolulu)
State Export	808 548-3048
Consumer Complaints	*
Ombudsman	*

Other U.S. Government Offices

Internal Revenue Service	808 546-2803
Farmer's Home Administration	808 961-4781 (Hilo)
Department of Commerce	808 546-8694 (Honolulu)
Department of Energy	808 548-2306 (Honolulu)
Department of Labor, Wage/Hour Division	213 688-4957 (Los Angeles)
Occupational Safety and Health Administration	800 546-3157 (Honolulu)

International Trade Administration
  State Office   808 546-8694 (Honolulu)
                                      808 548-3048
  Federal Information Centers   808 546-8620 (Honolulu)

IDAHO   Region X

Small Business Administration

Management Assistance
  Boise   208 334-1780

Financial Assistance
  Boise   208 334-1696

Veterans' Affairs Officer
  Boise   208 334-1780

Women in Business Representative
  Boise   208 334-1096

State Offices

  Small Business Program   208 334-1096
  Loan Information   208 334-2470
  Permits and Licensing   208 334-3598
  Procurement Information   *
  Department of Revenue   208 384-3159 (Boise)
  State Export   *
  Consumer Complaints   *
  Ombudsman   *

Other U.S. Government Offices

  Internal Revenue Service   800 632-5990; 208/336-1040 (Boise)
  Farmer's Home Administration   208 334-1730 (Boise)
  Department of Commerce   503 221-3001 (Portland, OR)
  Department of Energy   208 334-3800 (Boise)
  Department of Labor,
    Wage/Hour Division   503 221-3057 (Portland, OR)
                                   206 442-4482 (Seattle, WA)
  Occupational Safety and
    Health Administration   208 384-1867 (Boise)
  International Trade Administration 801 524-5116 (Salt Lake City, UT)
  Federal Information Centers   *

ILLINOIS *Region V*
Small Business Administration

Management Assistance
Chicago	312 353-4528
Springfield	217 492-4767

Financial Assistance
Chicago	312 353-4528
Springfield	217 492-4767

Veterans' Affairs Officers
Chicago	312 353-5125
Springfield	217 492-4416

Women in Business Representatives
Chicago	312 353-5031
Springfield	217 492-4416

Small Business Development Centers
Chicago	312 670-0434
Kane/DuPage/DeKalb	815 753-1243
Macon County	217 424-6297
S. Cook County	312 543-5000
S. Illinois	618 453-3307
S.W. Illinois	618 692-2929

State Offices

Small Business Program Illinois Department of Commerce and Community Affairs—Small Business Development Center Network	312 793-6885 (Chicago)

800 252-2923 |

Loan Information:
Illinois Industrial Development Authority	618 997-6382 (Marion)
Illinois Department of Commercial and Community Affairs	312 793-6304 (Chicago) 217 782-1458 (Springfield)
Procurement Information	217 782-4705
Minority Business	312 793-6885
Department of Revenue	800 252-8972; 217 782-3336 (Springfield)
State Export	312 793-2086
Consumer Complaints	*
Ombudsman	*

Other U.S. Government Offices

Internal Revenue Service	800 972-5400; 312 886-4609 (Chicago)
	800 972-5400; 217 492-4288 (Springfield)
Farmer's Home Administration	217 398-5235 (Champaign)
Department of Commerce	312 353-4450 (Chicago)
Department of Energy	217 785-2009 (Springfield)
Department of Labor, Wage/Hour Division	312 775-5733 (Chicago)
	217 492-4060 (Springfield)
	312 238-8832 (Bridgeview)
Occupational Safety and Health Administration	312 891-3800 (Calumet City)
	312 896-8700 (North Aurora)
	309 671-7033 (Peoria)
	312 631-8200 (Niles)
International Trade Administration	312 353-4450 (Chicago)
Federal Information Center	312 353-4242 (Chicago)

INDIANA   *Region V*

Small Business Administration

Management Assistance

Indianapolis	317 269-7264
South Bend (BO)	219 236-8361

Financial Assistance

Indianapolis	317 269-7272
South Bend (BO)	317 269-7272

Veterans' Affairs Officer

Indianapolis	317 269-7284

Women in Business Representatives

Indianapolis	317 269-7278
	317 269-2073

State Offices

Small Business Program	317 634-8418

Loan Information:

Corporation for Innovation Development	317 635-7325 (Indianapolis)
Procurement Information	*
Department of Commerce	800 824-2476 (Indianapolis)

Department of Revenue	317 633-6442 (Indianapolis)
State Export	317 793-8845
Consumer Complaints	800 382-5516
Ombudsman	317 232-3373
High Tech	317 635-3058

Other U.S. Government Offices

Internal Revenue Service	800 382-9740; 317 269-6326 (Indianapolis)
Farmer's Home Administration	317 269-6415 (Indianapolis)
Department of Commerce	317 269-6214 (Indianapolis)
Department of Energy	317 232-8940 (Indianapolis)
Department of Labor, Wage/Hour Division	317 269-7163 (Indianapolis) 219 234-4045 (South Bend)
Occupational Safety and Health Administration	317 269-7290 (Indianapolis)
International Trade Administration	317 269-6214 (Indianapolis)
Federal Information Centers	**883-4110 (Gary/Hammond) 317 269-7373 (Indianapolis)

IOWA *Region VII*

Small Business Administration

Management Assistance

Cedar Rapids	319 399-2571
Des Moines	515 284-4760

Financial Assistance

Cedar Rapids	319 399-2571
Des Moines	515 284-6091

Veterans' Affairs Officers

Des Moines	515 284-6090
Cedar Rapids	319 399-2571

Women in Business Representatives

Des Moines	515 284-4762
Cedar Rapids	319 399-2571

Small Business Development Centers

Ames	515 294-8069
Cedar Falls	319 273-2696
Des Moines	515 271-2655
Iowa City	319 353-5340

State Offices

Small Business Program	515 281-8310; 800 532-1216

Loan Information: **515 281-4058**

Iowa Product Development Corporation	515 281-3925 (Des Moines)
Procurement Information	515 281-3089
Department of Revenue	515 281-5996
State Export	515 281-3655
Consumer Complaints	*
Ombudsman	515 281-3592
High Tech	515 294-3420

Other U.S. Government Offices

Internal Revenue Service	800 362-2600, ext. 4964
	515 284-4964 (Des Moines)
Farmer's Home Administration	515 284-4663 (Des Moines)
Department of Commerce	515 284-4222 (Des Moines)
Department of Energy	515 281-4420 (Des Moines)
Department of Labor, Wage/Hour Division	515 284-4625 (Des Moines)
Occupational Safety and Health Administration	515 284-4794 (Des Moines)
International Trade Administration	515 284-4222 (Des Moines)
Federal Information Centers	515 284-4448 (Des Moines)
	800 532-1556 (Other Iowa locations)

KANSAS   *Region VII*

Small Business Administration

Management Assistance

Wichita	316 269-6273

Financial Assistance

Wichita	316 269-6571

Veterans' Affairs Officer

Wichita	316 269-6273

Women in Business Representative

Wichita	316 269-6426

Small Business Development Centers

Emporia	316 343-1200
Hays	913 628-4000

Lawrence	913 864-3117
Manhattan	913 532-5529
Overland Park	913 888-8500
Pittsburg	316 231-7000, ext. 435
Topeka	913 295-6305

State Offices

Small Business Program	913 296-3480
Loan Information	*
Procurement Information	913 296-2376
Minority Business	913 296-3480
Department of Revenue	913 296-0351 (Topeka)
State Export	913 296-3483
Consumer Complaints	800 432-2310
Ombudsman	*
High Tech	913 296-3480

Other U.S. Government Offices

Internal Revenue Service	800 362-2190; 316 263-2161 (Wichita)
Farmer's Home Administration	913 295-2870 (Topeka)
Department of Commerce	816 374-3142 (Kansas City, MO)
Department of Energy	913 296-2496 (Topeka)
Department of Labor, Wage/Hour Division	816 374-5721 (Kansas City, MO) 402 221-4682 (Omaha, NE)
Occupational Safety and Health Administration	316 267-6311, ext. 644 (Wichita)
International Trade Administration	816 374-3142 (Kansas City, MO)
Federal Information Centers	913 295-2866 (Topeka) 800 432-2934 (Other Kansas locations)

KENTUCKY *Region IV*
Small Business Administration

Management Assistance
Louisville	502 582-5976

Financial Assistance
Louisville	502 582-5973

Veterans' Affairs Officer
Louisville	502 582-5976

Women in Business Representative
Louisville   502 582-5976

Small Business Development Centers
Bowling Green   502 745-2901
Frankfort   502 564-2064
Highland Heights   606 572-6558
Lexington   606 257-1751
Morehead   606 783-2077
Murray   502 753-4134
Somerset   606 678-8174

State Offices

Small Business Program   502 564-2064
Loan Information   502 564-4554
Procurement Information   502 564-2064
Department of Revenue   502 564-8054 (Frankfort)
State Export   502 564-2170
Consumer Complaints   800 432-9257
Ombudsman   502 564-4270

Other U.S. Government Offices

Internal Revenue Service   800 428-9100; 502 582-6259
                                          (Louisville)
Farmer's Home Administration   606 233-2733 (Lexington)
Department of Commerce   502 582-5066 (Louisville)
Department of Energy   606 252-5535 (Lexington)
Department of Labor,
    Wage/Hour Division   502 582-5226 (Louisville)
Occupational Safety and
    Health Administration   502 564-2300 (Frankfort)
International Trade Administration   502 582-5066 (Louisville)
Federal Information Center   502 582-6261 (Louisville)

LOUISIANA   Region VI

Small Business Administration

Management Assistance
New Orleans   504 589-2354
Shreveport (POD)   318 226-5196

Financial Assistance
New Orleans   504 589-2705
Shreveport (POD)   318 226-5196

Veterans' Affairs Officer
New Orleans   504 589-5976

Women in Business Representative
New Orleans   504 589-2288

Small Business Development Centers
Baton Rouge   504 342-5366
                                     504 388-6282
Lafayette   318 231-5745
Lake Charles   318 477-2520, ext. 531
Monroe   318 342-2129
New Orleans   504 948-4944; 286-6663
Ruston   318 257-3537
Shreveport   318 797-5022

State Offices

Small Business Program   504 342-5366

Loan Information: **504 342-5367**
                                     504 342-5382 (Baton Rouge)
Procurement Information   504 922-0074
Minority Business   504 342-6491
Department of Revenue   504 389-6667 (Baton Rouge)
State Export   504 342-5388
Consumer Complaints   800 272-9868
Ombudsman   *
High Tech   504 342-5361

Other U.S. Government Offices

Internal Revenue Service   800 362-6900; 504 589-2488 (New
                                       Orleans)
Farmer's Home Administration   318 473-7920 (Alexandria)
Department of Commerce   504 589-6546 (New Orleans)
Department of Energy   504 342-4594 (Baton Rouge)
Department of Labor,
    Wage/Hour Division   504 589-6171 (New Orleans)
Occupational Safety and
    Health Administration   504 589-2451 (New Orleans)
                                     504 923-0718 (Baton Rouge)
International Trade Administration   504 589-6546 (New Orleans)
Federal Information Center   504 589-6696 (New Orleans)

MAINE   *Region I*

Small Business Administration

Management Assistance
Augusta   207 622-8242

Financial Assistance
Augusta   207 622-8378

Veterans' Affairs Officer
Augusta   207 622-8378

Women in Business Representative
Augusta   207 622-8383

Small Business Development Centers
Augusta   207 622-6345
Bangor   207 942-6389
Caribou   207 498-8736
Machias   207 255-3313
Portland   207 780-4423

State Offices

Small Business Program   207 289-2656
Loan Information   207 289-2656 (Augusta)
Procurement Information   *
Department of Revenue   207 289-3695 (Augusta)
State Export   207 623-5700
Consumer Complaints   *
Ombudsman   *

Other U.S. Government Offices

Internal Revenue Service   800 452-8750; 207 622-6171, ext. 466
                             (Augusta)
Farmer's Home Administration 207 866-4929 (Orono)
Department of Commerce   207 623-2239 (Augusta)
Department of Energy   207 289-3811 (Augusta)
Department of Labor,
   Wage/Hour Division   207 780-3344, ext. 344 (Augusta)
Occupational Safety and
   Health Administration   203 244-2294 (Hartford, CT)
                             207 622-6171 (Augusta)
International Trade Administration 617 223-2312 (Boston)
Federal Information Centers *

MARYLAND   *Region III*
Small Business Administration

Management Assistance
Baltimore   301 962-2233

Financial Assistance
Baltimore   301 962-2150

Veterans' Affairs Officer
Baltimore   301 962-2150

Women in Business Representative
Baltimore   301 962-2233

State Offices

Small Business Program   **800 654-7336; 301 269-2621

Loan Information:
Enterprise Zones   301 269-2624
Short-term working capital for
companies with procurement
contracts   301 659-4270
Industrial Development Financing
Authority (not for retail or
service businesses)   301 659-4262
Established businesses   301 828-4711
Procurement Information   *
Minority Business   301 383-5555
Montgomery County—Steve Ames   301 984-0999
Department of Revenue   301 267-5981 (Annapolis)
State Export   301 269-2621
Consumer Complaints: Telephone
Consumer Hotline, Inc.   800 332-1124
Ombudsman   *

Other U.S. Government Offices

Internal Revenue Service   800 492-0460; 301 962-2222
                                     (Baltimore)
Farmer's Home Administration   302 573-6694 (Newark, DE)
Department of Commerce   301 962-3560 (Baltimore)
Department of Energy   301 383-6810 (Baltimore)
Department of Labor,
Wage/Hour Division   301 962-2265 (Baltimore)
Occupational Safety and
Health Administration   301 962-2840 (Baltimore)

International Trade Administration   301 962-3560 (Baltimore)
Federal Information Center   301 962-4980 (Baltimore)

MASSACHUSETTS *Region I*

Small Business Administration

Management Assistance
Boston   617 223-7991
Springfield   413 536-8770

Financial Assistance
Boston   617 223-3125
Springfield   413 536-8770

Veterans' Affairs Officer
Boston   617 223-3293

Women in Business Representative
Boston   617 223-3212

Small Business Development Centers
Amherst   413 549-4930
Boston   617 734-1960
Chestnut Hill   617 969-0100, ext. 4092
Fall River   617 673-9783
Lowell   617 458-7261
Salem   617 745-0556
Springfield   413 737-6712
Worcester   617 793-7615

State Offices

Small Business Program   800 632-8181; 617 727-4005

Loan Information:
New and expanding high-tech
  businesses with high
  employment and growth
  potential   617 723-4920
Community Development
  Corporation Programs   617 742-0366
Business expansions   617 536-3900
Industrial finance   617 451-2477
Procurement Information   800 632-8181; 617 727-4005
Minority Business   617 727-8692
Department of Revenue   617 727-4393 (Boston)
State Export   *

Consumer Complaints	*
Ombudsman	*

Other U.S. Government Offices

Internal Revenue Service	800 392-6288; 617 223-5177 (Boston)
Farmer's Home Administration	413 253-3471 (Amherst)
Department of Commerce	617 223-2312 (Boston)
Department of Energy	617 727-4732 (Boston)
Department of Labor, Wage/Hour Division	617 223-6751 (Boston)
Occupational Safety and Health Administration	617 890-1239 (Waltham) 413 781-2420, ext. 522 (Springfield)
International Trade Administration	617 223-2312 (Boston)
Federal Information Center	617 223-7121 (Boston)

MICHIGAN   *Region V*

Small Business Administration

Management Assistance

Detroit	313 226-6075 313 226-7947 (SCORE)
Marquette (BO)	906 225-1108

Financial Assistance

Detroit	313 226-6075
Marquette (BO)	906 225-1108

Veterans' Affairs Officer

Detroit	313 226-3627

Women in Business Representative

Detroit	313 226-4276

Small Business Development Centers

Detroit	313 577-4431
Houghton	906 487-2470
Kalamazoo	616 383-8594
Mount Pleasant	517 774-3736

State Offices

Small Business Program	517 373-9039

Loan Information:

Emphasis on high-tech and growth industries	517 373-4330 (Lansing)

Community and private industrial
    development   517 373-6378
Procurement Information   517 373-8430
Department of Revenue   517 373-2910 (Lansing)
State Export   517 373-6390
Consumer Complaints   800 292-4204
Ombudsman and licensing
    information   800 232-2727; 517 373-6241
High Tech   517 373-0638

Other U.S. Government Offices

Internal Revenue Service   800 462-0830 (Detroit)
                                      800 482-0670 (Other cities)
Farmer's Home Administration   517 372-1910, ext. 272 (East Lansing)
                                      616 456-2337 (Grand Rapids)
Occupational Safety and Health
    Administration   313 226-6720 (Detroit)
International Trade Administration   313 226-3650 (Detroit)
Federal Information Centers   313 226-7016 (Detroit)
                                      **451-2628 (Grand Rapids)

MINNESOTA   Region V

Small Business Administration

Management Assistance
Minneapolis   612 349-3574

Financial Assistance
Minneapolis   612 349-3559

Veterans' Affairs Officer
Minneapolis   612 349-3565

Women in Business Representative
Minneapolis   612 349-3544

Small Business Development Centers
Bemidji   218 755-2754
Brainerd   218 828-5344
Duluth   218 726-7250
Mankato   507 389-2963
Marshall   507 537-7386
Moorhead   218 236-2289
St. Cloud   612 255-3215
St. Paul   612 647-5840
Winona   507 457-2150

State Offices

Small Business Program	800 652-9747; 612 296-5011
Loan Information	*
Procurement Information	612 296-6949
Department of Revenue	612 296-3781 (St. Paul)
State Export	612 297-4659
Consumer Complaints	*
Ombudsman	*
Licenses	612 296-0617
High Tech	612 341-2222

Other U.S. Government Offices

Internal Revenue Service	800 652-9062; 612 725-7320 (St. Paul)
Farmer's Home Administration	612 725-5842 (St. Paul)
Department of Commerce	612 725-2133 (Minneapolis)
Department of Energy	612 296-8899 (St. Paul)
Department of Labor, Wage/Hour Division	612 725-6108 (Minneapolis)
Occupational Safety and Health Administration	612 725-2571 (Minneapolis)
International Trade Administration	612 349-3338 (Minneapolis)
Federal Information Center	612 349-5333 (Minneapolis)

MISSISSIPPI   *Region IV*

Small Business Administration

Management Assistance
Jackson	601 960-4378

Financial Assistance
Biloxi	601 435-3676
Jackson	601 960-4378

Veterans' Affairs Officers
Jackson	601 960-4378
Biloxi	601 435-3676

Women in Business Representative
Jackson	601 960-5328

Small Business Development Centers
Jackson	601 982-3825
Long Beach	601 868-9988
University	601 232-5001

State Offices

Small Business Program	601 982-6457
Loan Information	*
Procurement Information	*
Minority Business	601 353-6855
Department of Revenue	601 354-6262 (Jackson)
State Export	601 359-3444
	800 468-1158 (In state toll free)
Consumer Complaints	800 222-7622
Ombudsman	*

Other U.S. Government Offices

Internal Revenue Service	800 241-3868; 601 969-4526 (Jackson)
Farmer's Home Administration	601 969-4316 (Jackson)
Department of Commerce	601 960-4388 (Jackson)
Department of Energy	601 961-2733 (Jackson)
Department of Labor, Wage/Hour Division	601 960-4347 (Jackson)
Occupational Safety and Health Administration	601 960-4066 (Jackson)
International Trade Administration	601 960-4388 (Jackson)
Federal Information Center	*

MISSOURI *Region VII*

Small Business Administration

Management Assistance
Kansas City	816 374-5868
Springfield (BO)	417 864-7670
St. Louis	314 425-6600

Financial Assistance
Kansas City	816 374-3416
Springfield	417 864-7670
St. Louis	314 425-6600

Veterans' Affairs Officers
Kansas City	816 374-5868
St. Louis	314 425-6600
Springfield	417 864-7670

Women in Business Representatives
Kansas City	816 374-3416
St. Louis	314 425-6600

Small Business Development Centers

Kansas City	816 926-4572
Rolla	314 341-4559
St. Louis	314 534-7232
Springfield	417 836-5680

State Offices

Small Business Program	314 751-4982
Loan Information	314 751-2686
Procurement Information	*
Department of Revenue	314 751-2151 (Jefferson City)
State Export	314 751-4855
Consumer Complaints	800 392-8222
Ombudsman	816 274-6186
High Tech	314 751-3222

Other U.S. Government Offices

Internal Revenue Service	800 392-4200; 314 425-5661 (St. Louis)
Farmer's Home Administration	314 442-2271, ext. 3241 (Columbia)
Department of Commerce	314 425-3302 (St. Louis)
	816 374-3142 (Kansas City)
Department of Energy	314 751-4000 (Jefferson City)
Department of Labor, Wage/Hour Division	314 425-4706 (St. Louis)
	816 374-5721 (Kansas City)
Occupational Safety and Health Administration	816 374-2756 (Kansas City)
	314 425-5461 (St. Louis)
International Trade Administration	816 374-3142 (Kansas City)
Federal Information Centers	800 982-5808 (Area Codes 816 and 417)
	800 392-7711 (Area Code 314)
	816 374-2466 (Kansas City)
	314 425-4106 (St. Louis)

MONTANA   *Region VIII*

Small Business Administration

Management Assistance

Helena	406 449-5381
Billings (POD)	406 657-6047

Financial Assistance
Helena   406 449-5381
Billings   406 657-6047

Veterans' Affairs Officer
Helena   406 449-5381

Women in Business Representative
Helena   406 449-5381

State Offices

Small Business Program   406 444-3923
Loan Information   406 444-4324
Procurement Information   406 444-2575
Minority Business   406 444-4723
Department of Revenue   406 444-2460 (Helena)
State Export   406 444-4380
Consumer Complaints   800 332-2272
Ombudsman   *
Licensing/Ombudsman   406 444-3923
High Tech   406 444-3923

Other U.S. Government Offices

Internal Revenue Service   800 332-2275; 406 443-2320 (Helena)
Farmer's Home Administration   406 587-5271, ext. 4211 (Bozeman)
Department of Commerce   307 778-2220 (Cheyenne, WY)
Department of Energy   406 449-3780
Department of Labor,
    Wage/Hour Division   801 524-5706 (Salt Lake City, UT)
Occupational Safety and
    Health Administration   406 657-6649 (Billings)
International Trade Administration   303 837-3246 (Denver, CO)
Federal Information Center   *

NEBRASKA   Region VII

Small Business Administration

Management Assistance
Omaha   402 221-3604

Financial Assistance
Omaha   402 221-3622

Veterans' Affairs Officer
Omaha   402 221-3626

Women in Business Representative
    Omaha   402 221-3626

Small Business Development Centers
    Chadron   308 432-4451
    Kearney   308 234-8344
    Lincoln   402 472-3276
    Omaha   402 554-3291
    Wayne   402 375-2004

State Offices

    Small Business Program   402 471-3774
    Loan Information   *
    Procurement Information   *
    Department of Revenue   402 471-2581 (Lincoln)
    State Export   402 471-4668
    Consumer Complaints   *
    Ombudsman   402 471-2035
    Patent Development Program   402 471-3786

Other U.S. Government Offices

    Internal Revenue Service   800 642-9960; 402 221-3504 (Omaha)
    Farmer's Home Administration 402 471-5551 (Lincoln)
    Department of Commerce   402 221-3664 (Omaha)
    Department of Energy   402 471-2867 (Lincoln)
    Department of Labor,
       Wage/Hour Division   402 221-4682 (Omaha)
    Occupational Safety and
       Health Administration   402 221-9341 (Omaha)
                        308 534-9450 (North Platte)
    International Trade Administration 402 221-3664 (Omaha)
    Federal Information Centers   402 221-3353 (Omaha)
                        800 642-8383 (Other Nebraska
                           locations)

NEVADA   *Region IX*

Small Business Administration

Management Assistance
    Las Vegas   702 388-6611
    Reno (POD)   702 784-5268

Financial Assistance
    Las Vegas   702 388-6611
    Reno (POD)   702 784-5268

Veterans' Affairs Officer
Las Vegas   702 385-6611

Women in Business Representative
Las Vegas   702 385-6611

State Offices

Small Business Program   702 885-4420
Loan Information   702 323-3033
Procurement Information   *
Department of Revenue   *
State Export   *
Consumer Complaints   800 992-0900
Ombudsman   *

Other U.S. Government Offices

Internal Revenue Service   800 492-6552; 702 784-5521 (Reno)
                                       702 385-6291 (Las Vegas)
Farmer's Home Administration   801 524-5027 (Salt Lake City, UT)
Department of Commerce   702 784-5203
Department of Energy   702 886-5157 (Carson City)
Department of Labor,
   Wage/Hour Division   602 261-4224 (Phoenix, AZ)
Occupational Safety and Health
   Administration   702 883-1226 (Carson City)
International Trade Administration   702 784-5203 (Reno)
Federal Information Center   *

NEW HAMPSHIRE   Region I
Small Business Administration

Management Assistance
Concord   603 224-4041

Financial Assistance
Concord   603 224-4041

Veterans' Affairs Officer
Concord   603 224-4041

Women in Business Representative
Concord   603 224-4041

State Offices

Small Business Program   603 271-2391
Loan Information   *

Procurement Information   *
Department of Revenue   603 271-1110 (Concord)
State Export   603 271-2591
Consumer Complaints   *
Ombudsman

Other U.S. Government Offices

Internal Revenue Service   800 582-7200
Farmer's Home Administration   802 223-2371 (Montpelier, VT)
Department of Commerce   617 223-2312 (Boston, MA)
Department of Energy   603 271-2711 (Concord)
Department of Labor,
    Wage/Hour Division   207 780-3344, ext. 344 (Portland,
                                              ME)

Occupational Safety and Health
    Administration   603 224-1995 (Concord)
International Trade Administration 617 223-2312 (Boston, MA)
Federal Information Center   *

NEW JERSEY   *Region II*

Small Business Administration

Management Assistance
Camden (POD)   609 757-5183
Newark   201 645-2434

Financial Assistance
Camden   609 757-5183
Newark   201 645-2434

Veterans' Affairs Officer
Newark   201 645-3251

Women in Business Representative
Newark   201 645-6491

Small Business Development Centers
Lincroft   201 842-1900
Newark   201 648-5621
New Brunswick   201 545-3300
Trenton   609 586-4800
Vineland   609 691-8600

State Offices

Small Business Program   609 984-4442

Loan Information:

High Tech	609 984-1671
General Business Loans	609 282-1800; 609 984-4442
Procurement Information	609 984-4442
Minority Business	609 292-0500
Department of Revenue	609 292-7592 (Trenton)
State Export	201 648-3518
Consumer Complaints	800 792-8600
Ombudsman	609 292-0700
High Tech	609 984-2444

Other U.S. Government Offices

Internal Revenue Service	800 242-6750; 201 645-6478
Farmer's Home Administration	609 259-3136 (Robinsville)
Department of Commerce	201 645-6214 (Newark)
Department of Energy	201 648-3904 (Newark)
Department of Labor,	
Wage/Hour Division	201 645-2279 (Newark)
	609 989-2247 (Trenton)
Occupational Safety and Health	
Administration	201 645-5930 (Newark)
	201 359-2777 (Belle Mead)
	201 288-1700 (Hasbrouck Heights)
	609 757-5181 (Camden)
	201 361-4050 (Dover)
International Trade Administration	609 989-2100 (Trenton)
Federal Information Centers	201 645-3600 (Newark)
	**523-0717 (Patterson/Passaic)
	**396-4400 (Trenton)

NEW MEXICO   Region VI

Small Business Administration

Management Assistance

Albuquerque	505 766-3588

Financial Assistance

Albuquerque	505 766-3430

Veterans' Affairs Officer

Albuquerque	505 766-1145

Women in Business Representative

Albuquerque	505 766-1143

State Offices

Small Business Program   505 827-6204

Loan Information:

New Mexico Research and
  Development Institute
358 Pinon Building
1220 South St. Francis Dr.
Santa Fe, New Mexico 87501
Business Development
  Corporation   505 827-6207
Procurement Information   *
Minority Business   505 827-6324
Department of Revenue   505 988-2290 (Santa Fe)
State Export   505 827-6200
Consumer Complaints   *
Ombudsman   *
Licensing   505 827-6318

Other U.S. Government Offices

Internal Revenue Service   800 527-3880; 505 243-8641
                                            (Albuquerque)
Farmer's Home Administration   505 766-2462 (Albuquerque)
Department of Commerce   505 766-2386 (Albuquerque)
Department of Energy   505 827-5950 (Santa Fe)
Department of Labor,
  Wage/Hour Division   505 766-2477 (Albuquerque)
Occupational Safety and Health
  Administration   505 766-3411 (Albuquerque)
International Trade Administration   505 766-2386 (Albuquerque)
Federal Information Center   505 766-3091 (Albuquergue)

NEW YORK *Region II*

Small Business Administration

Management Assistance
Albany (POD)   518 472-6300
Buffalo (BO)   716 846-4517
Elmira   607 733-3358
Melville (BO)   516 454-0750
New York City   212 264-4314
Rochester (POD)   716 263-6700
Syracuse   315 423-5376

Financial Assistance
Albany (POD)	518 472-6300
Buffalo (BO)	716 846-4301
Elmira	607 733-4686
Melville (BO)	516 454-0750
New York City	212 264-1480
Rochester (POD)	716 263-6700
Syracuse	315 423-5364

Veterans' Affairs Officers
Buffalo	716 846-5664
Elmira	607 734-2673
Melville	516 454-0750
New York City	212 264-3525
Syracuse	315 423-5364

Women in Business Representatives
Buffalo	716 846-4517
Elmira	607 734-3358
Melville	516 454-0750
New York	212 264-4349
Syracuse	315 423-5386

Small Business Development Center
Albany	518 473-1228

State Offices

Small Business Program	212 949-9300 (New York City)
	518 474-7756 (Albany)
Loan Information	212 578-4150; 212 949-9300
Procurement Information	212 949-9300; 518 474-7756
Minority/Women in Business	212 949-9288; 518 473-0137
Department of Revenue	800 342-3536 (tax kit)
	518 457-7177 (Albany)
State Export	212 309-0500
Consumer Complaints	212 488-7530; 212 577-0111
Ombudsman	212 949-9300
Licensing	800 342-3464; 518 474-8275
High Tech	518 474-4349

Other U.S. Government Offices

Internal Revenue Service	800 343-9000 (Albany)
	800 462-1560 (Buffalo)
	212 264-3310 (New York City)
Farmer's Home Administration	315 423-5290 (Syracuse)

Department of Commerce	716 846-4191 (Buffalo)
	212 264-0634 (New York City)
Department of Energy	518 473-4083 (Albany)
Department of Labor,	
Wage/Hour Division	716 846-4891 (Buffalo)
	516 481-0582 (Long Island)
	212 264-8185 (New York City)
	212 298-9472 (Bronx)
	518 472-3596 (Albany)
Occupational Safety and Health	
Administration	212 264-9840 (New York City)
	518 472-6085 (Albany)
	315 423-5188 (Syracuse)
	716 263-6755 (Rochester)
	914 946-2510 (White Plains)
	716 846-4881 (Buffalo)
	516 334-3344 (Westbury)
International Trade Administration	716 846-4191 (Buffalo)
	212 264-0634 (New York)
Federal Information Centers	**463-4421 (Albany)
	716 846-4010 (Buffalo)
	212 264-4464 (New York City)
	**546-5075 (Rochester)
	**476-8545 (Syracuse)

NORTH CAROLINA   *Region IV*

Small Business Administration

Management Assistance
Charlotte   704 371-6563

Financial Assistance
Charlotte   704 371-6563

Veterans' Affairs Officer
Charlotte   704 371-6577

Women in Business Representative
Charlotte   704 371-6587

State Offices

Small Business Program	919 733-6254
Loan Information	*
Procurement Information	919 733-7232
Minority Business	919 733-2712

Department of Revenue	919 829-4682 (Raleigh)
State Export	919 733-7193
State Export	919 737-3793
Consumer Complaints	*
Ombudsman	*
High Tech	919 549-0671

Other U.S. Government Offices

Internal Revenue Service	800 822-8800; 919 378-5620 (Greensboro)
Farmer's Home Administration	919 755-4640 (Raleigh)
Department of Commerce	919 378-5345 (Greensboro)
Department of Energy	919 733-2230 (Raleigh)
Department of Labor, Wage/Hour Division	704 371-6120 (Charlotte) 919 755-4190 (Raleigh)
Occupational Safety and Health Administration	919 755-4770 (Raleigh)
International Trade Administration	919 378-5345 (Greensboro)
Federal Information Center	**376-3600 (Charlotte)

NORTH DAKOTA *Region VIII*
Small Business Administration

Management Assistance
| Fargo | 701 237-5771, ext. 131 |

Financial Assistance
| Fargo | 701 237-5771, ext. 131 |

Veterans' Affairs Officer
| Fargo | 701 237-5771 |

Women in Business Representative
| Fargo | 701 237-5771 |

State Offices

Small Business Program	701 224-2810
Loan Information	701 224-5600
Procurement Information	*
Department of Revenue	701 224-2770 (Bismarck)
State Export	701 224-2810
Consumer Complaints	800 472-2927
Ombudsman	*
Rural Development	701 237-7502

Other U.S. Government Offices

Internal Revenue Service	800 342-4710;
	701 237-5771, ext. 5140 (Fargo)
Farmer's Home Administration	701 255-4011, ext. 4781 (Bismarck)
Department of Commerce	402 221-3664 (Omaha, NE)
Department of Energy	701 224-2250 (Bismarck)
Department of Labor,	
Wage/Hour Division	303 837-4405 (Denver, CO)
Occupational Safety and Health	
Administration	701 255-4011, ext. 521 (Bismarck)
International Trade Administration	402 221-3664 (Omaha, NE)
Federal Information Center	*

OHIO   *Region V*

Small Business Administration

Management Assistance
Cincinnati	513 684-2817
Cleveland	216 522-4180
Columbus	614 469-5548

Financial Assistance
Cincinnati	513 684-2814
Cleveland	216 522-4191
Columbus	614 469-6860 or 2359

Veterans' Affairs Officers
Cincinnati	513 684-2814
Cleveland	216 522-4194
Columbus	614 469-2351

Women in Business Representatives
Columbus	614 469-5548
Cincinnati	513 684-2814
Cleveland	216 522-4195

State Offices

Small Business Program	800 282-1085; 614 466-4945

Loan Information
800 282-1085
614 466-4945

Loans funded by public	
employees' retirement system	614 466-2085
Procurement Information	800 282-1085; 614 466-4945
Department of Revenue	614 466-7910 (Columbus)
State Export	216 522-4750 (Cleveland)
	614 466-5017

Consumer Complaints   800 282-0515
Ombudsman   *
Licensing   800 248-4040
High Tech   614 466-3887

Other U.S. Government Offices

Internal Revenue Service   800 424-1040; 216 522-3414
                                   (Cleveland)
                                 800 424-1040; 513 684-2828
                                   (Cincinnati)
Farmer's Home Administration   614 469-5606 (Columbus)
Department of Commerce   513 684-2944 (Cincinnati)
                                 216 522-4750 (Cleveland)
Department of Energy   614 466-1805 (Columbus)
Department of Labor,
   Wage/Hour Division   513 684-2942 (Cincinnati)
                                 614 469-5677 (Columbus)
                                 216 522-3892 (Cleveland)
Occupational Safety and Health
   Administration   216 522-3818 (Cleveland)
                                 513 684-3784 (Cincinnati)
                                 614 469-5582 (Columbus)
                                 419 259-7542 (Toledo)
International Trade Administration 513 684-2944 (Cincinnati)
Federal Information Centers   **375-5628 (Akron)
                                 513 684-2801 (Cincinnati)
                                 216 522-4040 (Cleveland)
                                 **221-1014 (Columbus)
                                 **223-7377 (Dayton)
                                 **241-3223 (Toledo)

OKLAHOMA   Region VI

Small Business Administration

Management Assistance
Oklahoma City   405 231-4491

Financial Assistance
Oklahoma City   405 231-4301

Veterans' Affairs Officer
Oklahoma City   405 231-4301

Women in Business Representative
Oklahoma City   405 231-4491

Small Business Development Center
Durant   405 924-0121, ext. 431

State Offices

Small Business Program   405 521-2401
Loan Information   *
Procurement Information   *
Department of Revenue   405 521-3125 (Oklahoma City)
State Export   405 521-3501
Consumer Complaints   800 522-8555
Ombudsman   *

Other U.S. Government Offices

Internal Revenue Service   800 962-3456; 405 272-9531
                                      (Oklahoma City)
                                    918 583-5121 (Tulsa)
Farmer's Home Administration   405 624-4250 (Stillwater)
Department of Commerce   405 231-5302 (Oklahoma City)
Department of Energy   405 521-2995 (Oklahoma City)
Department of Labor,
   Wage/Hour Division   918 581-7695 (Tulsa)
Occupational Safety and Health
   Administration   918 518-7676 (Tulsa)
                                    405 231-5351 (Oklahoma City)
International Trade Administration   405 231-5302 (Oklahoma City)
Federal Information Centers   405 231-4868 (Oklahoma City)
                                    **584-4193 (Tulsa)

OREGON *Region X*
Small Business Administration

Management Assistance
Portland   503 221-3441

Financial Assistance
Portland   503 294-5220

Veterans' Affairs Officer
Portland   503 294-5200

Women in Business Representative
Portland   503 294-5102

State Offices

Small Business Program   503 373-1200

Loan Information	503 378-4111
	503 373-1215
Procurement Information	*
Minority/Women-owned Business	503 378-1250
Department of Revenue	503 378-3184 (Salem)
State Export	503 229-5625
Consumer Complaints	800 452-7813
Ombudsman	*
High Tech	503 373-1200

Other U.S. Government Offices

Internal Revenue Service	800 452-1980; 503 221-3960
	(Portland)
Farmer's Home Administration	503 221-2731 (Portland)
Department of Commerce	503 221-3001 (Portland)
Department of Energy	503 754-3004 (Corvallis)
Department of Labor,	
Wage/Hour Division	503 221-3057 (Portland)
Occupational Safety and Health	
Administration	503 221-2251 (Portland)
International Trade Administration	503 221-3001 (Portland)
Federal Information Center	503 221-2222 (Portland)

PENNSYLVANIA   *Region III*

Small Business Administration

Management Assistance
Harrisburg (BO)	717 782-4405
Philadelphia	215 596-5834
Pittsburgh	412 644-5441
Wilkes-Barre	717 826-6495

Financial Assistance
Harrisburg (BO)	717 782-3846
Philadelphia	215 596-5889
Pittsburgh	412 644-5442
Wilkes-Barre (BO)	717 826-6498

Veterans' Affairs Officers
Harrisburg	717 782-3846
Philadelphia	215 596-5842
Pittsburgh	412 644-5442
Wilkes-Barre	717 826-6464

Women in Business Representatives
| Philadelphia | 215 596-5823 |
| Pittsburgh | 412 644-5441 |

Small Business Development Centers

Bethlehem	215 861-3980
Clarion	814 226-2626
Erie	814 871-7370
Lewisburg	717 524-1249
Loretto	814 472-7000, ext. 231
Middletown	717 948-6031
Philadelphia	215 898-1219, 787-7282
Pittsburgh	412 624-6435
Scranton	717 961-7588
Wilkes-Barre	717 824-4651, ext. 222

State Offices

Small Business Program	717 783-5700

Loan Information:

State Department of Commerce	717 787-4147
Pennsylvania Milrite Council	717 783-7408
Pennsylvania Industrial Development Council	717 787-3300
Pennsylvania Capital Loan Fund	717 787-3300
Procurement Information	717 783-8893
Minority Business	717 783-1127
Department of Revenue	717 787-8201 (Harrisburg)
State Export	717 787-7190 or 6500
Consumer Complaints	*
Ombudsman	*
High Tech	717 783-5053

Other U.S. Government Offices

Internal Revenue Service	800 242-0240 (Western)
	800 462-4000 (Eastern)
	412 644-6504 (Pittsburgh)
	215 597-0512 (Philadelphia)
Farmer's Home Administration	717 782-4476 (Harrisburg)
Department of Commerce	412 644-2850 (Pittsburgh)
	215 597-2866 (Philadelphia)
Department of Energy	717 783-8610; 800 822-8400 (Harrisburg)
Department of Labor, Wage/Hour Division	717 782-4539 (Harrisburg)
	412 644-2996 (Pittsburgh)
	215 597-4950 (Philadelphia)
Occupational Safety and Health Administration	215 597-4955 (Philadelphia)
	412 644-2905 (Pittsburgh)
	717 826-6538 (Wilkes Barre)

	717 782-3901 (Harrisburg)
	814 453-4531 (Erie)
International Trade Administration	215 597-2866 (Philadelphia)
	412 644-2850 (Pittsburgh)
Federal Information Centers	215 597-7042 (Philadelphia)
	**821-7785 (Allentown)
	412 644-3456 (Pittsburgh)
	**346-7081 (Scranton)

PUERTO RICO   *Region II*

Small Business Administration

Management Assistance
San Juan   809 753-4572, 4683, 4978

Financial Assistance   *

Veterans' Affairs Officer
San Juan   809 753-4519

Women in Business Representative
San Juan   809 753-4519

State Offices

Small Business Program	809 724-0542
Loan Information	809 726-2525; **726-4675
Procurement Information	*
Department of Revenue	809 724-9000
State Export	809 725-7254
Consumer Complaints	809 725-7555
Ombudsman	809 724-7373

Other U.S. Government Offices

Internal Revenue Service	*
Farmer's Home Administration	809 753-4308 (San Juan)
Department of Commerce	809 753-4555, ext. 555 (San Juan)
Department of Energy	809 727-0154 (Santurce)
Department of Labor,	
Wage/Hour Division	809 753-4463 (San Juan)
Occupational Safety and Health	
Administration	809 753-4457 (Hato Rey)
International Trade Administration	809 753-4555, ext. 555 (San Juan)
Federal Information Center	*

RHODE ISLAND   *Region I*
Small Business Administration

Management Assistance
Providence   401 528-4583

Financial Assistance
Providence   401 528-4586

Veterans' Affairs Officer
Providence   401 528-7500

Women in Business Representative
Providence   401 528-7500, ext. 4583

State Offices

Small Business Program	401 277-2601, ext. 21
Loan Information	401 277-2601, ext. 13
Procurement Information	401 277-2601, ext. 24
Minority Business	401 277-2601, ext. 26
Department of Revenue	401 277-2934 (Providence)
State Export	401 277-2601
Consumer Complaints	*
Ombudsman	401 277-2080

Other U.S. Government Offices

Internal Revenue Service	800 662-5055; 401 528-5200 (Providence)
Farmer's Home Administration	413 253-3471 (Amherst, MA)
Department of Commerce	401 277-2605 (Providence)
Department of Energy	401 277-3370 (Providence)
Department of Labor, Wage/Hour Division	401 528-4378 (Providence)
Occupational Safety and Health Administration	401 528-4669 (Providence)
International Trade Administration	617 223-2312 (Boston, MA)
Federal Information Center	**331-5565 (Providence)

SOUTH CAROLINA   *Region IV*
Small Business Administration

Management Assistance
Columbia   803 253-5298

Financial Assistance
Columbia   803 253-5374

Veterans' Affairs Officer
Columbia   803 253-5377

Women in Business Representative
Columbia   803 253-5377

State Offices

Small Business Program   803 758-7804
Loan Information   803 758-2094
Procurement Information   803 758-3150
Department of Revenue   803 758-2217 (Columbia)
State Export   803 758-3351
Consumer Complaints   800 922-1594
Ombudsman   *
High Tech   803 758-3208

Other U.S. Government Offices

Internal Revenue Service   800 241-3868; 803 765-5278
                                        (Columbia)
Farmer's Home Administration   803 765-5876 (Columbia)
Department of Commerce   803 765-5345 (Columbia)
                                        803 677-4361 (Charleston)
                                        803 235-5919 (Greenville)
Department of Energy   803 758-5794 (Columbia)
Department of Labor,
   Wage/Hour Division   803 765-5981 (Columbia)
Occupational Safety and Health
   Administration   803 765-5904 (Columbia)
International Trade Administration   803 765-5345 (Columbia)
Federal Information Center   *

SOUTH DAKOTA   *Region VIII*

Small Business Administration

Management Assistance
Sioux Falls   605 336-2980, ext. 231

Financial Assistance
Sioux Falls   605 336-2980, ext. 231

Veterans' Affairs Officer
Sioux Falls   605 336-2980

Women in Business Representative
Sioux Falls   605 336-2980, ext. 231

State Offices

Small Business Program	605 773-5032
Loan Information	605 773-3181
Procurement Information	605 773-3405
Minority Business	605 773-4906
Department of Revenue	*
State Export	*
Consumer Complaints	800 592-1865
Ombudsman	*
Rural Assistance Program	605 688-4147

Other U.S. Government Offices

Internal Revenue Service	800 592-1870; 605 225-9112 (Aberdeen)
Farmer's Home Administration	605 352-8651, ext. 355 (Huron)
Department of Commerce	402 221-3664 (Omaha, NE)
Department of Energy	605 773-3603 (Pierre)
Department of Labor, Wage/Hour Division	303 837-4405 (Denver, CO)
Occupational Safety and Health Administration	605 336-2980, ext. 425 (Sioux Falls)
Federal Information Center	*

TENNESSEE   *Region IV*

Small Business Administration

Management Assistance
Nashville	615 251-5881

Financial Assistance
Nashville	615 251-5881

Veterans' Affairs Officer
Nashville	615 251-7176

Women in Business Representative
Nashville	615 251-5888

State Offices

Small Business Program	615 741-5020
Loan Information	*
Procurement Information	615 741-1035
Minority Business	800 342-8420; 615 251-7291 (Nashville)
Department of Revenue	615 741-2801 (Nashville)

State Export	615 741-5870
Consumer Complaints	800 342-8385
Ombudsman	*
High Tech	615 741-5070

Other U.S. Government Offices

Internal Revenue Service	800 342-8420; 615 251-7291 (Nashville)
Farmer's Home Administration	615 251-7341 (Nashville)
Department of Commerce	901 521-3213 (Memphis)
	615 251-5161 (Nashville)
Department of Energy	615 741-6677 (Nashville)
Department of Labor, Wage/Hour Division	615 251-5452 (Nashville)
	615 525-7176 (Knoxville)
Occupational Safety and Health Administration	615 251-5313 (Nashville)
International Trade Administration	901 521-4826 (Memphis)
	615 251-5161 (Nashville)
Federal Information Centers	**265-8231 (Chattanooga)
	901 521-3285 (Memphis)
	**242-5056 (Nashville)

TEXAS   Region VI

Small Business Administration

Management Assistance

Austin (POD)	512 482-5288
Corpus Christi (BO)	512 888-3306
Dallas	214 767-0605
El Paso	915 541-7560
Ft. Worth (BO)	817 870-5457
Harlingen	512 423-8934
Houston	713 660-4420
Lubbock	806 743-7481
Marshall (POD)	214 935-5257
San Antonio	512 229-6270

Financial Assistance

Austin (POD)	512 482-5288
Corpus Christi (BO)	512 888-3331
Dallas	214 767-0605
El Paso	915 541-7586
Fort Worth (BO)	214 767-0605
Harlingen	512 423-8934

Houston	713 660-4453
Lubbock	806 743-7466
Marshall (POD)	214 935-5257
San Antonio	512 229-6250

Veterans' Affairs Officers

Corpus Christi	512 888-3304
Dallas	214 767-0605
El Paso	915 541-7560
Harlingen	512 423-8934
Houston	713 660-4409
Lubbock	806 743-7481
San Antonio	512 229-6280

Women in Business Representatives

Corpus Christi	512 888-3302
Dallas	214 767-0382
El Paso	915 541-7590
Harlingen	512 423-8934
Houston	713 660-4460
Lubbock	806 743-7471
San Antonio	512 229-6250

State Offices

Small Business Program	512 472-5059
Loan Information	512 472-5059
Procurement Information	512 472-5059, ext. 654
Minority Business	512 472-5059
Department of Revenue	*
State Export	512 472-5059
	713 229-2578 (Houston)
State Export	512 472-5559
Consumer Complaints	*
Ombudsman	512 472-5059
High Tech	409 845-0538

Other U.S. Government Offices

Internal Revenue Service	800 492-4830; 512 397-5314 (Austin)
	713 226-5142 (Houston)
	214 767-1428 (Dallas)
Farmer's Home Administration	817 774-1301 (Temple)
Department of Commerce	713 226-4231 (Houston)
	214 767-0542 (Dallas)
Department of Energy	512 475-5407 (Austin)
Department of Labor, Wage/Hour Division	214 767-6294 (Dallas)

	817 334-2678 (Fort Worth)
	512 888-3156 (Corpus Christi)
	713 226-4304 (Houston)
	512 229-6125 (San Antonio)

Occupational Safety and Health
   Administration   713 226-4357 (Houston)

806 762-7681 (Lubbock)
512 397-5783 (Austin)
817 334-5274 (Fort Worth)
512 425-6811 (Harlingen)
214 767-5347 (Irving)

International Trade Administration   214 767-0542 (Dallas)
Federal Information Centers   **472-5494 (Austin)

**767-8585 (Dallas)
817 334-3624 (Fort Worth)
713 229-2552 (Houston)
**224-4471 (San Antonio)

UTAH   Region VIII

Small Business Administration

Management Assistance
  Salt Lake City   801 524-3212

Financial Assistance
  Salt Lake City   801 524-3215

Veterans' Affairs Officer
  Salt Lake City   801 524-5800

Women in Business Representative
  Salt Lake City   801 524-5800

Small Business Development Centers
  Cedar City   801 586-4411
  Logan   801 750-2283
  Salt Lake City   801 581-7905

State Offices

Small Business Program   801 533-5325

Loan Information:
  High Tech, R&D, Emerging
    Businesses   801 533-6899
  New Product Development   801 583-4600
  Funding through state employees'
    pension fund   801 355-3884
  Procurement Information   801 533-4000

Minority Business	801 965-4208
Department of Revenue	801 328-5111 (Salt Lake City)
State Export	801 533-5325
Consumer Complaints	801 530-6601
Ombudsman	*

Other U.S. Government Offices

Internal Revenue Service	800 662-5370; 801 524-5767 (Salt Lake City)
Farmer's Home Administration	801 524-5027 (Salt Lake City)
Department of Commerce	801 524-5116 (Salt Lake City)
Department of Energy	801 533-5424 (Salt Lake City)
Department of Labor, Wage/Hour Division	801 524-5706 (Salt Lake City)
Occupational Safety and Health Administration	801 524-5080 (Salt Lake City)
International Trade Administration	801 524-5116 (Salt Lake City)
Federal Information Centers	**399-1347 (Ogden)
	801 524-5353 (Salt Lake City)

VERMONT *Region I*

Small Business Administration

Management Assistance

Montpelier	802 229-9801

Financial Assistance

Montpelier	802 229-0538

Veterans' Affairs Officer

Montpelier	802 229-0538

Women in Business Representative

Montpelier	802 229-0538

Small Business Development Centers

Brattleboro	802 257-7967
Burlington	802 656-2990
Montpelier	802 223-2389
Rutland	802 773-3349
St. Johnsburg	802 748-8177
Winooski	802 656-4420

State Offices

Small Business Program	802 828-3221
Loan Information	*

Procurement Information   *
Department of Revenue   802 828-2509 (Montpelier)
State Export   802 828-3221
Consumer Complaints   800 642-5149
Ombudsman   *

Other U.S. Government Offices

Internal Revenue Service   800 642-3110; 802 951-6370
       (Burlington)
Farmer's Home Administration   802 223-2371 (Montpelier)
Department of Commerce   617 223-2312 (Boston, MA)
Department of Energy   802 828-2768 (Montpelier)
Department of Labor,
   Wage/Hour Division   617 223-6751 (Boston, MA)
Occupational Safety and Health
   Administration   603 224-1995 (Concord)
International Trade Administration   617 223-2312 (Boston, MA)
Federal Information Center   *

VIRGINIA *Region III*

Small Business Administration

Management Assistance
Richmond   804 771-2410

Financial Assistance
Richmond   804 771-2765

Veterans' Affairs Officer
Richmond   804 771-2765

Women in Business Representative
Richmond   804 771-2765

State Offices

Small Business Program   804 786-3791
Loan Information   *
Procurement Information   *
Minority Business   804 786-5560
Department of Revenue   804 770-4494
State Export   804 786-3791
Consumer Complaints (State
   agencies only)   800 552-9963
   Telephone Consumer Hotline, Inc. 800 332-1124
Ombudsman   *

Other U.S. Government Offices

Internal Revenue Service	800 552-9500; 804 771-2289 (Richmond)
Farmer's Home Administration	804 771-2451 (Richmond)
Department of Commerce	804 771-2246 (Richmond)
	703 560-6460 (Fairfax)
Department of Energy	804 745-3305 (Richmond)
Department of Labor, Wage/Hour Division	804 771-2995 (Richmond)
Occupational Safety and Health Administration	804 782-2864 (Richmond)
International Trade Administration	804 771-2246 (Richmond)
Federal Information Centers	**244-0480 (Newport News)
	804 441-3101 (Norfolk)
	**643-4928 (Richmond)
	**982-8591 (Roanoke)

WEST VIRGINIA   *Region III*

Small Business Administration

Management Assistance

Clarksburg	304 623-5631
Charleston (BO)	304 347-5220

Financial Assistance

Clarksburg	304 623-5631
Charleston (BO)	304 347-5220

Veterans' Affairs Officers

Clarksburg	304 623-5631
Charleston	304 347-5220

Women in Business Representatives

Clarksburg	304 623-5631
Charleston	304 347-5220

Small Business Development Centers

Athens	304 384-3115
Charleston	304 346-9471; 245-1298
Parkersburg	304 424-8277

State Offices

Small Business Program	304 348-2960
Loan Information	304 348-3650
Procurement Information	304 348-2960
Department of Revenue	304 348-2071 (Charleston)

State Export	304 348-2234
Consumer Complaints: Telephone	
Consumer Hotline, Inc.	800 332-1124
Ombudsman	*

Other U.S. Government Offices

Internal Revenue Service	800 543-7200;
	304 422-8551, ext. 1255
	(Parkersburg)
Farmer's Home Administration	304 599-7791 (Morgantown)
Department of Commerce	304 343-6181, ext. 375 (Charleston)
Department of Energy	304 348-8860 (Charleston)
Department of Labor,	
Wage/Hour Division	304 343-6181, ext. 448 (Charleston)
Occupational Safety and Health	
Administration	304 343-6181, ext. 420 (Charleston)
International Trade Administration	304 347-5123 (Charleston)
Federal Information Centers	*

WASHINGTON   *Region X*

Small Business Administration

Management Assistance

Seattle	206 442-5534
Spokane	509 456-3786

Financial Assistance

Seattle	206 442-4518
Spokane	509 456-5346

Veterans' Affairs Officers

Seattle	206 442-5645
Spokane	509 456-5346

Women in Business Representatives

Seattle	206 442-8404
Spokane	509 456-3786

Small Business Development Centers

Bellingham	206 676-3896
Pullman	509 335-1576
Spokane	509 456-4259

State Offices

Small Business Program	206 753-5614
Loan Information	206 753-2219

Procurement Information   *
Minority Business   206 753-4243
Department of Revenue   *
State Export   206 464-6283
Consumer Complaints   800 552-0700
Ombudsman   *
Licensing   800 562-8203
High Tech   206 753-5614

Other U.S. Government Offices

Internal Revenue Service   800 732-1040; 206 442-5515 (Seattle)
Farmer's Home Administration   509 662-4353 (Wenatchee)
Department of Commerce   206 442-5615 (Seattle)
Department of Energy   206 754-0725 (Olympia)
Department of Labor,
    Wage/Hour Division   206 442-4482 (Seattle)
Occupational Safety and Health
    Administration   206 442-7520 (Washington)
International Trade Administration   206 442-5616 (Seattle)
Federal Information Centers   206 442-0570 (Seattle)
                                     **383-5230 (Tacoma)

WISCONSIN   *Region V*

Small Business Administration

Management Assistance
Eau Claire   715 834-1573
Madison   608 264-5117
Milwaukee   414 291-1095

Financial Assistance
Eau Claire   715 834-1573
Madison   608 264-5261
Milwaukee   414 291-3941

Veterans' Affairs Officers
Madison   608 264-5261
Milwaukee   414 291-1473

Women in Business Representatives
Madison   608 264-5516
Milwaukee   414 291-3941

Small Business Development Centers
Eau Claire   715 836-5811
Green Bay   414 465-2167
Kenosha   414 553-2047

La Crosse	608 785-8782
Madison	608 263-2221
Milwaukee	414 224-4758
Oshkosh	414 424-1541
Stevens Point	715 346-2004
Superior	715 346-2004
Whitewater	414 472-3217

State Offices

Small Business Program	608 266-0562

Loan Information:

High Tech, New Product	608 266-7968
MESBIC	608 266-8380
Development Fund/General Purposes	414 271-5900
Energy related employing unemployed youth	608 256-1620
Community Development Projects	608 266-0590
503-Certified Development Corporation	
Wisconsin Business Development Finance Corporation	*
Procurement Information	608 266-2605
Minority Business	608 267-9550
Department of Revenue	608 266-1961 (Madison)
State Export	608 266-1767
Consumer Complaints	800 362-3020
Ombudsman	608 266-0562
Permit Information	800 HELP-BUSiness
Legislative Hotline	800 362-9696
High Tech	608 266-1018

Other U.S. Government Offices

Internal Revenue Service	800 452-9100; 414 291-3302 (Milwaukee)
Farmer's Home Administration	715 341-5900 (Stevens Point)
Department of Commerce	414 291-3473 (Milwaukee)
Department of Energy	608 263-1662 (Madison)
Department of Labor, Wage/Hour Division	414 291-3585 (Milwaukee)
	608 264-5221 (Madison)
Occupational Safety and Health Administration	414 291-3315 (Milwaukee)
	414 734-4521 (Appleton)

International Trade Administration   414 291-3473 (Milwaukee)
Federal Information Center   608 271-2273 (Milwaukee)

WYOMING   *Region VIII*
Small Business Administration
Management Assistance
Casper   307 261-5761

Financial Assistance
Casper   307 261-5761

Veterans' Affairs Officer
Casper   307 261-5761

Women in Business Representative
Casper   307 261-5761

State Offices

Small Business Program   307 777-7287

Loan Information:
Industrial Development Corp.   307 234-5351
Procurement Information   *
Department of Revenue   307 777-7971
Consumer Complaints   *
Ombudsman   *

Other U.S. Government Offices

Internal Revenue Service   800 525-6060;
                                    307 772-2220, ext. 2162 (Cheyenne)
Farmer's Home Administration   307 265-5550, ext. 5271 (Casper)
Department of Commerce   307 778-2220, ext. 2151 (Cheyenne)
Department of Energy   307 766-3362 (Laramie)
Department of Labor,
    Wage/Hour Division   303 837-4405 (Denver, CO)
                                    801 524-5706 (Salt Lake City, UT)
Occupational Safety and Health
    Administration   303 234-4471 (Lakewood, CO)
International Trade Administration   303 837-3246 (Denver, CO)
Federal Information Centers   *

Index